The Unbound Book

# The Unbound Book

Edited by

*Joost Kircz and Adriaan van der Weel*

AMSTERDAM UNIVERSITY PRESS

Cover design: Studio Jan de Boer, Amsterdam
Layout: Trees Vulto DTP en Boekproductie, Schalkwijk

Amsterdam University Press English-language titles are distributed in the
US and Canada by the University of Chicago Press.

ISBN        978 90 8964 600 2
e-ISBN    978 90 4852 221 7 (pdf)
e-ISBN    978 90 4852 222 4 (ePub)
NUR        615

# Table of contents

# The book unbinding

Adriaan van der Weel and Joost Kircz

Digitisation – and the mediatisation resulting from it – is extending its hold on society at an unprecedented rate. This goes for all mediums and all modalities, including the modality of text, which is the subject of this book. Change of such a pervasive nature, and even magnitude, in itself may be nothing new, but certainly the rate of change that we are witnessing, and the acceleration of the rate of change, are unprecedented. The consequences of the digitisation of our textual discourse cannot yet be fathomed, but they are likely to be more far-reaching than we can imagine.

The vast amount of serious thinking about the subject, and the staggering number of publications devoted to it, should not surprise us. With its tremendous ramifications digitisation is not just a catalyst of change, it is a catalyst of thinking *about* change, and about the acceleration of change. While acknowledging that it cannot pretend to final verdicts on matters of such consequence, this volume proceeds from the perceived need for a deep and continuing conscious engagement with these remarkable processes of change and the forces that underlie them in order to appraise where we stand and where we are heading. To that end it collects a number of insightful essays about important issues that need to be pondered as authors, the book trade, and consumers migrate to digital modes of writing, publishing, and reading.

With the exception of small pockets of hardcore audiophiles, few people today listen to recorded music in analogue form. Music is downloaded or streamed – and increasingly subscribed to rather than bought. Physical carriers such as CDs are fast disappearing, and with them – or so it would appear – the sense that material ownership of the product and its contents matters. Film and video, too, are now produced and consumed almost exclusively in digital form. Historically text was the first modality, or datatype, after numbers to have been made machine readable. Yet perhaps surprisingly, books have so far proved remarkably resistant to such wholesale digitisation. That is not to say that we have not witnessed spectacular digital development in the world of textual communication over the last decade: first email, then websites, blogs, and social media have enriched us with their distinct features – notably increasing interactivity. However, most of this has not so much replaced the existing world of paper, but extended it, augmenting the total output of text demanding our attention as readers. This development has given new currency to the age-old concept of information overload.[1]

The present volume contains a selection of papers from the Unbound Book conference held in The Hague and Amsterdam, 21-23 May 2011.[2] It addresses the question of what the digital revolution might mean for conventional paper books. It is not about blogs, web sites, social media, email, and all those other new text forms with which the Web is teeming – although it is important to keep that backdrop in mind. It is especially about the digital future of the long-form text popularly designated by the term 'book' – ebooks, book apps, and other screen-based digital forms in which the book may be read – in terms of its content and shape.

The conference's working title was 'What is a book?' One of the prominent challenges resulting from the analogue-digital textual hybridity in which we currently find ourselves is to define what we are even talking about when we use the words 'book', 'reading', and 'literacy' in a digital context. Whatever way one wants to look at it, the digital book has drifted a long way from the material commodity that we have known as a book for centuries, which is discussed in this volume by Baggerman and Kovač. One view could be that the term 'book' ought to be reserved for the product of a particular technology, print, just as 'codex' is reserved for its manuscript predecessor. This stance has the attraction of presenting the digital incarnation of the book more or less as a clean slate. Why clip the wings of our imagination before we even attempt to break free from the unnecessary ballast of centuries? Certainly we could adhere strictly to the existing definition and outlaw many if not all digital incarnations of the book as being insufficiently book-like. This view stresses the discontinuities between paper and screen. By contrast, the notion of cultural continuity presents the most natural way to attempt to understand change. Stretching – or at least attempting to stretch – the existing definition acknowledges the continuities between the analogue book that we have grown up with and the new digital forms that we experiment with today. This collection judiciously does a bit of both.

Although often problematised, the conventional book never used to be a particularly worrisome concept in itself. It is only in comparison with new concepts currently developing that we have begun to question it. Not unlike Molière's Monsieur Jourdain's discovery that he has been speaking prose all his life without knowing it, books were never linear until hypertext made them so (and then only so long as footnotes, glosses, indices, and other technologies of the printed book were not reinterpreted retrospectively as means to promote non-linear readings). Similarly, the fixity of the book as we now recognise it was never problematic until the perceived flexibility of the digital text made it so. On the contrary, printing has often been celebrated as a major victory of fixity over the vicissitudes of manuscript transmission. But then again, could hypertext ever have been thought of as non-linear without the example of print?

Reading in the digital sphere will be seen to gain, if not indeed a new meaning, then at least a host of new connotations. Beyond the possibility of consuming the text in the conventional sense, the technological possibilities of the digital form are of course very different. In the essays here collected we will find canonical solitary engagement with the text supplemented by 'social' forms of reading and see how technology emphatically foregrounds itself in the reading experience. Indeed, the 'industrial' forms of reading that may be performed by the computer have a very tenuous relationship to what we have always understood by the term.

That the concept of literacy needs to evolve along with the transition from paper to digital is obvious, but how is not immediately clear. The reader's capability of manipulating a device is probably not part of it. Cutting open the pages of a book, or charging the battery of one's tablet are auxiliary skills that each have their own charm, but they are only a remote part of literacy. Nor is literacy simply the capacity to perform the 'technical' act of reading, in the sense of the brain recognising meaningful patterns of characters forming words forming sentences forming paragraphs, and so on. For a definition of literacy to be usable in a digital context it should include not only the ability to understand the mediated nature of the process of reading but also to understand the role of the medium itself in the transmission of meaning. How vastly different the role of the digital medium is in this respect is what this book sets out to explore.

As far as conventional print is concerned, digital technology has of course long been used as an aid in the production of books in their familiar tangible paper form. It was when digital technology became part of a network of linked computers that it began to constitute a fully digital communications circuit all the way from author to reader. From its inception in the 1990s the World Wide Web in particular brought digital dissemination and digital reading within wide popular reach. The explosion of digital text forms caused by the Web has not yet come to an end, and the flood of digital texts is only growing. There is no reason to suspect that this flood will diminish in the foreseeable future either, as more and more people make use of the irresistible opportunity to be publicly heard.

With all our other media consumption – of radio, television, film, music, games, and so on – migrating inexorably to the digital screen along with so much text, is it likely that the paper book, resilient though it has shown itself thus far, will stay behind for much longer? Indeed, can the book *afford* to stay behind much longer without becoming irrelevant? If the curiously disembodied, almost ghostlike nature of digital text forms gives rise to a faint feeling of alienation, isn't this balanced by an even stronger sense of opportunity? However you look at it, the new digitality would only appear to make available new ways of communicating emotions, of transferring knowledge, of delivering enjoyment. What was it in the first place that caused the paper form of the book to hold out for so long against the digital 'logic' that has all other mediums and modalities so firmly in its grip?

In the course of the last half century or so, quite a number of initiatives to introduce the digital book have foundered – or at least met with remarkably little popular success. Michael Hart, who regarded his Project Gutenberg as the earliest e-book venture, dates its beginning back to his keying in the United States Declaration of Independence on the University of Illinois' mainframe back in 1971. But despite its pioneering fame it has always remained a marginal phenomenon. No doubt one major reason was that the texts concerned were mainly out-of-copyright ones, but their spartan presentation (initially as simple ASCII files only) did not add to their appeal as reading texts, while the absence of suitable reading devices was probably a factor also.

Since Ted Nelson published his book *Literary Machines* in 1980, many minds have been fascinated by the concept of hypertext literature. Prominent among those who have contributed to its creation are people like David J. Bolter, John B. Smith, and Michael Joyce, co-creators in the mid-1980s of the Storyspace software that inspired the writing of a number of hypertext fictions. In 1987 Apple started bundling HyperCard, an early hypertext, multimedia, and visual programming environment, with its computers. Though an Electronic Literature Organization was officially founded in 1999 'to promote and facilitate the writing, publishing, and reading of electronic literature', it has never found much favour with the general reader.

In the current collection two contributions take up the hypertext issue. Florian Cramer observes a rather surprising reversal in the relationship between the book as a paper and as a digital medium. He sees print books displaying interesting experimental characteristics in, for example, graphic design, while e-books appear to have settled on highly conventional linear formats. Cramer discusses some of the fundamental reasons for why hypertext has not found wider favour – and why the hypermedia electronic book culture envisioned in the 1990s likely will never come to pass. Technological instability appears to be the key issue here. Joost Kircz and August Hans den Boef suggest that the chief problem with hypertext has been that it was never properly implemented technically, notably by not making use of the possibility to type links semantically in such a way that the reader knows how to interpret the material provided in the link target. They argue that, given a practical solution to this problem, there are many highly feasible applications for hypertext, especially in a scholarly and educational environment.

On the hardware side, the e-book did not fare much better. Alan Kay devised his Dynabook concept – a forerunner of today's tablet, aimed in particular at children – as early as 1968, but it never progressed past the prototype stage. At the 1991 Frankfurt Book Fair, seven years after the CD-ROM was introduced, Sony presented the first 'electronic book reader', the Data Discman, based on that technology. It used small, eight cm CD-ROMs for its 'books' and was aimed at students and international travellers, but it was taken off the market only a few years later. The first e-book reader to be sold in commercial quantities, the Rocket e-book, was similarly presented at the 1997 Frankfurt Book Fair by Nuovo Media, but again it did not survive its introduction for very long. Not until the e-paper (also called e-ink) technology went into commercial production in 2004 could e-book readers move out of the gadget sphere.

Though other manufacturers had begun to market e-paper readers, the break-through came with the Amazon Kindle of 2007. This is no doubt owing to the seamless shopping experience presented by Amazon, clearly inspired by Apple's astounding success with its iTunes store. If there is any lesson to be learned from the history of the e-book in terms of both hardware and software – and this should give us pause for thought – it is that any success it has met with can be attributed to relentless marketing more than catering to any existing demand. We have already observed that consumers have at best shown a lukewarm response to digital book reading. Given that publishers, at least outside the academic sphere, have also not been among the avid advocates of digital books, the major impetus for what growth we can observe has in fact originated with the big technology companies: Amazon with its Kindle infrastructure, Apple with its recent iPad and iBookstore, and Google with its unsurpassed book digitisation project. Even then, the figures so far remain modest, especially outside the English speaking world. Uptake of digital reading is highest in the US, with near 15 percent of turnover deriving from e-books in 2011, while Europe is staying behind with the UK at six per cent, the Netherlands at 2.4 per cent, and Germany at less than three per cent.

Despite national differences, the overall level of awareness and popular-ity of digital reading is clearly rising, and equally clear is a general sense of the import of current developments. However, a matching level of insight into the nature and impact of these developments keeps eluding us. There is an unabating stream of publications on the subject, but much of this is in the nature of com-ment rather than analysis and real insight. This is understandable, and probably largely unavoidable, not because we don't think hard enough about it, or because insufficient resources are devoted to the questions, but simply because it is diffi-cult to take sufficient distance from developments that keep overtaking us at such unprecedented speed.

In terms of the development of hardware and software, Siemens and Koolen et al. in their contributions present a very useful analysis of the actual empirical progress being made in the development of the e-book. As the history of technol-ogy makes amply clear, inventing is not a linear process. Thinking up the idea for an invention is one thing; the lengthy and tortuous process by which the inven-tion's social uses and usefulness are being gradually discovered is quite another. It is an unpredictable process, and one that takes time. Siemens and Koolen assume the sensible position that this obviously lengthy process can be sped up and influenced by better harnessing recent usability research on both hardware and software. Systematic analysis of such research (including notably work on user interfacing) should reduce the inefficiency of contingency and happenstance of technological discovery (Jónasdóttir 2012).

It has to be acknowledged that insight is also hampered by the clash of partisan, highly ideological points of view that the subject seems time and again to invite. Anyone remotely interested in authorship, publishing, and reading will have a hard time avoiding the recurring heated debates on the digitisation of books. Technosceptics and technophiles can be regularly observed at loggerheads in a dialogue of the deaf. This is not something to pass over lightly. Mediums change the way we think: they create a framework (or *habitus*) for understanding the world. They 'change our textual mind' (Van der Weel 2011a). Knowing that the changes that are upon us are epochal, but not knowing how exactly they will express themselves – and thus how they will affect us – causes understandable anxiety.

This book has the ambition to present a more dispassionate appraisal in the face of the heated debates on the subject of digital textuality one may encounter any day on Internet forums, blog posts, discussion lists, and so on. As editors we are not committed to a particular stance, though individual authors may be. We neither take the position that the digital future spells the end of a Golden Age of the Book, nor shrug off the book as a relic from a bygone era while impatiently awaiting a Golden Digital Future. We simply observe that even as digital developments occur fast – and are clearly unstoppable – the book is still prominently amongst us. We believe that people still live as *homo typographicus* in the Order of the Book, and that we cannot begin to understand the present transformations, let alone the future, without a thorough historical consciousness. For the Order of the Book is the product of centuries.

Indeed, the paper book's long history and the resulting typographic habituation, apart from being the cause of a fair amount of controversy as to the significance of the digital revolution, probably constitute a fundamental reason why the digital book has been so slow to find favour with readers – quite apart from the reasons already suggested. Over the centuries the paper book has been perfected as a reading machine, and people have been socialised as book users to such an extent that they rarely reflect on what it is and does. It does what it is supposed to do remarkably well, and few people have felt an urgent need for change.

As already suggested, a historical perspective is particularly useful in appraising the extent to which digital developments are turning a thoroughly familiar world of books and reading upside down. As this process is taking its course, we find that books and reading represent a largely unspoken set of cultural norms (a *habitus* in Bourdieu's terms). As Arianne Baggerman shows in her contribution, these norms can be made more visible and explicit by means of a comparison with what is about to replace them. Our familiar textual world was always book-lined, and books were predictably – and therefore comfortably – tangible, present, permanent, and linear by nature. As such, books could, for example, serve as *lieux de mémoire*, both for the stories they contain and for anything that the user associates with them, privately, or in common with others.

Whatever it may be in the process of becoming (and that is by no means clear), digital text by contrast is decidedly protean and elusive. It is certainly no longer tangible, present, permanent, and linear.

When all we had to access information was paper, besides the human brain (and perhaps microfilm), there was a premium on ordering it so as to stave off everthreatening chaos. Linearity is one of the most fundamental ordering principles.

The computer as an access interface to the world's textual resources is putting an end to that. The Control+F key combination efficiently cuts through order and chaos alike. Whether or not hypertext has a future as a form of non-linear communication, now that the notion of linear text has been technologically subverted, it is possible that in the longer run textual linearity will be regarded as merely one mode of representation. Historically it may be found to have been tightly but contingently bound up with oral communication – by definition linear, because it is time based – and the printed book – essentially linear, though it can be used in non-linear ways. This leads to the question to what extent textual linearity was always a simplification, or even idealisation, of reality. At the very least linear textuality must be regarded as merely one of many possible representations of knowledge and culture. In scholarly and scientific research, for example, visualisations, which are non-linear, are increasingly common alternative representations, as are infographics in news media.

As Alain Giffard suggests, while the book's interface over time melted away into the background, the digital interface (at least for now) is placing itself firmly in the foreground. The digital interface does not even primarily deal with the text itself, but with the means of accessing the text (the approach to the text). Selection and gaining access went from acts that precede the reading act to acts that are firmly embedded in the act of reading itself. With the reader permanently submerged in a sea of texts, reading is a matter of constant selection: deciding which fragments are relevant; which links are to be followed. This introduces an extra layer in the medial interface of digital (online) reading. The implication is an increasing responsibility for the reader.

If Giffard has already called attention to what he terms the 'industrial' side of our everyday digital reading, there is, as Bernhard Rieder explains, an even more industrial side to digital reading in the form of Big Data processing. Digital book forms allow us to deal with text numerically and statistically, yielding different kinds of knowledge. Replacing the human reader by a machine, sophisticated forms of pattern recognition and statistical analysis can extract knowledge from machine-readable textual data that is not (or only with great difficulty) available from human reading. In turn, this suggests different research questions to ask and generates alternate forms of output. Machine-produced, the results can be instantly graphed, mapped, and visualised in all sorts of ways rather than communicated through linear text requiring painstaking analysis by human researchers.[3]

In these various ways digital textuality affects us cognitively by transforming reading as an intellectual practice. But as Anne Mangen suggests in her contribution, the reader's cognitive performance may also be affected by the haptics of handling the material substrate from which texts are read. People may be reading (and writing!) more than ever before, but we need to ask ourselves *how* they read. Technology is not transparent, and the technologies of paper and screen each offer distinctly different 'affordances' that are suspected to affect cognitive engagement with the text. One of the affordances of the screen is the potential of performing the reading activity on the network, and notably in a Web 2.0 environment, so it makes a huge difference socially what substrate people read from. In this context, too, Mangen stresses the need to ask ourselves about the possible cognitive consequences.

Just as digitisation affects the way we relate intellectually and cognitively to the book as individuals, it has fundamental social and economic effects. What will happen with the book as a communication device, and with the book trade as a cultural industry is the subject of Miha Kovač's contribution. As Kovač sets out to show, the book trade is already undergoing major upheavals, and ineluctably heading for further change. Many if not most of the changes are entirely accidental: the unintended 'side' effects of digitisation, such as the fact that length and print run cease to play a determining role in publishing; that the digital file format instigates very different ownership relations than does the physical book; that consumers who have invested in an e-reading device, especially the Kindle (although it is likely that the Kobo reading infrastructure will have the same effect), appear to be reading more English language books. In publishing, the value chain changes as a consequence of the 'disintermediation' of traditional links: Amazon for example acts as publisher, wholesaler, and bookseller rolled into one. Though bookshops are beginning to disappear from the street – assuming for the moment that reading will survive in the increasingly mediatised, multimedial, and multimodal user experience – buying books will not disappear. It will instead be mediatised by moving online. Online the act of buying is of course easily 'socialised', through 'I just bought ...' buttons and such like. In this, bookselling follows the wider trend of mediatisation (and attendant socialisation) of human interaction with the world, which is also exemplified by reading, as we shall see below.

Many critics have drawn attention to the ways in which Web 2.0 may compromise privacy. Reading online forms an interesting case in point, as Kovač personally discovered. When his iPad had failed to switch off while it was charging overnight with the Kobo reader application running, the next morning he found himself the recipient of a congratulatory email awarding him with the 'best in bed award' for reading three nights in a row and for reading more than three hours during the night.

The privacy issue mentioned by Kovač would, if anything, become even more relevant if reading, too, were to become more actively socialised, as Bob Stein argues it should in his contribution. In an indirect sense this is already common practice, with people widely making use of social networks to report on their reading activities. But Stein proposes building a digital infrastructure for the express purpose of exchanging reading experiences and annotations directly between readers, who may be far flung. The usefulness of such an exchange particularly in an educational setting is obvious. Stein's expectation is that digital connectivity of this kind, especially in a Web 2.0 context, will lead to a greater sense of (virtual) community at large. In this respect technology is often regarded as a force for a better world, with echoes of a post-capitalist utopia. As we saw earlier, digitisation of other modalities has already led to a dwindling importance of ownership, for example; it is certainly not unthinkable that this may also happen in the case of books.

Fascination with the un-paper-like potential of the new medium is, understandably, widespread. Creating new 'digital objects' can only be done with an open mind to the inherent possibilities of the digital medium. It involves the moulding of meaning within the constraints of a medium, using its particular expressive capabilities. Someone cutting some meaning in stone would think twice before picking up a hammer and chisel. Using unwieldy material such as stone or birch bark, popular in parts of Tsarist Russia, will lead to short intense messages. In the case of the computer people can afford to rattle on and let the reader decide what is relevant. This places greater emphasis on the interface as a filtering mechanism. The materiality of the expression is closely related to the form and so has a major influence on the content of a work. But other factors are at play. How the digital possibilities will be used in any given instance will depend essentially on four factors:

1   the technological nature of the substrate (e-ink as a technology has, at least currently, different possibilities than tablets and other backlit screens);
2   the nature of the work and the intention of the author;
3   economic considerations; and, last but not least,
4   users' demands or needs.

(1) Today we often hear the mantra that it is only 'content' that matters, while form is contingent. This is clearly untenable. The physicality of ownership is what made the metaphor of devouring a book's contents (as explored by Baggerman) speak so powerfully to the imagination; it is what enables one to make the text truly one's own, literally as well as figuratively. True, one might argue that, even if there is some substance to this, it has no bearing on the textual content, on the actual words being published, which after all remain the same across substrates. But even if this were so, there are other ways in which the immaterial nature of the digital text as well as the material nature of the digital substrate affects the way we experience digital textuality. For example, digital technology not only *enables* multimodality and different lengths for example, but quite possibly even *favours* enhancement and other, especially shorter, lengths. If fixity versus flux, linearity versus non-linearity, closure versus open-endedness matter as textual characteristics, then form matters.

(2) The e-book revolution may have been slow in starting, but it is accelerating. Anyway digital reading has already become normal as a result of the popularity of social media, email, blogging, etcetera. As digital reading becomes more widespread, replacing paper-based reading, this might naturally lead to authors experimenting with new ways of communicating literature and other texts. Indeed, technological innovation might well result in genre innovation. If an

'enhanced' digital book (the generic term for objects that make use of the range of digital possibilities) were created by an author, it might not be instantly clear in what category it fits, and whether we would like to call it a book or something else, but we could at least agree that it is a new 'creative product' of some sort. If, on the other hand, a publisher or editor was responsible for a new, enhanced edition of an existing work, it might be argued that this produced a fundamental departure from the original creative expression, regardless of whether we agree to still call it a book.

(3) Digital technology not only enables but often actively favours the use of other modalities besides text such as sound and still and moving images. Certainly one of the effects of this convergence is a greater number of possible ways to disseminate knowledge besides text, especially visualisation in scholarship and science. But it has to be borne in mind that producing audio, visual, and film material of a decent quality is not cheap. Economic considerations thus limit the technological potential of the digital medium.

(4) Apart from economic considerations, there is the more fundamental question: *should* a novel be presented as if it were a film? *Doctor Zhivago* as a novel has a distinctly different impact than the movie. They are two different expressions of a story line. Ultimately the crucial question is surely: what techniques and devices might answer to user's needs? Reference works have always been among the first to be successfully digitised. A bird catalogue would be electronically enhanced by audio files with the various bird songs, next to text and pictures. A second enhancement might be short videos with the flight patterns. This not only makes sense from a technological perspective, and is economically feasible, but it also enhances the books' usefulness to the reader. Similarly, in educational and scholarly texts, the book is used as a tool. Designers have to provide the digital equivalent of making dog ears, writing in the margins, underlining, etc. They have to match the characteristics of a present-day genre with technological possibilities. In the final analysis it seems likely that authors will follow users more than blaze a trail themselves, as they are dependent on the readers' favour.

At the onset of the digital deluge books had evolved into perfect reading machines. If we start using screen technology, it is one thing to identify what we lose in the process (which is a natural human tendency), but quite another and, it might be argued, an ultimately more fruitful one to identify how that screen technology might shape the activities that we always used paper for. Screen technology is likely to determine our learning and entertainment habits. Awareness and eventually new insights are essential if we are to have any hopes of influencing the direction in which screen technology can develop.

As scholars, what can we do in the face of the amazing speed with which the digital revolution is taking place? We can define concepts, conceptualise, taxonomise, ontologise, devise a vocabulary, and, last but not least, analyse with iron discipline. That is what the thoughtful essays that make up this book set out to do.

## Acknowledgements

The essays that follow, with the exception of Alain Giffard's, which was especially commissioned, originated in the Unbound Book conference held in The Hague and Amsterdam, 21-23 May 2011. All presentations are available on video via the website http://e-boekenstad.nl/unbound/, which also hosts all blogs on the conference. They appear, again with the exception of Alain Giffard's, in the order in which they were presented in the conference. This conference was a joint project of: Create-IT Applied research centre at the Hogeschool van Amsterdam, the Institute for Network Cultures, and the department of Book and Digital Media Studies, Leiden University.

This volume would not have been possible without a great deal of help. First of all we would like to thank the other members of the conference organising committee, Morgan Currie and Geert Lovink. To make the conference financially possible we could depend on the generous sponsorship of Stichting Lezen, Brill Publishers, Gottmer Uitgevers Groep, Boom Uitgevers, Nbd/biblion, OCLC, CPNB, SIOB, Van Duuren Media/Yindo, Springer, Public Library Amsterdam (OBA), National Library (KB), Museum Meermanno, Letterkundig Museum, Virtueel Platform, Mondriaan Foundation and the SIA-RAAK grant for the Amsterdam E-book City project (# 2009-14-3H). We thank them all.

Last but by no means least, we thank our tireless copy-editor Morgan Currie, and gratefully acknowledge the helping hands of Mariya Mitova and Ruud Hisgen.

*Leiden and Amsterdam*
*Adriaan van der Weel and Joost Kircz*

### Notes

1   As Ann Blair convincingly argues in *Too much to know: Managing scholarly information before the modern era* (2010), we moderns are not the first to be affected by the condition.
2   See http://e-boekenstad.nl/unbound/index.php/program/.
3   In his article 'Conjectures on world literature' (2000), Franco Moretti terms this sort of data analysis 'distant [as against "close"] reading'. He elaborates on the concept in *Graphs, maps, trees: Abstract models for literary history* (2005).

**Celsius Library Wallpaper[1]**

# 'I read the titles on the spines and remember'

## *The unbound reader of the future*

Arianne Baggerman

What is a book? Answering this simple question has recently become an almost impossible task. As digital technologies are developing faster and faster, our ideas and definitions have to be updated on a daily basis. Or have we already reached the point where the question must be reframed? Should we ask ourselves: What *was* a book?

Recently I have become more and more aware of the increasing gap between technological development and scholarly insight, with the latter lagging ever more behind. Publications in the field of the digital book, and more generally the Internet and World Wide Web, have an even shorter durability than the digital content they discuss.

I will give two examples. Two years ago I attended a lecture by Hans Willem Cortenraad, the director of the Dutch Centraal Boekhuis. The Centraal Boekhuis is the Dutch national logistic service centre linking publishers and booksellers (Cortenraad 2009). This institution has been storing and distributing books for 135 years. Books made of paper of course. But the director saw great possibilities in making this center a distributor of e-books as well. He had these expectations less than a year before the introduction of Apple's iPad. Now, two years later, the plans of the Centraal Boekhuis have been overtaken by reality. Apple is becoming a main distributor of e-books, charging a much higher percentage of the retail price (30 percent) than the Centraal Boekhuis ever has (Haakman 2011). And Apple does much less than the Centraal Boekhuis, whose trucks are still a well-known sight on Dutch roads – but for how much longer?

Similarly, some years ago the idea that paper books and e-books would co-exist peacefully was widely held. It was thought that paper books and e-books could be two partly overlapping, complimentary domains. Anthony Grafton, for example, concluded his otherwise very critical book *Codex in crisis* in 2008 with the optimistic prediction that digitisation projects 'will illuminate, rather than eliminate, the unique books and prints and manuscripts that only the library can put in front of you. For now, and for the foreseeable future, if you want to piece together the richest possible mosaic of documents and texts and images, you'll have to do it in those crowded public rooms where sunlight gleams on varnished tables, as it has for more than a century, and knowledge is still embodied in millions of dusty, crumbling, smelly, irreplaceable manuscripts and books' (Grafton 2008, 60). His idea in 2008 that the future of the book would be the best of two worlds has nevertheless proved to be too optimistic. As Grafton himself was soon to discover, e-books would rapidly replace rather than supplement paper books.[2]

In the world of Dutch University libraries, too, the terms 'de-selection' and 'off-site storage' have become as familiar as 'digital durability'. 'Because that's what happens: the books gradually disappear from the library because most scholarly information can be consulted via "the Internet", stored "in the cloud".' This quote does not come from one of the critics of digitisation a few years ago but is actually the opening sentence of the UKB (the association of the Dutch University Libraries and the National Library) Policy Plan published recently under a title that is meant to be neither ironic nor pessimistic but rather triumphant: *The scientific libraries on their way to 'the cloud'*. This publication announces the plan to expand the retention policy for paper journals to the book collections as well: 'Point of departure in this may be that the shared collections of all the libraries will store at least one printed copy' (*De wetenschappelijke bibliotheek*, 2011).[3]

For me as a historian, this is the right moment to look again at some of the old arguments of those who in the past decade have propagated digitisation, and then to ask the question, are their arguments still viable – if they ever were? Many arguments of those who were in favour of e-books have evaporated into thin air.

Data carriers of digital content have a durability of five years at the most, Alberto Manguel wrote fifteen years ago (Manguel 1996, 78). Strangely enough, durability has hardly developed since. It's still a 'challenge' both technically and economically, which could be the reason why this important aspect is never discussed, as Jan Ferrari and Nanette Pfiester conclude in a recent article on the subject (Ferrari and Pfliester 2011, 77-78). A recent Dutch report, *Toekomst voor ons digitaal geheugen* ('Future for our digital memory') (2010), confirms that preservation of digital information still is a major problem. This report does not make any predictions about the solution to this problem. In *Digitizing Collections: Strategic Issues for the Information Manager*, Lorna M. Hughes makes 'preservation' the first in her list of what she calls the wrong motives for digitisation. Preservation is a wrong motive, 'because digital formats are not suitable for preservation at this time [...] A digital "master copy" is not a "preservation master"' (2004, 51-52). Other incorrect arguments from her list include the desires 'to save space' and 'to save money'. As yet 'digital durability' is only an attractive sounding alliteration, and the expectation of the advocates of digitisation some years ago that this problem would be solved in the nearby future has not come true.

Another example of an argument for digitisation which has been overtaken by the facts is that e-books are supposedly better for the environment than books made of paper. This argument has lost its value since we know that Google and such companies are heavy users of energy, while at home computers and other electronic devices consume more and more energy. Google's servers require half a watt in cooling for every watt they use in processing. Their newly built data centre in Dallas, for example, 'can be expected to demand about 103 megawatts of electricity – enough to power 82,000 homes' (Strand 2008, 64). Randall Stross (2009, 19) points out that in 2006 data centres across the U.S. already used more energy than all the nation's television sets put together. When e-books and e-articles are home-printed the energy costs and environmental costs (toner, paper) rise enormously compared to paper books. Paper books are in all respects more durable than e-books. Recycling old books is certainly better for the environment than recycling old e-book readers or iPads.

The rhetoric of the debate on e-culture, especially on the side of the pros, is also rapidly wearing out. A good example of this phenomenon is a study by Mark Bauerlein, titled *The dumbest generation: How the digital age stupefies young Americans and jeopardizes our future* (2008). The author is a former director of research and analysis at the American National Endowment for the Arts. He calls a long list of witnesses for the prosecution. For instance, it has become clear that the great investment by the American government in ICT did not result in a more intelligent generation – on the contrary. Traditional knowledge is vanishing, but new skills needed to make use of modern information technology and to search the Internet are equally lacking among young people. The author's main complaint, however, is the limitless optimism of politicians and opinion leaders about the skills that young people will develop while playing computer games. The tone of this book, published in 2007, is today dated. Who still believes in a new 'generation Einstein'? Which parent still believes that computer games contribute to the education of their children? Which teacher still thinks that hours spent on Internet will raise the IQ of the pupils? Even the facts that Bauerlein mentions are now dated, after the introduction and widespread uptake of the smartphone and blackberry. What is more, the discussion itself has changed: it is no longer a discussion for or against digital culture, but the question, how can we preserve some of the content and values of traditional culture in a digital environment?[4] The digital culture no longer needs any defense; it is there already. Still, the future remains unpredictable, and enthusiasm for digitalism today resembles the enthusiasm for nuclear power in the 1960s. There is also another resemblance: the dangers are unknown or ignored.[5]

The effects and tendencies sketched by Bauerlein in 2007 are also visible in the Netherlands. Since 2000 the Dutch government has invested large sums in the digitisation of our cultural heritage, the collections of archives, museums, libraries, and in making these more accessible to young people. This is done by creating stylish websites and weblogs, by twittering, and by creating all kinds of web communities and forums in the field of culture. At the same time much of the government budget for education is spent on ICT in schools. In 2010 the number of computers in secondary schools was five times higher than 15 years ago: one computer for every four pupils (Schols, Duimel and De Haan 2011, 91). Recently the Netherlands Institute for Social Research published a report on the use of the Internet for cultural purposes among teenage school children (ibid).[6] The outcome of this study is devastating. I will give a few examples. Two per cent of these children visited the website 'cultuurplein.nl' (culture square); the same percentage visited the website 'geheugen van Nederland' (The memory of Holland). Only 'museumkennis.nl' (museum knowledge) has a higher score: three per cent (ibid 38). It turned out that one factor is all-important for participation in culture among teenagers. This is the physical environment: museums, theaters, libraries, or concert halls that parents take their children to (ibid 79-80, 83-84, 124). These parents' investments also determined the participation of their children in digital culture; they were the few who visited the cultural websites mentioned.

The use of ICT in schools has no significant influence on the participation of pupils in culture. I cite the report: 'It is remarkable that this research shows that the intensity of education in the field of culture or ICT does not contribute to the intensity with which students seek content on Internet, make contact or even create new media content.' The creation of new content by Internet users was always one of the hobbyhorses of the gurus of the new digital age. However, a teenager who writes and performs music and puts a clip on YouTube is a *rara avis*, an exceptionally rare bird, the report concludes (ibid 114). The same report also dismantles another vision of the future often sketched by digital believers to silence their opponents: older generations, the so-called 'digital immigrants', cannot judge the effect of digital culture on younger generations, often called 'digital natives' (ibid 70). The idea was that 'digital natives', those who grew up with the Internet, would not have the negative effects common among the older generation, such as loss of concentration or problems with multi-tasking. The recent report points in the opposite direction: the ICT capabilities of young people are in general worse than those of their parents. They usually have no idea of the basics of digital technology and are hardly capable of doing an adequate Internet search. Only a minority of young people have developed digital skills. Few teenagers know how to install an anti-virus program, execute a complicated Internet search, check information found on the Internet, or make an on-line comparison between products. Their fathers do this better. Surprisingly, most teenagers (57 per cent) agree that their digital capabilities are overrated by adults (ibid 84). Strangely enough, the University Library of Amsterdam ignores this insight and states in an official policy declaration of 2011, 'Especially Bachelor students are well trained in being distracted while reading because of the many applications of pc, laptop, or tablet' (Berkhout 2011, 16). This is one of the arguments used to transform the university library into a social meeting place or modern 'village square', no longer centred around the reading room, but around a cafe. This transformation of university libraries can be seen around Europe.

E-books are not durable and not good for the environment; the discussion between pros and cons is only of historical interest, and the so-called generation Einstein has been dismissed. In the meantime, digitisation is a run-away train thundering forward – but certainly not toward the destination that was originally announced. However, so much money and energy is invested and so many people are depending on the great digital project that no one wants to hear anything about less desirable side effects. Unfortunately, research into the effects of digitalism on the human mind and behaviour takes years. For governments to formulate and implement a policy on the issue takes even more time.

Maybe it is time to re-invent the book.

This probably was the reasoning by the Samsung company, which has announced the introduction next year of the paper phone. I quote from the announcement: 'an advanced "thin-film" flexible paper computer (…) This computer looks, feels and operates like small sheets of interactive paper.' You can use it by 'flipping the corner to turn pages, or writing on it with a pen. You fold or bend the page to move forward in a book. Now, with this device, you can do that on your phone, too' (Haptic 2011). The inventor of this new gadget in computer land – computers, mobile phones, televisions shaped in the form of bound interactive sheets made of graphene – has the firm belief that, 'This is the future. Everything is going to look and feel like this within five years.'[7] Here we see a return to the bound book with pages that can be turned. Including, of course, all the functions that are now in a smart-phone.

At first sight this is very efficient, but it is precisely the multimedial quality that makes this new e-paper-phone/book under construction inferior to the traditional book made of paper. The link with the Internet disrupts the concentration that the paper book facilitates. Physical books favour long-form attention, and thus long-form discursive texts and arguments.[8] This is the essence of the argument made by Nicholas Carr in his recent *The shallows: What the Internet is doing to our brains*. Linear reading, which is the reading of printed books, Carr says, stimulates creativity, critical thinking, and profundity. The Internet, by contrast, stimulates primary functions, such as hand-eye-coordination, quick reflexes, and the processing of visual information. Carr's rather cautious conclusions are founded on recent research in neuroscience. These studies show a great lack of concentration among young 'digital natives' compared to older 'digital immigrants' (2010, 141-142). The strengthening of primary functions is relatively small. Young 'digital natives' are sponges that absorb irrelevant information. This is confirmed by the above-mentioned and even more recent Dutch report, which concludes that since children are in general less at home in the world of ICT than their fathers, they profit less from the possibilities offered by the Internet.

The new digital book with digital paper probably will have lots of apps, but one application will be missing: an app that stimulates the concentration of the reader, an app that counters the multi-mediality of the e-book. Libraries will return to an earlier stage: rooms with e-book-readers, expensive and thus chained, like the books in Renaissance libraries. Library rooms can meanwhile be redone with fashionable wallpaper, printed with the spines of books, the newest hot thing among designers.[9]

Let's examine which crucial properties of the paper book should be saved in the development of the electronic book. In light of this new development, the reappearance of the book, this question is all the more urgent. It is clear that first of

**The Andrew Martin Library wallpaper**

all, one property of the new medium should go: multi-mediality. Also the possibility to change published texts constantly should disappear. A text should have a standard version, like the printed paper book. An author or an editor is allowed to change texts, of course, but digital books should also have the property to be published formally as a first or, say, revised second edition, etc. The idea of published standard texts is an essential element in the development of (Western) culture, and this cornerstone should not be lost. An e-book standard-text should be at least as durable as a paper edition. This quality should be preserved, as books are the collective memory of our culture.

My research has, in addition to this, shown that paper books are equally important for the personal, individual memory of men and women. Paper books have played an essential role in the formation of a sense of individuality ever since their introduction centuries ago. New e-books should have the potential to answer to this need. This argument has so far not been brought forward in the discussion, and therefore I will sketch, with the help of some examples, the way Dutch readers in the eighteenth, nineteenth, and twentieth centuries remembered their lives with the help of their books.

Dutch memoirs and autobiographies of this era are full of fond memories of reading and often point out the formative role books played during childhood and teenage years. The metaphors these readers use for the act of reading are significant. They did not simply read their books – they devoured them, absorbed them, and sucked them in. The early twentieth century politician Ferdinand Domela Nieuwenhuis, for example, had strong memories of the 'great *History* by Schlosser in 18 volumes (...). Loaded with all these bound volumes, I carried my loot with great joy to the quarter where I used to work' (1910, 14). Later on his favorite book was *The Life of Jesus* by Feuerbach: 'and after I had devoured the compelling books of Ludwig Feuerbach, yes, devoured is the right word, because they were a new revelation on for me, and I had to break with many of the old traditions'. J.H. Schaper, a politician from a later generation, remembers the 'great joy' he felt when he bought at a market 60 issues of the Dutch translation of Adolf Steckfus's *History of the world* for only 35 cents. He tells his readers that he was very fond of this work and 'devoured' its content (1933-1935, 16). The cherished memories of the former schoolteacher Aegidius Timmerman about his juvenile reading are very physical as well. He too used to 'devour' his books (1983, 25). Man of letters Just Havelaar was not driven by hunger for books, but thirst, and he soaked them up: 'Yes, the way we soaked the word of Van Deijssel up in those days: that was real reading!' (1926, 47) The eighteenth-century politician Boudewijn Donker Curtius describes his passion for books as even more than hungry or thirsty. From an early age on he vigorously 'fell to his books' (Van Boven 2010, 37).

In the memory work of these autobiographers, their books function as stepping-stones for their minds. That is why books are not only remembered for their content but in their full materiality – taste, smell, weight, dog-ears, and other signs of former readers, etc. The childhood memories of Willemine Mees, born in 1887, for instance, are bound 'to a very old and worn book of fairy tales' (n.d.). Pedagogue Jan Ligthart could remember vividly the tracts handed out at Sunday school, 'some were matte, others were printed on glossy paper, some with, some without prints, small and large' (1950, 118). As in the cases of Nieuwenhuis and Schaper there is a strong physical element to his interactions with his books: 'Just like my sister with her doll's dresses, I played with my books'. Remembering the 'old, well-thumbed volumes of *Graphic* and *Art journal*' in the bookshelves of his father helped man of letters Aart van der Leeuw to bring back his childhood years: 'These were the most faithful friends of my childhood. The bindings, cracked and torn loose, showed that they were old companions, but the thousands of tears and scribbles inside them revealed how much they suffered from my love and treatment. The pages were all the more dear to me because of these signs of intimacy. I rustled these papers through my fingers going from one print to the other' (1914, 28). Railway engineer Gerrit Middelberg remembers exactly how he found his first book in a foreign language 'in our book rack' and how it looked: 'it was a well-bound book with nice illustrations' (n.d.). Mathilde Berdenis van Berlekom, suffragette, tells her readers about the 'big book chest' in the upstairs room with a 'strange smell', where she discovered a treasure of 'old books in brown covers, including novels by Dickens' (n.d.). Public servant Frederik Nagtglas remembers vividly how, in the year 1845, for the first time he bought a book at an auction, 'a nice, parchment-bound copy of the *Hollandsche spectator*' (1977, 54). Femina Muller remembers how much she was impressed by a performance of Vondel's famous play Gijsbrecht van Amstel, and that the same evening she read and re-read 'the old edition of [Vondel's] tragedies, in a parchment-bound book in two volumes' (1907, 52).

Those relics from the past existed not only in the minds of their former readers; they were often still around in their material form. These books were frozen memories, waiting for the right occasion to reunite with their former readers. Such occasions could be the removal of bookcases for new homes, or rearranging the order of shelves after having received new books as presents for a birthday or for Christmas. Eventually, children's books were moved to the attic, waiting for a second life in the hands of a new generation of young readers. Nagtglas and his brothers and sisters, for instance, read novels 'already read to shreds' by their mother, with the result that those books were 'even more worn out than before'. Apie Prins explored the book case of his father: 'he had a lot of books by Jules Verne, gilt-edged, and the works of Darwin, which I had to read, [...], and Goethe and Schiller complete [...], and the *Odyssey*, in Greek with wonderful letters, and the *Winkler Prins [Encyclopaedia]* and *Don Quixote*, and *Gulliver's travels*, and *Mazeppa* with illustrations, and a lot more' (1958, 108). The father of the later physician Hendrik Burger anticipated his children's love of reading. In his study he kept a 'colossal book chest with green curtains; on the lowest shelf there were also books that could be read by children. The most favorite of these books was *The book of the Cape*, Kolbe's description of the Hottentot people, a book that used to be placed on a chair as long as a child was not tall enough to be seated at the table for reading' (1949, 18). As a child, the later journalist Alexander Cohen discovered in the attic 'a book chest made of white wood, of which I hid the key, to prevent my father from doing so; there were among other books a Shakespeare in a popular illustrated edition, Heine's *Buch der Lieder*, *Ivanhoe*, *Waverley*, *Kenilworth*, and *Red gauntlett*; Thier's *Histoire du Consulat et de l'Empire* [...], *De drie musketiers* [The three musketeers], [...]'. In this attic with all these books he was, as he says, 'in his kingdom'. 'After choosing one book or another, I climb another ladder to the most remote and safe part of the house, a platform under the rafters' (1936, 33-34). The 'sanctuary' of Jan Ligthart was even smaller, a light shaft in the kitchen with a perimeter of one meter. This 'little room' was his private library where he hoarded all his treasures, mainly tracts from Sunday school, which he carefully catalogued. Because of his father's defenselessness against an insistent salesman, this little library was constantly enlarged with mostly still uncut books and journals. 'There I lay down, near the light window, looking at the dark plates of the *Bijbelsch magazijn voor alle standen* and the hunting scenes from *De aarde en haar volken*'. Years later Ligthart found them back 'in some raisin boxes of rough whitewood. Then I repossessed them. And they have not left me since.' At the time Ligthart was writing, his childhood books had acquired a new function; they had become the 'favourite picture books' of his grandchildren.

In the memory of autobiographers books are much more than content alone, the only property advocates of digitising projects today are aware of. The strong interrelation of bound paper books with personal identity also becomes clear in the bookish way autobiographers sometimes describe themselves – 'I went to school like a duodecimo edition of my father' (Timmerman 1983, 61) – and in the titles of many nineteenth-century autobiographies: 'book of life'.[10] For many generations books in their full physical appearance were a haven of rest and tranquility, a tool for the development of empathy, and in the end, a memory palace.

Or to say it differently: 'There was something calming in the reticence of all those books, their willingness to wait years, decades even, for the right reader to come along and pull them from their appointed slots. *Take your time*, the books whispered to me in their dusty voices. *We're not going anywhere*' (2010, 12). This is a quote from Nicholas Carr's book *The shallows* of 2010.[11] To illustrate this special and not easy to define quality of physical books, I can quote the memoirs of the popular Dutch eighteenth-century writer Gerrit Paape: 'I am surrounded by my paper and useful friends. Each moment they are ready to suit me (…) Sometimes I place myself in total tranquility in front of my bookcase. I read the titles on the spines and remember, while reading them, the content of each book. In this way I let them perform in review, without exhausting my people (…) No king or prince can be so happy with his regiments of soldiers, as I am with my books' (1792, 147).

The bound paper books these historical readers inherited or bought served as an extension of their personal, individual memory. That phenomenon is completely different from farming out memory to computers and providers, which weakens the memory function in the human brain and consequently will result in a loss of identity (Baggerman 2011a, 19-20; 2011b, 455-541). Books in their material form have always functioned as a supplement to our memory and a challenge and improvement of our personal memory skills at the same time.

The book of the future should have extensive durability; it should support the concentration of its readers, should contain unchangeable standard-texts, and should have that wonderful quality of becoming part of the memory palace of its individual readers. These requirements may seem too much to ask. However, I suggest a simple solution: the book of the future will be bound and printed in ink on paper. Simply for practical reasons. Paper and ink prevent miscommunication and stimulate concentration. Printed pages are better for the environment than computers and e-readers. Paper is cheap and durable. Books made of paper and ink published during the last five centuries form our collective and individual memory, and, as even Bill Gates, chairman of Microsoft, had to admit, reading bound paper books is much more agreeable than digital reading: 'Reading off the screen is still vastly inferior to reading of paper. Even I, who have these expensive screens and fancy myself as a pioneer of this Web Lifestyle, when it comes to something over about four or five pages, I print it out and I like to have it to carry around with me and annotate. And it's quite a hurdle for technology to achieve to match that level of usability' (Darnton 2009, 69).

## Notes

1   Image from http://orcunceyhan.deviantart.com/art/Celsus-Library-wallpaper-99971708 30-10-2011.

2   In 2010, Grafton had all the alarm bells ringing when the London Warburg Library was threatened with closure, a unique collection based on the Hamburg library of Aby Warburg, rescued from the hands of the Nazis in 1933 to become part of the University of London in 1944. Forty per cent of the books from this collection are not available in the British Library, Grafton stresses in his article in *The New York review of books* (Grafton and Hamburger 2010).

3   About the policy on deselection of the Dutch university libraries see also: http://www.ukb.nl/activiteiten/deselectie.html and http://www.ukb.nl/organisatie/algemenestukken/2010 u ji_Bewaarbeleid.pdf. In the world of public libraries the question is no longer which books have to be deselected, but which libraries do we have to close? According to the Vereniging van Openbare Bibliotheken (Association of Public Libraries), of the more than thousand Dutch public libraries more than three hundred will be closed. The number of libraries in the city of Rotterdam for example will be reduced from 21 libraries to six ('Sluiting bibliotheken is een sociale ramp', 2011).

4   On pp. 168-89 of his recent book *Changing our textual minds: Towards a digital order of knowledge* (2011a), Adriaan van der Weel lists numerous examples of the extensive social consequences of the rapid uptake of the digital (textual) media.

5   See also Tenner (1996). Of biased and irresponsible public management in recent years many more examples could be given, such as willfully ignoring risks at the introduction of the Euro.

6   Research into the digital cultural participation of 12 to 18-year-olds was conducted in 2008 among 1592 students from 167 classes from 32 secondary schools. That was before the rise of smart phones and tablets.

7   From 'Press Release: Revolutionary new paper computer shows flexible future for smartphones and tablets' (2011).

8   Compare the argumentation of Adriaan van der Weel, 'De lezer ontletterd' (2011b, 26-31).

9   For example the Andrew Martin library wallpaper: http://www.occa-home.co.uk/andrew-martin-library-wallpaper.

10  Examples: *Bladen uit het levensboek eener Israelietische*, bewerkt door C.F. Verschoor, 's-Gravenhage, 1915; Simon Hendrik Buytendijk, *Bladen uit mijn levensboek* Nijkerk, [1905]; Abraham Meijer, *Ik zal gedenken. Bladen uit het levensboek*, Amsterdam, 1876; Christiaan Antoon Oudemans, *Losse bladen uit het leven van den generaal Oudemans*, [Amsterdam], [ca. 1880]; Jan-Hendrik Schimmel, *Jan-Willem's levensboek*. Losse bladen, verzameld door H.J. Schimmel, Schiedam, 1896; Carel Vosmaer, 'Bladen uit een levensboek' in: *Eenige schetsen*, Amsterdam, 1860; J.H.F. van der Wall, 'Bladen uit mijn levensboek', *Bataviaasch Nieuwsblad*, 4.12.1926-29.4.1927; Johannes Kuiper, *Wonderlijke leidingen Gods, en Iets uit mijne latere levensjaren: eene bladzijde uit mijn levensboek Bergumerheide*, 1898, 3e ver-

meerderde druk; Johannes Jacobus van Oosterzee, *Uit mijn levensboek voor mijne vrienden*, Utrecht, 1882.

11  Compare the comment on this quote of Lorcan Dempsey (OCLC Chief Strategist and Vice President Programs and Research) on his weblog after his visit of the Annual RLG Partnership Symposium 2010, 'When the books leave the building: The future of research libraries, collections and services': 'It seems they [the books] lied. While many of the books will remain on the shelves for some years to come, it is clear that the exodus has begun. The books are leaving the library' (2011).

# What a book was and what remains

*Thoughts about the future of trade publishing*

Miha Kovač

## An anecdotic approach: Riders of the lost data

I started to write these lines on a hot July afternoon in 2011 in the cafe of the Barnes and Noble bookstore in Georgetown, Washington, D.C. I have known the shop for a long time. I first entered it sometime in the 1990s, and after 2004 I started to return to it on an almost-yearly basis. Back then, the shop – as were all Barnes and Noble bookstores – was considered a huge innovation in bookselling, with a rather unpleasant effect on the rest of the book trade. With its theme-park megastores, an unprecedented number of new titles put on sale, and huge discounts, Barnes and Noble – together with Borders – was often accused of killing small and independent booksellers.

Fifteen years later, in the summer of 2011, the world turned upside down not only for these two bookselling companies but also for the whole book industry: due to bad management, the rise of Internet sales, and the advent of e-books, Borders was on the way to bankruptcy and Barnes and Noble was considered to be one of the last bastions of the shrinking brick-and-mortar book trade.

On that hot July day, the scars of the fight between digital and analogue could be seen both in the bookstore and in its cafe. On the ground floor of the shop, the best place at the entrance was taken by a stand selling Nooks, Barnes and Noble's state-of-the-art e-book reading devices. In the rest of the shop, stationery, toys, music, and DVDs were squeezing out printed books that defensively occupied only one-third of the ground floor and about half of the second and third. In the cafe, some customers had books on their tables. The rest, however, were reading on iPads, Nooks, Kindles, and laptops, very obviously taking advantage of the free Internet access in the shop.

Back home, in my beloved Slovenian backyard, bookshops were still running their business as usual. In the spring of 2011, on a 20-minute walk from the main Ljubljana railway station to the university where I teach, I regularly passed four bookshops. When I returned to the railway station via the Mladinska Knjiga publishing house where I spent the rest of my working day, I encountered three more, not to mention the huge newly refurbished building of the main city public library. Not only visually but also statistically, everything seemed to be quite ok with the Slovene book trade in summer 2011: library loans were up in comparison with

2010, and in the first half of 2011, book sales were down only five per cent in comparison with 2010 – not bad, keeping in mind the fact that Slovenia's economy was in the midst of a recession that hit the European periphery a bit later than its metropolitan centres.

However, as I was writing these lines, the future of the Slovene book trade was as uncertain as it was in the more developed world. In the main Ljubljana bookshop, which stocks around 70,000 titles, about half of the books on sale were in English. A rough estimation, based on the data of the biggest Slovene book retailer, is that books in English represented around 15 to 20 per cent of all Slovene book sales in brick and mortar bookshops. Although based only on anecdotal evidence, thanks to the secrecy of Amazon and other e-book providers about their sales numbers, it was obvious that sales of e-books in English were also slowly gaining momentum in my part of Europe in 2011, taking customers away from brick-and-mortar bookstores. Rather paradoxically, for somebody who from early childhood on spent all his life surrounded by printed books, I was most likely one of the first Slovene Kindle adopters. I shifted all my English book purchases from print to digital in 2009 – a logical consequence of the fact that e-books in English were cheaper than the same titles bought in print format in Slovene bookstores. Soon I was followed by my daughter and many of my academic and publishing colleagues, acquaintances, and friends – and very likely by many other Slovene readers of books in English.

All in all, it seemed only a matter of time before this shift to digital reading would start to influence Slovene brick-and-mortar book sales. Keeping in mind both the fact that Slovene bookshops operate on tight margins and the relatively high percentage of English books sold in Slovene bookshops, losing even half of these sales would be enough to cause trouble for a significant number of Slovenian bookshops.

As Slovenia, like many other European countries, has high Internet penetration and high proficiency in English, it is very likely that similar processes were taking place in other parts of continental Europe as well.[1] At the Digital Book World conference in Frankfurt in October 2011, for example, Michael Tamblyn, vice president of Kobo, stressed that in continental Europe, sales of e-books in English were up 300 per cent in their store in 2010-2011. It therefore made sense to assume that sales of e-books would accelerate in 2012-2013, when the biggest global players were supposed to open e-bookstores in a variety of European languages.

But what is happening to our minds and hearts throughout these processes? Will the advent of e-books and marginalisation of p-books merely change publishing business models? Or will the shift from print to digital – supported by the rise of English as the second-biggest language in the world that makes books in English a viable alternative to books in local languages – change the ways we think and cause an identity shift in continental Europe as more and more people become bilingual readers? And do people who read e-books make meaning out of their reading matter in different ways from people who read only p-books? Are we perhaps living in an era of radical change in information retrieval and dissemination processes similar to what happened in Europe with the advent of print five hundred years ago? Indeed, do we know what is/was a printed book, what printed books do to our minds and hearts, and what remains of all this in the turbulent times of digital transition we live in?

## Three ways to define a book

Jean-Pierre de Tonac, who edited and prepared for publication Umberto Eco's and Jean-Claude Carrière's debate on the future of the book, tried to define the book not only by language and length of the text (as did Eco and Carrière) but by the specific way of reading that the book invokes. In particular, he outlined the differences between linear reading and hypertext:

> But what is a book? And what will change if we read on screen rather than by turning the pages of a physical object? Old fashioned habits, perhaps. A certain sense of the sacred that has surrounded the book in a civilisation that has made it our holy of holies. A peculiar intimacy between the author and reader, which the concept of hypertextuality is bound to damage. A sense of existing in a self-contained world that the books, and along with it, certain ways of reading, used to represent (De Tonac in Eco and Carrière 2011).

It is worth noting de Tonac's loose language while trying to determine differences between linear and hypertextual reading: old fashioned habits will 'perhaps' be lost with the end of the printed book, intimacy between the author and reader is 'peculiar', and the printed book as a self-contained world invokes 'certain' ways of reading – as if de Tonac suspects that differences between reading printed and digital books have an effect both on the content of the message and on the reader. At the same time, he is unable to think about these effects and processes using more specific attributes and adjectives than 'peculiar', 'perhaps', and 'certain', leaving the meaning of these words to be filled in by the reader. On such a basis, it is impossible to start a more in-depth discussion on what is a book.

The reverse of such loose debates on what is a book is a definition that focuses predominantly on a book as a physical object, and as such tries to be mathematically exact. At the June 2008 conference of the Society for the History of Reading, Authorship and Publishing at Oxford Brookes University, in a session titled 'Is there a history of the future of the book?', in his talk about UNESCO and encyclopaedic book definitions, Ruediger Wischenbart demonstrated that throughout the last two hundred years,

> ... it is striking how the same formal elements – a certain number of pages, the purpose of the content being public, and almost always, the fact of the binding

and therefore the limits of a book imposed by its beginning and end – are stated by each definition, while the book's tradition, its cultural role in bringing in a certain quality or sophistication of content, the matter of copyright, the industry around creation and production of books, and many more aspects, are all omitted (Wischenbart 2008).

In other words, what remained unanswered – both in debates of leading European intellectuals about the end of the book and in encyclopaedic definitions of the book – was what the book does as a communication device and how it does what it does. It is as if a magic spell made all those clever people who wrote and read books throughout last 200 years unable to see the peculiarities of their main communication tool, not to mention that only a few were able to see that the book as a physical object has an impact on the structure of communicated content.[2]

But what happened that all of a sudden all these flaws in definitions of the book became visible and debated at conferences on books? Is it only the visual difference between printed books and e-book readers that made such questions legitimate and old ways of defining a book obsolete? In other words, did the move from print to digital enable us to see a set of peculiarities of printed books to which we were blind for the last five hundred years? Or are we dealing with broader shifts in communication paradigms that walk hand in hand with deeper changes in the mentalities of our era?

Let us therefore start with a basic question, namely what a printed book as a communication device does.

## The book as a communication device

At least at first glance, the answer seems to be obvious: the printed book is a device for storing and disseminating information and knowledge – in short, a container of knowledge (see for example Wischenbart 2008) in which a variety of navigation tools are used in order to organise and make accessible the stored information (for more on this see Cope and Phillips 2007). What further characterises p-books is that information stored in them is predominantly in textual or textual/visual form and – as stressed by Eco in debate with Carrière – that the text in them is longer than, for example, information in papers and magazines (for more on this see Eco and Carriere 2011, Kindle edition, 3304-14). This applies to a huge variety of p-book genres: a cookbook or a book on gardening contains more information than a single recipe or a gardening tip published in a daily paper or on the web. A novel is longer than a short story, and a scientific monograph is usually longer and more complex than a single research paper. All these different genres invoke different reading practices. Mangen (2008) and Hillesund (2010) stress that reading a scholarly text requires studious immersion, and reading a novel invokes a more emotional immersion, while browsing through a gardening book or a cookbook invokes more fragmented reading than in the case of fiction and scholarly books.

In short, a printed book is a communication device empowered with navigation tools, used for transmitting longer texts that invoke a variety of different reading practices. In order to further describe how the book does what it does we shall look at the ways in which publishing processes determine format and content of texts stored in printed books and how they influence the meanings of what is read. From this point on, we will shift to the more technical vocabulary of publishing studies and predominantly rely on Genette's concepts of epitext and peritext.

## Formats and marketing of the book

As shown in Gerard Genette's *Paratexts* (1987) and as analysed by Claire Squires in *Marketing literature* (2007), readers' choices are heavily influenced by the paratexts: the visual and physical appearance of a printed book, including design of the front and back cover, blurbs, the name of the author, dedications and inscriptions, prefaces, title of the book, etc. (called peritext by Genette); and by the retail, social, and personal contexts in which the book is put on sale, marketed, and read (epitext).[3] Such effects of paratext on readers were empirically proved at the turn of the twentieth century, when research funded by two British trade publishing houses, Paragon and Penguin, showed that in trade publishing, the cover, i.e., a central part of the peritext, was the key factor in decisions to buy or not to buy the book (Douglas 2008, 130). Furthermore, research commissioned by Orion Publishing emphasised that a good cover 'will encourage the consumer to pick up a book, and the consumer is then five times more likely to buy' (Phillips 2008, 177). In short, at least in trade publishing, the reader's first decision to take a look at the book has little to do with its content: it's the look of the physical book that sparks the first impulse to read or buy it.

This indicates that peritexts and epitexts of printed books attract the reader's attention in a different way than their e-counterparts. At the time of writing, narrative e-books didn't have similarly visually attractive covers as p-books (and in case of e-editions of gardening books and cookbooks, tourist guides, coffee-table books, and health manuals, there was no artwork embodied in the materiality of the book) that would persuade customers to buy them on impulse as is the case with printed books. Furthermore, in classical bookshops customers find books they didn't expect to discover. Metadata of e-books – accompanied with suggestions of other readers – do help in finding books from a specific field more quickly and more precisely than browsing in a brick bookshop but (again, according to anecdotal evidence, as no serious research has been done on this) hints from other readers rarely cause a customer to buy a book from a genre he or she never looks at. As such, marketing tools in an e-book environment diminish the role of surprise and randomness in searching. In 2011 in American bookstores, the reluctance of book readers to give up such accidental browsing led to a practice known as show-rooming: in autumn 2011 a survey conducted by Codex Group revealed that 39 per cent of people who bought (either print or digital) books from Amazon in the last 30 days said that they looked at the book in a brick-and-mortar bookshop before buying it online – as if the marketing power of online retailing and of e-paratext couldn't compete with its analogue and brick-and-mortar counterpart.[4]

Switching back to the language of publishing studies, due to economic and technological differences between e- and p-books, filtering and marketing processes in the e-book retail environment are different from filtering and marketing processes in brick bookstores. Click bookstores don't allow customers to become engaged in unintended shopping for titles in unfamiliar genres in the same way as do brick bookstores, nor can e-books persuade customers to look at them by the mere beauty of their cover or artwork. Besides the fact that, at the time of writing, software didn't allow e-versions of illustrated books to adapt to different screen sizes of colour reading devices in the same way as text-only e-books, the strength of paratext (and in the case of illustrated books, the strength of their layout and design), might be one possible explanation why sales of illustrated e-books and enhanced illustrated e-books haven't gained momentum yet and why as recently as autumn 2011, sales of illustrated printed books were actually growing in us brick bookstores (Shatzkin 2011). According to us Bookstats data, in 2010 e-books comprised 13.4 per cent of adult fiction sales, 3.9 per cent of adult non-fiction, and 1.8 per cent of children's book sales. Enhanced e-books were only around .01 per cent of all book sales (Publishers Lunch 2011).

In other words, the marketing process through which the fleeting attention of the customer is changed into real interest for a book, and then into desire and the action of buying it, is different in the world of narrative p-books than in the world of narrative e-books, and very different in the world of illustrated books. Put more colloquially, given the same content, it is much more difficult to fall in love at first sight with a digital file than with its embodiment as a printed book. Consequently, the reader's decisions about what books to buy and what to read are different in an e-environment than in its analogue counterpart.

## Formats and the symbolic value of the book

Furthermore, in many cases, the visibility and materiality of a printed book have a significant value for its owner. As Van der Weel stresses, 'Besides the material and instrumental value attached to books, books also carry an important symbolic meaning, especially as carriers of knowledge (both religious and secular), and culture… Even a sense of identity might be said to attach to books; hence the persistence of the old saw "show me your book case, and I will tell you who you are". What is important in all these cases is the *visibility* of books, resulting from their materiality, and the obvious ownership relation projected by this visibility' (Van der Weel 2010a).

These p-book-related identities can vary from religious to political, cultural, and ethnic. It is hard to imagine a devoted Christian without a Bible at home, or a true-believing communist (although a rare and almost extinct species these days) without at least one book by Karl Marx on the bookshelf. Additionally, at least smaller nations in Europe link their identity strongly to men and women of letters who wrote in their national languages: being a Slovene, for example, almost requires owning a book of poems by the nineteenth-century romantic poet France Prešeren, who is considered to be one of the founding fathers of the modern Slovene language.

On the other hand, fandom as a more contemporary identity phenomenon relates to a specific book genre instead of the language in which the book is written and as such doesn't require the author to have the same national identity as the reader. Nevertheless, ownership of printed books still matters. Regardless of the fact that in 2011 in the US fiction bestsellers were selling better in e- than in p-format, *Dance with dragons*, the fifth part of George R.R. Martin's *Songs of ice and fire* saga, for example, was selling better in print than in e-format on the first day of the publication in July 2011, clearly indicating that fans wanted to have a physical copy of the book as a part of their Martin collection in their home libraries (Publisher's Lunch 2011). A month earlier, on the other side of Atlantic, during his visit to Poland and Slovenia, Martin attracted thousands to autograph sessions.[5] It is worth mentioning that in Ljubljana, about half of his fans came with English books that were around 30 per cent cheaper than Slovene translations, as if the language of the book they owned and read mattered less than its price. This would have been an outrageous gesture in the eyes of nineteenth and twentieth century Slovene nationalists. I also noticed a fan who turned up with a Kindle. That Martin signed the back of the device using a waterproof pen clearly showed that it's the physical object and not the digital file that carries symbolic value for its owner.

## Education and symbolic capital of printed books

According to research conducted by M.D.R. Evans et al. (2010), having a home library of printed books heavily influences the educational success of children. 'Children growing up in homes with many books get three years more schooling than children from bookless homes, regardless their parents' education, occupation and class', they conclude. 'This is as great an advantage as having university educated rather than unschooled parents, and twice the advantage of having a professional rather than an unskilled father.'

As their research was based on data from the 1990s, when e-books were not yet a serious factor in publishing, they couldn't ask whether an e-book library stored in smartphones or in e-book readers of unskilled parents has the same positive effect on their offspring as a home library of printed books. Neither did available data allow them to see whether a home library full of fantasy and pulp fiction in paperback (in countries where paperbacks existed) had the same effect on education of the children as a library full of more 'snobby, literary, prestigious' hard cover books (Thompson 2010, 35, 37). As a result, we don't know whether printed books as such brought with them symbolic capital that positively influenced children's education, or whether some particular types and genres of books had a richer effect than others.

However, in spite of all these unanswered questions, it is clear that at least in the last decade of the twentieth century, printed books still carried significant symbolic capital.

On the other hand, the immateriality of e-books, their inability to establish an ownership relation projected by their visibility, and their lower prices, will undoubtedly generate lower symbolic capital for e-books in comparison to their printed counterparts. An interesting research question for future historians both of the book and of literature will therefore very likely be how much of an author's symbolic capital was generated variously by the materiality of the book and by the publisher's financial outlay (i.e., by the fact that somebody was willing to invest a significant amount of money to produce and disseminate the author's work).

All this of course remains to be seen – as remains to be seen what such transformations of the book's symbolic capital mean for education and for personal and national identities linked to printed books.

## Book formats and book institutions

With the advent of e-books, it became obvious that both the content of the printed book and its form were closely related to the technology and economy of printing and bookbinding. Simply put, throughout the twentieth century, printing technology didn't allow for the printing of works longer than, say, 1000 pages and shorter than 48; additionally, the economy of printing made financially unsustainable all books that were printed in runs of fewer than 500 to 1000 copies. As a consequence, only those books were published for which the publisher assumed that at least 500 copies would be sold, and which were not longer than 1000 pages and not shorter than 48 pages. These two simple rules – together with limited space on the shelves of brick-and-mortar bookshops – triggered a complicated set of editorial and publishing practices that filtered book content, determined the length of fiction and non-fiction books, and in a way made life easier for readers as only the texts selected by publishers became publicly accessible. Huge quantities of texts written by wannabe authors simply didn't find their way to regular book trade channels.

Furthermore, the professions of publishers, booksellers, and librarians came into being because printed books are complex products to create, physically produce, filter, ship, distribute, market, disseminate, and store. In 2010, for example, the number of professional attendees at the Frankfurt book fair was around 300,000. This global armada of book people produced, marketed, and disseminated books; furthermore, they – very often as an unconscious side effect of their activities – also promoted printed book as a medium and consequently enforced book-reading habits. Never mind how fiercely they competed, quarrelled, or even hated each other, the end effect of their efforts was beneficial to all of them as they helped to create and maintain spaces of book-buying and reading and – through a chain of bookshops and public libraries – made the book and book-reading visible parts of urban landscapes.

In short, in the book business, a set of self-regulated business practices, professions and institutions appeared through which printed books were filtered, produced, marketed, sold, stored, disseminated, and read. Although this was not their primary goal, all these activities and institutions supported and maintained reading practices and influenced the content of the printed books. In Claire Squires' words, in the world of print, the transformation of text into a marketable product called a book 'entails overlapping interpretations, incomplete translations, and a continual shifting of meaning from text to written and consumable object and back again' (Squires 2007, 57).

Now what will happen with all these institutions and professions if e-books take over? And what will happen with the book as a medium if some of these institutions and professions go away?

## Disintermediation: New formats and new institutions?

In 2011, there was only one fair and clear answer to this question: we don't know, as it hasn't happened yet. Nevertheless, it was obvious that the end of the printed book would seriously change not only the urban landscape and the publishing professions, but also the very notion of the book. The reasons for such conclusion are as follows.

In an e-environment, technological and economic pressures that in p-publishing triggered the rise of book professions, determined filtering processes, and the size and length of printed books, are disappearing. First, e-book technology and the economy of e-publishing allow publication of titles that would sell even a single copy; second, there are no upwards or downwards limits to the number of pages; and third, the limitations posed by the number of metres of shelf space in brick-and-mortar bookshops became irrelevant with the advent of e-book stores with unlimited storage capacity.[6]

The consequences of these changes are threefold. Firstly, in the US new book genres such as Kindle Singles have appeared that don't follow classical conventions regarding the length of narrative books.[7] Secondly, some fiction authors have discovered that in an e-environment, they don't need publishers anymore. The most successful among them, such as John Locke, became self-publishing millionaires[8] who hired editorial staff to help them edit their work and – at least in Locke's case – marketed their books by themselves thanks to the marketing experience they had generated in their previous careers.[9] And thirdly, Amazon as the biggest global e-bookseller started to publish e-books and act as a publisher, as did some agents. If these current American trends continue and spread to Europe, the authors, publishers, agents, and e-booksellers of narrative books might globally merge into a new kind of book profession, and some of the intermediaries that exist in the analogue publishing process might be cut out.

But will they? Will e-publishing destroy the entire p-book infrastructure together with bookshops and libraries around the globe, or might these transformation processes slow down? And is such disintermediation of publishing global and unavoidable, or is it predominantly an American phenomenon that could be avoided in the rest of the world merely by deciding to publish e-books on a smaller scale?

In order to answer these questions, we should take a look at three additional sets of trends in the cultural and social environment of the contemporary publishing industry, both supporting and reversing the marginalisation of p-books.

## Global English, controlled reading, and book preservation

At least in continental Europe, an e-supportive trend is the rise of English as a global language. As there is no hard data on the number of people who speak English as a second language and read and buy e-books in English, the evidence is only anecdotal, such as Tamblyn's statement already quoted about the 300 per cent rise of sales of English e-books in continental Europe. In this context, an educated guess might lead to the conclusion that if Pareto's law applies to buyers of English books in continental Europe, a switch of the top 20 per cent of book buyers from print to digital might mean an 80 per cent drop in sales of printed English books. At least for those bookshops in the urban centres of Amsterdam, Ljubljana, and Copenhagen that stock 30 to 40 per cent of books in English, this might have quite unpleasant consequences. If this will be the case, it might represent an important turning point in economic history: for the first time, an overseas competitor will cause a serious problem to an entire industry without physically setting foot in the territories where the battle takes place, achieving all this with products that were not even primarily intended for sales in those territories.

At the time of writing, the growth of English as a second language, and with it the growth of English reading as an e-book accelerating process, seems to be unstoppable. In the long run, however, the economic turmoil in Europe might have some unexpected consequences for the future cultural development of the continent about which I don't dare to speculate.

Counter-trends that might work in favour of print publishing seem to be more controversial and difficult to spot. Let me mention first one obvious example, preservation, then one controversial, the need for privacy. The existence of e-books relies on the supply of electricity, and it is common sense that, similar to a limited number of copies of manuscripts on paper in existence, a limited number of information clouds in which e-books are stored is by definition more exposed to natural and human disasters than hundreds of copies of the same printed book stored in a variety of private, public, and special libraries in different geographic locations. Not to mention that any failure in electricity supply would make all the books in clouds temporarily inaccessible: in short, if we want to store book content safely for a longer period, it still makes a lot of sense to print it.

Privacy, of course, is different matter: while reading an e-book either on a dedicated device or on a tablet, one can simultaneously communicate about what one is reading via social networks such as Twitter or Facebook. Furthermore, e-book-sellers that sell dedicated reading devices and tablets know for each and every customer which books he or she purchases, at which time of the day the user of the device is reading, at what pace the pages are turned, how long he or she reads at a time, what he or she underlines, and what kind of footnotes are made.

In short, e-reading is controlled and public in comparison with reading on paper. At this point it is of course difficult to speculate if such visibility and controllability of previously private reading, together with distractions caused by communicating about the reading experience via social networks, will lead back to print a significant number of book readers once they become fully aware of all this, or if the wish for greater visibility of our private doings is in fact becoming part of our newly born digital mentality and is as such in fact speeding up the digital transformation.

## Conclusion: Indeed, what is a book and what does it do?

If we upgrade the definition of the book in chapter 2.0 on the basis of everything said above, we could describe the printed book as a highly preservable information tool that throughout its materiality and visibility invoked a set of different private and uncontrolled reading practices, influenced by marketing and symbolic effects that were executed through the book's epitext and peritext by a variety of book institutions run by an armada of book professionals.

In the digital world, almost all book marketing and reading practices, together with the symbolic capital of the book, seem to be changing. With these changes the definition of the book is changing too – although more slowly than expected. The fact that in Europe in 2011 e-books were still lagging behind p-books both in terms of preservability and marketing could be seen as a proof that Eco was right when stressing that the printed book as an information device became almost perfect throughout the last 2000 years and as such could not be terminated over night (Eco and Carrière 2011). Therefore, the printed book could be understood as 'part of our second nature' (Kovač 2008) – and destroying a device that became both perfect and part of our second nature requires more than just a few years. It cannot be done only by one or two globally expanding companies. Controversial trends that both support and slow down the global spread of e-books described above seem to confirm this conclusion.

Inside the book business, such controversies are reflected in the fact that in terms of sales and marketing, e-books were to a significant extent parasitically dependent on the peritext and epitext of printed books. When this text was written, it was not clear whether the parasite would kill the host and simultaneously injure itself, or a symbiosis might appear in which p- and e-books would co-exist in a kind of dual economy. It makes sense to assume that in the latter case, book markets will continue to exist, and in the former, they will shrink significantly, until they either turn into something completely different or, just the opposite, e-books will become as preservable as p-books and an e-paratext will appear that allows better marketing practices than the paratext of printed books. Clearly, a happy ending is not guaranteed: when editing of this paper was finished by the end of 2011, the Barnes and Noble bookstore in Georgetown, in which I started to write it, was closed due to inability of the company to pay the rent. In such a context, it is not hard to imagine circumstances in which the disappearance of some book professions might significantly slow down the dissemination of book content, especially if we have in mind that – as shown by Nicholas Carr in *The shallows* – digital civilisation is not a place where immersed and concentrated reading and thinking thrives.

Regardless of the outcome, we can be sure of at least one thing: all scenarios described above will invoke different forms and meanings of reading materials than we knew in print civilisation. Even more, they might invoke a very different understanding of the book as has been described in this paper. Therefore, analysing the transition of the book industry from print to digital (and the behaviour of book professionals and authors in this process) and scrutinising differences between epitexts and peritexts of e- and p-books will be essential in understanding the changed mentalities of contemporary *homo digitalis*. Somewhere deep in these processes are hidden the answers to the questions that I regard as crucial for future book research – namely, how information devices and market forces that drive their production and dissemination interact with our ways of reading and with the way we make meaning out of the material we read.

With this, the contours and deeper meaning of contemporary book studies as a new research field are becoming visible, directing us to a way in which a more in-depth answer to the question 'what is a book, and what does it do to our hearts and minds' might become possible.

## Notes

1   For Internet penetration see http://www.internetworldstats.com.
2   There was of course Marshall MacLuhan, whose dictum 'the medium is the message' needs to be reconsidered in the context of the spread of e-books. Much less notorious Don McKenzie and his work seem to be a better starting point for more theoretical research to understand the consequences of a changed book format. For a recent survey of the implications of the shift to digital textuality see Van der Weel (2011a).
3   A high level of conceptual similarity exists between Thompson's publishing field and Genette's epitext. We leave for the future a more detailed examination of differences and similarities between these concepts.
4   For more on this see http://mediadecoder.blogs.nytimes.com/2011/12/04/book-shopping-in-stores-then-buying-online/.
5   For more on this see http://grrm.livejournal.com/.
6   For more on this see Kovač (2011).
7   A hypothesis for further research might be that Kindle Singles appeared not only because e-technology and the e-publishing economy allow them, but also because shorter texts somehow correspond with a shorter amount of time dedicated to reading in the digital age, as noted by the National Endowment of Arts longitudinal research on reading habits in US. Interestingly, NEA research in 2008 has shown a 3.5 per cent increase in literary reading, however, overall book reading went down 2.3 per cent, according to *Reading at risk*, NEA 2004, and *Reading on the rise*, NEA 2009, both available at http://www.nea.gov.
8   http://lethalbooks.com.
9   For more on this see Mike Shatzkin's blog on 26 June 2011, www.idealog.com, and Locke's own account of his success: http://www.amazon.com/Sold-Million-eBooks-Months-ebook/dp/B0056BMK6K.

# Social reading is no longer an oxymoron

Bob Stein

The word 'social', in the context of reading in the electronic environment, is used to signify a whole range of affordances available to readers, as well as writers. The discussion is often couched in terms that contrast the interactive experience of electronic reading with the straightforward, rather one-directional mode of reading physical books. So the term has tended to suggest a whole panoply of possibilities of dealing with text, such as the ability to annotate it in electronic reading devices and the aggregation of the annotations with those of other people, or discussing and reviewing books on social networking websites.

In the digital realm reading is being disrupted in all sorts of ways pertaining to a whole range of aspects: technical, social, and cultural. At the most obvious level, constraints on the incorporation of modalities are disappearing. Text is now regularly and rather seamlessly intertwined not only with images but also sound, video, and interactive elements. Next to that, instantaneous and global distribution is propelled as much by advancements in technology as by shifts in cultural mindset, such as the rise of the Open Access movement. At the same time, the nature of on-screen reading seems to facilitate a transition toward the disaggregation of text – linearity and finality are increasingly shed, as texts, not least by competing with other stimuli, disaggregate into smaller units and branch out into a multitude of directions. Writing is similarly impacted, so that in addition to a wide array of tools such as word processors, document-preparation systems, mind-mapping software, and so on, authors are increasingly able to engage with readers and to receive immediate feedback that might inform their writing while it is still in progress.

In this context, it is indeed tempting to claim that reading is no longer the absorbed, straightforward activity that it once was, that 'social reading is no longer an oxymoron' – because people can now do so many things with or around electronic texts instantly, and, with an audience of a virtually global reach, reading and writing are not any more the 'solitary' acts that they were in the age of print. In fact, it might be truer to say that social reading is not an oxymoron. Period. One of the lesser-acknowledged consequences of the shift of text production and consumption into the digital realm is that it throws the peculiarities of (using) physical books into sharper relief. Features of the book that have gathered no or little notice (what has often been referred to as the 'transparency' of the technology) now come to stand out, as discussions proliferate on the opportunities presented by the electronic environment as well as the indispensable features of traditional books.

The culture of the physical book as a final entity receiving the stamp of various types of institutional approval – from that of the publisher to those of libraries and universities – as it is being passed on from author to reader, has conditioned us to think of textual works as the embodiment or culmination of the finite acts of disengaged parties. Not only has the interaction between the various stakeholders in the lifecycle of the book been vastly understated, but also these acts have often been thought of as far less nuanced and complex than they actually are, which is a major reason why transferring them into the electronic environment can be so challenging. The experience of reading is not reducible to the intake of 'pure' content, nor is it accommodated or reflected simply by physical pages covered with words. As my friend and colleague James Bridle has pointed out by likening reading to going on a journey, the book is to a great extent a means of taking part in an event. And in this process of readers becoming part of an event, the book also has the important role of a medium of recording, taking into possession, and personalising that experience. The tendency to take over the blank spaces of pages and to alter their physical shape is akin to readers wanting to share thoughts on books that they have read with others, in that both can be considered aspects of one and the same urge – that of creating a sort of archive of experience:

> The books are subliming, they are going up into the air, and what will remain of them is our experiences. That experience is encoded in marginalia, in memory, and in data, and it will be shared because we are all connected now, and because sharing is a form of communal prosthetic memory (Bridle 2011b).

Socialness is thus an integral part of the reading experience, but its importance has tended to remain underestimated because this type of activity has traditionally taken place outside the space of the book itself – around the dinner table, or in book clubs, or on the pages of other publications in the form of reviews or references. When we are now finding ourselves at a stage where it is far more attainable to have the text and the activities accompanying reading within the same space, this presents an occasion that we think holds great value and great promise, and that we are determined to explore. Such attempts at making sense of the dynamic developments in reading habits and technology are beneficial if we seriously begin to fathom the opportunities presented by the digital medium and to conceptualise a new infrastructure of text production and consumption that would be in good service to the public. Even if in the attempt to envision a new type of reading or reading-related experiences, or to draw out new contours in greater specificity, we run the risk of arbitrariness and failing to account for nuances and subtleties, we can only benefit from a further inquiry into, and even contention of, any proposi-

tions put forth, as this would invigorate a much-needed discussion of a very pertinent, socially important topic.

Far from implying a resolute break with the past in favour of an overly optimistic future heralded by new technology, our experiments with social reading
acknowledge the significance of certain traditional practices, but with an eye on
the useful affordances of new technologies that may enhance or supplement them.
Probing the relationship between text and paratext at the heart of the social reading experiment can thus be seen as a continuation of a process inherent to the history of the book – that of conventionalising the apparatus within the space of the
text (Drucker 2011). Experimenting with modes of social reading as an integral
part of the transition of content creation and consumption online can be viewed as
part of the continuum of building upon a variety of models, as we strive to arrive
at an ever-more pertinent ecosystem of textuality: 'a new economy is being put in
place. It brings into coexistence, in a mobile way, a multiplicity of models, and of
modes of archiving and accumulation. And that's what the history of the book has
always been' (Derrida 2005, 17).


## 'Getting the book invented properly'

My work with the Institute for the Future of the Book, and, before this, with the
Voyager Company, can be said to have been centred around the idea of 'getting
the book invented properly'. The phrase comes from a promotional video produced for the launch of one of the first electronic books that Voyager made, *The
hitchhiker's guide to the Galaxy*. Douglas Adams wrote the copy for the advertisement himself, and in it, he beautifully captured the feeling of notions relating to
books and reading continuously being revisited and re-invented. The delightfully
humorous delivery notwithstanding, the intro makes an important point of the
fact that this process of critical reflection has been a recurrent one, going back in
time to the very first transformations of inscribing or reading 'technologies' such
as the arrival of the codex or the printing press and the ensuing repercussions (the
democratisation of communication, the expansion of conversation, etc.) ushered
in by each new development:

> Getting the book invented properly has been a long, hard slog for mankind. Earlier
> attempts have been dogged by hardware problems. The hardware was rock based,
> which meant that it was heavy, cumbersome, and, above all, very hard.
>
> Then someone had a bright idea: let's scrunch up a lot of trees, mash them into a
> nice pulp, flatten them out, dry them, write on them, and then, I don't know, roll'em
> up or something. It was a terrific success. Or, at least, a semi-terrific success. The
> scroll was much lighter, much softer, and a little bit easier to handle. Clearly, it was
> the 'I don't know, roll'em up or something' bit that needed some work.

New research brought a stunning new idea – why not cut up the rolls of paper, sew them up the middle and, I don't know, stick'em between a couple of bits of board or something.

This was the turning point. This new version of the book was fantastically easy to use. All you had to do, basically, was sit there. It really caught on. In fact, it caught on in such a big way, that soon everybody was writing down virtually anything they could think of and putting it in the books. Lots of them. Lots and lots of them. The whole business was getting out of control again. So, back to rock-based technology!

Someone had had a bright idea about what to do with silicon, which is scrunch it up, flatten it out, do a horrendous amount of other stuff to it, and then, I don't know, stick it in a PowerBook or something. It would be a crucial breakthrough. Now, however much people wrote, it could be turned into Voyager Expanded Book software, and the PowerBook could handle it. All things anybody liked about previous types of books – pictures, text, scrolling, page turning – could be modeled in software, and you can take as many books as you wanted, anywhere you liked.

Voyager Expanded Books – everything you liked about books, scrunched up into silicon, or something. Voyager Expanded Books – getting the book invented properly.[1]

The promo piece highlights, on the one hand, the dynamics between an attachment to the physical specifics of text carriers, which people almost inexorably seek to transfer or mimic in a new medium, and, on the other hand, the often unanticipated directions that new systems take and the social and cultural ramifications that also inevitably follow. A central feature in these evolutions, as Adams's interpretation implies, is the trial-and-error nature that seems to be inherent in many of the developments making up the history of the book.

The Institute for the Future of the Book has evolved out of a shared preoccupation with the characteristics, opportunities, and effects of digital developments in text production and consumption and a belief that through active participation and intervention in this transition we can steer the course of developments toward a greater social benefit. In what we are dealing with now, we are often confounded by the lack of words yet to describe certain concepts and processes, which often leads us to resort to the use of accepted terms in new contexts and to signify new things. Often when we are dealing with developments so current and in flux as to constitute a constantly moving target, it is through engaging practically with technology and new types of tools that we are afforded some insight into and understanding of these new phenomena, continuously groping for the right handles and the suitable language to reflect on these developments.

People have often asked me why I chose this particular name for our organisation, when the remit of the institute is clearly not (limited to) bound codices. Indeed, a designation like 'discourse' or 'human communication' might have been better suited to reflect the institute's core area of inquiry. Apart from the sheer allure that the word 'book' still holds in popular imagination (and – it should be mentioned –

the fact that it was, accidentally or not, under this particular moniker that the project received generous financial support from the MacArthur Foundation), a new ecology of text that as yet lacks matching new semantics necessitates a recourse to such established signifiers. It may take 50, perhaps 100, years before the new concepts with which we are dealing today have settled and we have the words for them. Until then, my approach is to keep adapting the definition of what a book is.

It all started for me in 1979, when I saw a video produced by the Architecture Machine Group Lab at MIT, in which a man in front of a computer demonstrates a new kind of reading software.[2] In the video he selects a word by touching the computer screen, which calls out a definition of that word. With another tap on the screen, he plays a video, embedded in the page alongside the text. This early demonstration of converging modalities marked for me the point when I started questioning my own idea of the book, until then limited to a page containing some text or, at most, text combined with images. The spark had certainly been lit then, but it was not until a couple of years later that I revisited this initial moment of revelation and started spending more time conceptually revising my idea of the book.

A consultancy job at the *Encyclopedia Britannica*, where I was tasked with setting up one of the first-ever electronic encyclopedias, led me to start seriously wrestling with the question of the essence of the book – what are the book's essential features, and what aspects of it can be enhanced, added to, or modified when it is no longer constrained materially? With the *Britannica* project, the idea was not simply to transfer images of the physical pages onto LaserDisc, but actually to make sure that the encyclopedia existed as bytes on the new carrier. Facing up to this challenge, which was at that time literally a foray into unexplored territory, I took upon visiting various media and technology labs in search of a methodology for properly digitising the physical volumes of content. In the course of my research, a sudden moment of clarity occurred – a conceptual breakthrough as to how the book does or could function and how the reader engages with it physically as well as culturally and socially. And this moment came when I stopped thinking of the physical nature of the book – of ink and bound pages – and started thinking about the way in which the book is used. In contrast to other media – TV and radio – available at that time, around 1981, books were the only one where the user was in actual and full control of the experience of the material: the time and pace of taking up the information, the direction, the iterations, and so on. In other words, books could be considered to be a type of 'random-access' medium, long before that term entered our usage and acquired the meaning that it now has in the field of computer science. I realised that, inexorably albeit gradually, microprocessors were going to be introduced into all of these producer-driven media, so that eventually users would be able to consume all the content actively, in the same way in which they were reading a book. Technology such as video discs, which came out in 1979, would enable people to 'read' a movie, for instance, stopping it and rewinding or fast-forwarding instantaneously.

## User-driven media

With the advent of the World Wide Web, a new need for reconceptualising the book insisted itself. At this point, in the early 1990s, the breakaway from the physical had reached a new level, when the container seemed to be all but completely disappearing. My attempt to wrap my head around this new rupture was aided by the grant from the MacArthur Foundation that went toward setting up the Institute for the Future of the Book. The Institute was established as an organisation dedicated exclusively to thinking about and talking about the book as an object and as an experience. It attempted to synthesise from ongoing conversations a vision of the production and consumption of textual matter that would be more in line with the networked age. The team at the first meetings of the institute consisted of young people in their early twenties who had grown up with the Internet and thus had a very different experience from mine, me being a publisher of the 'old school', in the business of making fixed objects. Our approach was, again, to work on the assumption that a combination of theoretical analyses and practical experimentation would move the discussion forward.

Not too long after these initial conversations, a new platform for reading and interacting with text was conceived. During lunch with author and media scholar McKenzie Wark, one day in 2006, he mentioned to me that he had written a draft for a new book, GAM3R 7H30RY (Wark 2006). He said that he had not signed a deal for it yet, and I asked him if he would be interested in putting the book up online. The idea appealed to him, so I went back to my colleagues at the Institute for the Future of the Book, and we soon set to work to find out how to present Ken's work online in the most fitting way. Prompted by the specificity of Ken's writing – instead of the usual pages, he had numbered his paragraphs, and each paragraph represented a largely self-sufficient and self-explanatory unit – we decided to render the text in such a way as to reflect this peculiarity. Finally, we ended up with a structure that resembled a stack of cards, with each card containing a paragraph. Convinced that the conversation around a text is an important part of any reading experience, we next thought about the way we could have discussions around these chunks of text. The team thought that if the comments were to appear at the bottom of the stack, it would be fairly cumbersome for users to connect a comment with the precise paragraph to which it refers. Therefore, we decided to move each comment next to the paragraphs with which it is associated, so that each paragraph would automatically change the comment stream.

With this technical setup, the text went online on BoingBoing (Doctorow 2006), and only within an hour or two, we watched a conversation emerge that was both exciting and illuminating. In the course of a few days, Ken went from following up on every single comment the moment it appeared, to assuming the role of a kind of moderator as he became more comfortable with the system. Finally he was starting to act much like a professor at a seminar does – he may know more than anybody else in the room, he may have set the subject, but he is trusting that the conversation as a whole is going to reach everybody's understanding. And we could see the same thing happening with the GAM3R 7H30RY project.

The project has been called 'an envelope-pushing endeavour in both form and content' (Doctorow 2006), and it received a lot of attention. Particularly notable was the interest expressed by a number of academics who thought they could use something similar for their teaching. Many of them wanted to work with a comparable system but for regular texts, not for paragraph-based material as was Ken's. It was with this feedback in mind that in 2008 we built something called the Commentpress – a plug-in for the popular blogging platform WordPress that allowed users to make comments on any paragraph of a page of electronic text, with the comments appearing next to the paragraph on which they have been made.

One of the first projects that showcased the Commentpress theme was *The Golden Notebook* project (Golden Notebook, n.d.), designed by James Bridle (Bridle 2011a). The idea was to have six different women who did not know one another beforehand and would tune in from different parts of the world, reading Doris Lessing's book online in the course of six weeks, sharing their thoughts in the margins as they did so. Thus, on the left-hand side was a page of text from the book, and on the right-hand side appeared the conversation that these women had on just that page of text.

Already upon launching the two experiments described above, I could sense the importance of their implications. The commenting function that proved so popular with the GAM3R 7H30RY project had been just a tweak, so to speak, in the way users comment on electronic text. In essence, what we had done was simply move user feedback up alongside the text. All the same for me this new arrangement represented a challenge to the entire notion of the hierarchical structure that traditionally characterises the relationship between authors and readers. This hierarchy, imposed by print, suddenly became a lot flatter when the core text and the readers' comments occupied the same visual space. It was, moreover, possible now to preserve continuity with aspects of traditional reading that we thought were valuable and ought to be transferred in the electronic environment, if also reconfigured to fit with the workings and aesthetics of the digital age. In this sense, *The Golden Notebook* project demonstrated unequivocally the viability of the asynchronous reading group: one did not have to be in the same room at the same time with people interested in discussing a particular work – thoughts about a text could be exchanged within a common space regardless of physical location or time zone.

## A book is a place

Gradually, as these experiments were taking place, my own idea of the book was boiling down to a single image – the image of the book as a place where readers and authors congregate. And in this space the roles of the two evolve to accommodate new expectations and needs. A different kind of author is increasingly going to be found – one whose commitment is not to engage with the subject matter on behalf of future readers, the proverbial lone figure toiling away in isolation with the readers at the back of his or her mind. Meanwhile, readers would no longer assume the role of passive recipients who years later get to see the final, polished product of creative labour. A new-school author is one who engages with readers within the context of the subject matter, making them part of the creative process throughout its progress.

What we are witnessing now can even be seen as a shift beyond a flattening of the hierarchy between author and reader and a move toward a qualitatively new mode of generating and thinking through ideas. Engaging in social reading-writing is a much more expedient way of thinking about complex issues, when bits and pieces that can be used toward their understanding are often at our disposal, scattered throughout the global network. Social reading thus adds up to a kind of harnessing of multiple resources available on the web to help us think through various problems, and it is reasonable to believe that the boundaries between reading and writing will continue to blur in the future, as (groups of) people assume the roles of both reader and writer in a system of participatory, active sense-making and knowledge production.

This vision by no means implies an overnight and all-sweeping change in attitudes and practices. Indeed, for many authors allowing outsiders into their creative process can still be an intimidating thought. Writers may find it difficult to think out loud or to change a modus operandi that has so far worked well for them. But for authors yet to be published, for young people who grew up with the Internet and social networking and who have lived their whole conscious lives in public, this is likely to be the *natural* way to write a book.

## A social book

What the Institute for the Future of the Book is currently busy with is constructing an entire ecosystem for publishing that assumes that books *are* places where people gather. It is both an open space for anybody who wants or has been selected to have a say about a piece of text and a platform for the exchange of thoughts within the framework where the text lives, a framework that provides context beyond which the coherence and dynamics of the conversation would dilute or dissipate. The idea of community that is integral to the social reading experience I am talking about thus depends crucially on the careful balance between openness and enclosure, enabling the formation of a 'domain of meaning'.[3]

There are aspects of the notion of the book thus described that are of greater specificity and that matter for its understanding. In the first place, it should be made clear that the social book – as well as all kinds of reading, it is our absolute belief – will live increasingly inside the browser. Mobile apps or proprietary, nonbrowser-based readers are not the way into the future. This conviction is borne out of decades of experience making CD-ROMs for Macintosh and Windows and all the varieties in between. The idea of having to prepare a book for every single mobile device that is out there, not to mention desktop computers, is just not feasible. Developments in software such as HTML5 now make it possible to create a book as beautiful as one would wish to and with all the interactivity one would like to put into it.

The further break-down of the concept of social reading into subcategories, or 'flavours', that follows is therefore to be taken with this basic assumption in mind. The classification below evolved out of a taxonomy I developed last year on social reading (Stein 2010); my initial reflections on the topic were made available online for open perusal and discussion (via Commentpress) on the Institute for the Future of the Book's website.

*Social means having a conversation with people you know in the margins of a book*
The reading platform currently being developed at the Institute for the Future of the Book is exclusively geared toward fostering lively, interactive, rich conversations around a piece of text. A click of the mouse enables the user to open a social layer of a certain online book, where interactions of all shapes and forms can take place. For instance, one can highlight a piece of text, put graphic marks on a page (anything from a vertical line to a dot, etc.) and attach comments to them, screen back the text to bring forth highlighted quotes or a comment, initiate or join a thread of comments, write notes that can be made either private or public, and so on. Social networking functionalities such as buttons to share a comment via Twitter or Facebook, are, of course, also integrated into the system.

*Social means having access to the comments of everyone else who is reading the same book you are reading*
The social aspect of reading depends directly on the availability of a pool of readers' comments at everyone's disposal, which can be further fine-tuned by a system of weighing for cogency or poignancy, for instance. And while a more liberal broad-access community may present a risk to the quality of the exchange, in an environment where users have their own profiles and can engage even further with a text and with other readers by participating in specific reading groups, a robustness of quality should emerge that would ensure that discussions remain meaningful.

*Social means being able to read an expert's gloss on a book*
Think about it this way: a group can be one person. One of the important elements of the social book is that a person's annotations have to be extractable. If one goes through a book and marks it up, one has to be able to take these comments out of the book and bring them elsewhere. Twenty years from now, my granddaughter might want to read my gloss on *Tale of two cities*, and she is probably not going to

have the same reader that I am using now. Therefore we need protocols that will make it possible for someone to go through a markup decades after it has been created. A lot of work has already been done in this direction – one example is the open protocol for annotations developed by James Bridle, which the Institute for the Future of the Book is committed to supporting, so that any comments made in a social book document will be exportable down the road.

With the backlog of thousands of years of analogue culture digitised, it will be increasingly important to have a guide through a book, someone who can lead the user through the important bits and explain why they are important. This can be many orders of magnitude better than a digest of the book – when you get to a bit that is interesting, you will be in the book, so you can just keep reading from that spot onward at will.

*Social means being able to engage with authors asynchronously or real-time 'in the book'*
A short while ago in the book reviews section of *The New York Times*, an ad appeared for a Random House book with a URL pointing to a place where it was possible to arrange for the author of the book to chat live with a reading group. We could easily imagine the benefits of this type of interaction, similar to the author tour, if it were taking place 'inside the book', alongside the text itself. There are a lot of authors, perhaps aside from the very big names, who have many reasons why they might join a readers' group and point to things in their books for them. A reader with an interest in crocheting, for instance, is likely to find access to the author of a book on that subject a very valuable opportunity. It would give them a chance, for instance, to inquire about difficult steps, get the author's opinion on the latest trends, and so on. Another example is a textbook that comes with a number of hours of tutoring by a person somewhere around the world who is knowledgeable in the subject. Thus it is not hard to imagine a social version of a book that would be interesting enough for readers to pay a small fee – three dollars, or five, or ten – in order to have it.

## Reading and writing

The history of the Institute for the Future of the Book and of all the projects that led to or emanated from it unequivocally affirm for me the importance of engaging with new technologies not only to arrive at practical solutions but also to think conceptually about new developments. Taking an active stance when it comes to technologies of inscription informs a critical assessment of their implications and, crucially, equips us to influence the course of their development. We are aware of the pitfalls of talking about an abrupt departure from the traditional, sustained narrative. At the same time, it is paramount to start thinking beyond certain limitations imposed by the order of print and to question the meaning that certain practices have held for us simply by virtue of having no alternative to them.

In traditional text production and consumption, reading and writing represented two distinct aspects of the process of creating a textual work, a dichotomy that persists to this day but is undergoing profound changes. It might be quite some time before we really start to figure out that the new forms of expression no longer presume that this boundary has the same significance it did in the era of print, but the importance of the arguments going on in the interstices, as it were, is clearly steering toward an intersection where reading and writing meet and inform and propel each other.

The main question before us at this point is how to enhance the experience of the long-form textual work via the possibilities of the electronic environment. In other words, we want to inquire into the ways that a group of people work on and think about a text together, so that this interaction is given the visibility and place within an ecosystem of reading that it deserves. We can take Wikipedia as an example of the flip side of this vision. The way Wikipedia is designed and functions ultimately highlights a piece of text, or, rather, the latest version of it – a version often deriving out of a consensus reconciling the views and comments of various authors/commentators. And although that text's shape changes to reflect the back-and-forth going on 'in the back', the discussions themselves, where in my opinion the truth is, still remain relegated to the background, and there is no easy way to get to them as yet.

It is far from trivial to reverse this type of design that backgrounds the conversation critiquing and shaping a piece of text. A lot of work has to go into making this part of the reading experience right. The amount of work that has gone into Wikipedia is astounding, and it would take an equally massive effort to put up an equivalent reading environment that really allows users to get into the argument that goes on in the interstices.

Yet finding a way to such a system holds a big promise. Readers have always been inclined to share or discuss their experience of works with others, and in the networked age this can be made possible on a global scale, asynchronously. The social layer is therefore where the value will be. With content becoming increasingly available for free online, whether legally through Open Access or as a result of piracy, a change in attitudes to the accessibility of textual matter is already taking root; it makes sense, therefore, to talk about business models along the lines of the following arrangement: readers can have access to a core text for free, but if they want to engage, they are going to have to pay to be part of a collective experience around this text.

Sustained narrative is, of course, not going to disappear – it has been, still is, and will be part of the academic curriculum as well as beyond it. At the same time, the technology we use to read these and other types of texts – a plethora of reading platforms, sharing buttons, and book review websites – have already invaded the space of reading and are having an impact, if not so much on the process of reading itself, then on the social activities surrounding it. I take it as our task to engage critically with these new affordances and question established practices, even if it means putting forth unorthodox ideas. 'Truth emerges in the course of struggle' goes one of my favourite quotes, attributed to Mao, and I am 100 per cent in favour of experiments that flip things upside down.

**Notes**

\*    Many thanks to Mariya Mitova for expertly bringing an extemporaneously narrated slide show into line with the exigencies of print.

1    Taken from a 1993 audio recording. An mp3 can be listened to here:
http://www.futureofthebook.org/blog/archives/2005/05/lost_recording_of douglas_adam. html.

2    This is what later became the MIT Media Lab. The video can be accessed online at http:// www.bookandbyte.org/Weel/MovieManual.mov.

3    'For instance, at the most abstract and fundamental level of meaning production, we know that the distinction between a mark and a non-mark, a signifying entity and an incidental trace, depends upon the force of a frame... Delimitation of domain creates meaning' (Drucker 2011).

# 81,498 words

## *The book as data object*

BERNHARD RIEDER

Is a digital library a machine or an institution? (Agre 2003)

## Introduction

After the entrance – or 'incursion' according to certain commentators – of Amazon.com into the book market in 1995, a second US company, Google Inc., has provoked strong reactions in the world of print in recent years. Already Amazon.com's business model and logistics relied heavily on certain features of networked computing, and the company became a poster child for a Web 2.0 imaginary of how to do business online. As *Wired*'s Chris Anderson (2004) famously argued, 'shelf space' had become virtually infinite for online sellers, enabling them to offer a larger catalogue than even the largest brick-and-mortar store. Tim O'Reilly (2005) lauded Amazon.com's strategy to make 'a science of user engagement' and to exploit 'user activity to produce better search results' by encouraging its customers to rate, comment, and browse, registering every purchase and every click, analyzing the data, and reordering rankings and navigational pathways accordingly. According to O'Reilly, it was this fixation on data that gave Amazon.com the critical edge over its competitors. Very much in line with the Web 2.0 catechism, Google Inc. set out in 2004 to carry the book's encounter with algorithms and databases a step further by announcing the plan to digitise *all the books ever published*. Together with book-oriented social networking platforms like LibraryThing or Goodreads, the two companies have become the main actors in a series of transformations that are set to affect how books are found, read, and understood. Google's ambitious goals and the company's track record when it comes to its self-assigned mission 'to organize information on a global scale in order to make it accessible and useful to all'[1] beg for particular analytical attention, and this paper will therefore concentrate on Google Books[2] as perhaps the most pervasive effort to *perform* the book as a data object.

Focusing on a set of specific questions related to books as digital documents, there are many important pieces of the larger puzzle that I will *not* take into account. I will neither retrace the story of the digitisation project led by the company from Mountain View since 2004, nor reference the debates that seem to arise after every announcement of yet another library agreeing to have its collections scanned. Issues concerning copyright and remuneration of authors and editors are equally beyond the scope of this chapter, and I will therefore leave the various legal initiatives that are currently seeking to clarify the relations between the different actors involved uncommented. Finally, I do not want to add to the discussion on whether a private American company should have the right to appropriate significant portions of foreign national heritage or not. While these matters are certainly very important, I would instead like to argue that services like Google Books raise certain fundamental questions about the organisation of knowledge in contemporary Western societies that deserve to be discussed in detail. For civilisations organised around writing, changes affecting the various techniques and practices surrounding the written word are bound to have important implications. And although it is very difficult to talk about these changes without slipping into overarching arguments or petty moralising, they deserve to be discussed and thought through.

A starting point for the argument I want to make could be a somewhat naïve question: what kind of *object* is a digital collection containing the full-text of more than ten percent of all books ever published,[3] a collection accessed by millions of people each day? Why would a company build such a collection and what is its 'value'? Is such a very large database simply the logical continuation of the library, a version that is perhaps more practical and easier to manage but ultimately comparable to the Library of Congress or other national libraries? Or, on the contrary, are there enough breaks and shifts to justify talking about the emergence of a new sort of object and, potentially, a new configuration of knowledge? To begin to account for these questions, it is useful to look more closely at this latest incarnation of the eternal dream to *capture* all the world's knowledge that is Google Books.

## The book, the algorithm, and the database

A description of any website is likely to be outdated the moment it is published. My goal is therefore to outline, through a review of its current form, the general ideas that guide Google's book platform. The core functionality consists, of course, in giving users access to the books that have been scanned by the company or provided, already in digital form, by a publisher. Depending on the different legal regulations, access can extend to all the pages, to some pages, to extracts, or to metadata only. Books that are in the public domain can generally be downloaded in PDF format or as a text file created from the images of scanned pages through automatic optical character recognition (OCR). Other features allow users to interact with books in different ways: a registered user can create his or her own 'library' made of 'shelves', which boils down to a relatively basic system of labelled lists; unsurprisingly, there is a powerful search engine that scouts both the metadata and the full text of books. This last feature leads up to the argument I want to put forward here: the processes of scanning and text recognition embed the book into a technological configuration that certainly includes the characteristics of both a catalogue and a reading device. But beyond these familiar elements lurks an industry-leading information system, a database consisting of the full-text content of the processed books complemented by a steadily growing set of supplementary information which is 'mined' by a variety of algorithms.

This extension points to a similar shift in search techniques that took place on the Web in the late nineties, namely the rise of the algorithmic full-text search engine, epitomised first by AltaVista and then by Google Search, to name only the most emblematic, and the fading of Web 'catalogues', such as the Yahoo Directory, which were compiled manually by human editors. The different ways of processing contents – manual cataloguing vs. automated crawling and indexing – imply, as a corollary, very different architectures of knowledge, i.e. different ways of ordering and relaying information. Indexing the full textual content of a document opens the door to automated processes that, in a sense, can be understood as ways of *reading* or *interpreting* – 'explaining the meaning of' (OAD) – a book. These processes imply a *particular* understanding of the book as a structured set of words, and they 'project' it in certain ways, both individually and as part of a larger corpus. It is therefore not surprising that Google Books offers, beyond the more traditional search functions, representations or 'views' of a title that are produced by algorithms harvesting the textual material. The cloud of words and word combinations that can be found under the 'common terms and phrases' heading on a book's overview page mobilises statistical techniques to find units that are particularly 'significant' for the work in question.[4] Each term is also a hyperlink that leads to a list of passages, taken from the scanned pages, where it can be found.

In keeping with the requirement of simplicity that characterises Google's philosophy when it comes to interface design, this feature is rather basic and more

able according Adam Smith analogy analysis of wealth animals appear archeological arrangement articulation basis become biology character Classical age Classical thought common Condillac constituted continuity culture Cuvier define Descartes designate Destutt Destutt de Tracy discourse domain Don Quixote economics eighteenth century elements empirical episteme epistemological established ethnology exchange existence experience express fact figures finitude foundation function fundamental given grammer guage hand human sciences ibid identities and differences individual labour Lamarck language laws linked Linnaeus living longer man's mathesis means metal mode modern thougt movement natural history never nineteenth century object ontology organic structure origin philology philosophy Physiocrats Port-Royal positivity possible production proposition psychoanalysis pure quantity question reflection relation represent resemblance revealed role root seventeenth signified signs similitude sixteenth century space speak species taxinomia taxonomy theory things tion transcendental truth verb visible Western culture whole words

Figure 1: The word cloud from Google Books for *The order of things* by Michel Foucault

understated than the various views and measures that Amazon.com provides in this area. The company is also not hesitant to remove a feature that does not empirically demonstrate its usefulness to users; the 'places mentioned in this book' feature, which generated a geographical map populated by the town names detected in the text, has thus disappeared in the latest redesign.

Google shows its technical prowess when it comes to linking a book with others and to connecting it with additional data sources. The 'popular passages' feature is particularly intriguing: it provides a list of phrases, taken from a selected title, that frequently appear in other books and, copyright permitting, directly links to the relevant pages. In addition, Google lists the references to a title that originate from the Web, from other books, and, via Google Scholar, from the world of scholarly publications. The strategy to invest broadly in harvesting a large variety of data clearly bears its fruits here. Finally, there are both editorial and user reviews, again taken from different data sources or directly submitted through an interface on the site.

All these features give rise to dense networks that connect (almost) any title to a multiplicity of documents and pieces of information. With reference to literary analysis, one could say that Google Books produces different types of *transtextuality*, often taking the material shape of a hyperlink, placing a text 'in an open or hidden relation to other texts' (Genette 1982, 7). The techniques *building* these relations have been developed in at least three distinct directions. First, the system generates a series of what Genette (1987) would call *paratextual* representations (alternative 'tables of contents', generated from the full text: clouds, lists, maps, text statistics, etc.), which aim, on the one side, at 'explaining' a book by providing an overview of the most 'significant' words, the most quoted passages, and so on, and, on the other, at establishing direct navigational entry points into the text. The goal is to *show* us and *direct* us to 'what matters' in the book, as seen through the lens of statistical calculation. Second, different forms of *intertextual* relations between works (direct citations, shared passages, etc.) are scouted for by another set of algorithms and, once again, transformed into both representations and opportunities for navigation. These techniques can go as far as comparing the statistical distributions of words between books and calculating similarity coefficients to indicate 'related' works. Third, Google Books and similar services add a *classificatory* layer that includes basic metadata (author, publication date, etc.) as well as subject classification, which is either based on traditional organisational systems such as the Dewey Decimal Classification or on collaboratively filtered folksonomies established from tags or lists. Algorithmic procedures based on concept extraction or document clustering are not (yet) common, but both Google and Amazon.com propose 'readability' scores that situate a book inside of the full corpus by expressing its difficulty in relation to other works. Whether these measures are actually *pertinent* or *useful* is a question that is beyond the scope of this article, but they perfectly reveal the eagerness to use calculations to express aspects that we would readily classify as 'cultural'.

| These statistics are computed from the text of this book. (learn more) | | | | |
|---|---|---|---|---|
| **Readability** (learn more) | | **Comparede with other books** | | |
| Fog Index: | 10.0 | 26% are easier | | 74% are harder |
| Flesh Index: | 67.2 | 22% are easier | | 78% are harder |
| Flesh-Kincaid Index: | 7.6 | 24% are easier | | 76% are harder |
| **Complexity** (learn more) | | | | |
| Complex words: | 10% | 27% are easier | | 73% are harder |
| Syllables per Word: | 1.5 | 23% are easier | | 77% are harder |
| Words per Sentence: | 15.5 | 41% are easier | | 59% are harder |
| **Number of** | | | | |
| Characters: | 466,299 | 57% are easier | | 43% are harder |
| Words: | 81,498 | 61% are easier | | 39% are harder |
| Sentences: | 5,413 | 68% are easier | | 32% are harder |
| **Fun stats** | | | | |
| Words per Dollar: | 13,697 | | | |
| Words per Ounce: | 9,611 | | | |

Figure 2: Amazon.com's text statistics for Victor Hugo's *The hunchback of Notre Dame*

Readability indices are calculated from the size of a title's vocabulary, the length and complexity of words and sentences, and other factors. The 'fun stats' show that such indices can be created from almost any information, in this case from the book's price and weight, in relation to the number of words it contains.

The transition from printed paper to electronic reader, at least for the moment, leaves the compositional logic of the book as a linear sequence of words, sentences, and chapters largely intact. The full-text book database however is set to treat it as a raw material that can be *deterritorialised* – reduced to textual atoms and their frequencies – and *reterritorialised* – reassembled into groupings of algorithms and interface elements that (re)frame it and make it navigable in different ways. Tables of contents and word indices have provided alternative ways of navigating a book for centuries, but the digital machinery clearly pushes much further in this direction. While electronic readers strongly affect the book as a commodity, online book platforms extract it further from its traditional *configuration* (bookstore, library, paper, reading chair, etc.) and place it into a new set of relations (database, algorithm, screen, interface, etc.).[5] There is an analytical distinction to be made between a cognitive component – the platform as 'vision machine' (Virilio 1988) that introduces layers of automated perception – and 'grammars of action' (Agre 1994) that, embedded in the interface, define modes of interaction and structure navigational pathways. As we have seen above, these two dimensions are deeply intertwined and although we still lack empirical confirmation, it seems clear that the practices of searching, browsing, reading, and understanding will all be affected by this pervasive change of 'device' (*dispositif*).

The question of whether these transformations represent a 'loss' or an 'enrichment' is clearly too full of cultural, political, and aesthetic *a priori* to treat it seriously here. It seems sensible, however, to remember that the famous expression 'ceci tuera cela', with which the archdeacon in Hugo's *The Hunchback of Notre Dame* (81.498 words!) laments the revolution in both knowledge and power associated with the printing press, is not a law of nature. The history of media has shown time and again that the addition of new devices and formats is rather a story of accumulation, negotiation, and diversification than one of replacement. The shift from an 'Order of the Book' to a digital 'Libroverse' is marked by continuities, discontinuities and a complicated set of unfolding *consequences* (Van der Weel 2011c). But even if the book is not on the verge of being killed off, it is important to note that the logic of the database and algorithm lodges it in new configurations, which not only allow for new practices of searching and reading but also imply shifts in collective and cultural forms of circulation and appropriation. It is therefore crucial to consider the economic motivations of a commercial company set on scanning tens of millions of books and on making them accessible in the specific ways I have discussed over the last pages. I will, again, focus on the computational exploitation of data and present it as a complex source of value.

## Why digitise millions of books?

Despite its 'mission' cited above, it is imperative to treat Google first and foremost as a publicly traded company, with a responsibility to its shareholders and 30,000 employees to make profits. This does not mean that (short-term) commercial goals are the only considerations taken into account by decision-makers. Google's stock structure[6] and considerable cash reserves provide its top executives with significant leeway to plan with the medium and long-term in mind. Business considerations are certainly crucial, but the company has also shown that it is willing to explore and develop opportunities that do not have a clear or immediate potential to generate revenues. In the case of Google Books, I would argue that there are at least three very obvious sources of (potential) income:

1   On the Web, every page served can be outfitted with ads. In short, the more pages served, the better. A very large collection of books represents, in a sense, valuable advertisement real estate. By providing a comprehensive and useful service, Google can further increase the number of pages – and thus ads – it delivers to users, thereby growing its 'circulation', to use a newspaper term. The company already serves ads with search results on Google Books and also pro-

vides links to online shops where users can purchase a title, earning a commission if a title is purchased.

2   Since the opening of the Google eBookstore[7] in the United States in late 2010 it is clear that Google intends to compete with online booksellers, including Amazon.com's Kindle Store and Apple's iBookstore. A very large number of books available for free can certainly help attract customers who can then be 'guided' to the commercial offer and perhaps be bound to the platform.[8]

3   Google seeks to present itself as – and indeed seeks to become – a one-stop counter for all informational needs and desires. A book service fits perfectly into this logic and promises to further reduce the frequency with which a user has to leave the Google universe to go to other sites. This not only helps with committing users to an ever expanding platform but also to realise significant economies of scale by sharing technological know-how (modules, algorithms, best practices, etc.) and infrastructure (data centers, data delivery facilities, etc.). We regularly underestimate the immense technological knowledge and engineering skill involved in building large-scale, high-performance Web systems and forget the competitive advantage Google has when it comes to both improving existing services and developing new ones.

In addition to these relatively straightforward elements – advertising, sales, network effects / economies of scale – it seems that the case of Google Books is particularly suited for discussing certain computational aspects whose potential value is a lot less obvious. The two central directions, here, are first the processing of the contents themselves and second the capture and analysis of interactions between users and books.

4   Although attempts to create software that would be 'intelligent' in the same way as human beings have so far proved unsuccessful, even very simple programs can perform functions that could be described as 'cognitive', functions that can provide significant cues in knowledge production processes. As Wendy Chun (2011) phrases it, software can create 'order from order', in the sense that algorithmic processing makes it easy to ascertain frequencies, patterns, and relationships in large amounts of data and to represent these as coefficients, lists, graphs, and other forms. The automatic creation, for example, of a concordance or index for a text – the main uses of computers in early 'digital humanities' from the 1950s onwards (Schreibman et al. 2004) – may seem banal, but the manual work required for such a task can be enormous, and indices are very helpful things after all. The functionalities of the Google Books service presented above are mostly based on relatively well-understood statistical techniques (counting words and collocations, calculating probabilities, comparing frequency distributions, etc.) that nonetheless produce results that can be inter-

esting and useful.[9] I would therefore like to propose to view the book database as a latent reservoir of knowledge that is at least partially exploitable by algorithmic approaches. At the moment, we are not yet able to assess fully what Jean-Claude Guédon (2008) called the 'computational potential' of these reservoirs, but it is certainly revealing that the contracts between Google and its partner libraries are generally quite favourable for both the libraries, in particular the European ones, and the end users, while strictly blocking other search engines from access to the digital files. Books have played a central role over the last centuries in organising the fundamental conversations a culture has with itself and with other cultures. They document the richness and diversity of human imagination and ingenuity. More than any other medium, books are at the very core of how we understand and invent ourselves. Even if only a fraction of this wealth can be harnessed by algorithmic means, there is enormous potential for all kinds of (commercial) applications.

From an economic standpoint, we can already see a set of areas where large book databases are starting to become valuable assets, beyond the immediate interest of end user services like Google Books. In the field of machine translation, for example, statistical techniques have proven their superiority over approaches based on language modelling, but large amounts of high-quality text data are needed to 'train' the systems. Having access to a large number of book titles in different translations is evidently very useful for keeping an edge in this competitive area – and Google progressively builds translation capabilities into many of its services, most recently into their online office suite Google Docs. Concept extraction and related fields are another area where high volumes of first-rate data are crucial for producing usable results. Already in the late 1950s, the information pioneer Hans-Peter Luhn showed how a basic statistical analysis of word adjacency could reveal conceptual relations inside text documents (Luhn 1959). The ability to build representations of thematic clusters or term relationships – in the form of semantic networks, thesauri, ontologies, and so on – is certainly not enough to fully attain the level of *meaning* in a non-superficial sense of the word, but it can go far in improving search results and providing a better overview for users. A research project associated with Google Books provides a third, and rather striking, example for illustrating the computational potential of a very large book database. By making their main research tool available to the public on the Google Labs site,[10] the project, going by the telling name 'culturomics',[11] has gained considerable attention. Using a (large) subset of Google Books as their dataset – in all 5.2 million titles in seven languages – the researchers have shown that it is possible to produce perspectives on cultural, political, social, and economic developments in society by analysing and visualising the frequency variations of 'word grams' over time (Michel et al. 2011).[12] The stated aim is to *measure culture*, and certain historical events such as Nazi censorship of Jewish authors do indeed show up very clearly in the data. My goal here is not to weigh in on Adorno's famous dictum, said when talking about his uneasy collaboration with Paul Lazarsfeld in the late 1930s, that 'culture might be precisely that condition that excludes a mentality capable of measuring it', but to point to the fact that serious efforts are underway to *make all this data talk* in one way or another. The particular performativity of the resulting *speech*, whether it will have intellectual merit or create significant economic value, remains largely to be seen. It is clear, however, that the data pool underlying Google Books is already one of the richest document collections on human history and culture ever compiled.

5   There is a second major element that has to be taken into account when investigating the computational potential of this collection, namely the 'capture' (Agre 1994) of how people actually interact with it, how they search, navigate, browse, and *read*. Computer interfaces can register every query, log every click, measure every timespan, and store every cursory mouse gesture; and, generally, they do. For users, the most visible application of statistical processing of interactions is in features like spell checkers or the different implementations of suggestion systems in Google's Web search engine and other services,[13] but potential uses can go much further. The data produced by capturing user interactions represent a significant addition to the book contents themselves, and they can be used to improve ranking mechanisms and classificatory structures, to evaluate functionality, and to personalise different site elements. More generally, the correlation of user profiles with book contents can produce data that represent 'paths of meaning' – word relations, semantic networks, etc. – derived from actual practice instead of mere text mining. These data 'speak' not only about books, but also about the intimate relationship that individuals and *cultures* – 'webs of significance' according to Geertz (1973) – entertain with these artifacts. The ability to better understand what people *do with books*, what they are looking for and how they read them, may end up being more valuable commercially than the contents themselves. The Google Flu Trends project is a practical example showing how a rather straightforward analysis of user data, in this case search queries, can be used to accurately predict outbreaks of disease.[14] This particular model can surely not be transferred 'as is' to just any other domain, but it gives us an idea of how real-world data can produce impressive results without any kind of elaborate processing. It is certainly not excessive to expect that the culturomics project's goal to 'measure culture' can easily be extended from books to interactions with books and from a purely historical perspective to the examination of current cultural trends.

The obvious commercial application of captured interactions, beyond improvements to the sites themselves, would be the further enrichment of user profiles for better ad targeting in the various Google services and partner sites. The current pricing system for advertisement, which determines the price an advertiser pays for a user click by means of keyword auctions, has the effect that the company has strong incentives to not only strive to serve *more* advertising but *better* advertising, i.e. advertising that leads to higher conversion rates and thus to a higher sales price for a click. It is hard to overstate the economic importance of user profiling for personalised ad placements, by far the most important source of revenue for Google. Targeting based on incredibly detailed accounts of user habits promises not only to increase the likelihood that a visitor purchases a product on the advertiser's site or to extend the duration of a visit, but also to reduce the level of 'ad resistance' by actually showing fewer but more 'relevant' ads to each user. In short, the high quality of data contained in books can help Google to both learn more about user interests and about the structures of meaning that exist in any culture.

## A new logistics of reading

Issues of privacy are certainly crucial in this context, but they are also highly visible, and I would therefore like to put forward an equally important but less visible question: which type of 'epistemic culture' (Knorr Cetina 1999), which ordering of knowledge, is favoured by the mechanisms that drive a service like Google Books? According to José van Dijck, '[k]nowledge is not simply conveyed to users, but is co-produced by search engines' ranking systems and profiling systems' (2010, 575), and we should therefore treat a large-scale book database as a 'knowledge system' (Van der Weel 2011c) that implies its own logic. Beyond the concrete techniques, this means that we have to examine the standards and principles that govern the selection and parameterisation mechanisms that decide how to 'show' a book, where to link, and in what order.

I would like to argue that the *problem* that these systems appear to respond to is not only that of a *representation* of knowledge (what is the world?), but also that of the *allocation of limited resources* (how to act in the world?). What book best fits a query? What is 'significant' in a book? What are the 'most closely related' books for a given title? In the end: what to read? The institutions that are traditionally invested in providing answers to these very questions – families, schools, libraries, mass media, churches, etc. – each operate according to their own principles, sometimes in collaboration, sometimes in conflict with one another. What online systems do is to add another logic to the pile, a logic that is somewhat different from the existing ones, however. Automated processes produce strange artifacts that may not seem all too different from taxonomies, dictionaries, reading lists, conceptual networks, or catalogues on the outside, but when it comes to looking at how informational units are selected and ranked, we find mechanisms that are much more akin to *pricing mechanisms* in markets than to the ways scholars, educators, librarians, or expert committees work. This argument needs to be explained more closely.

In neoclassical economic theory, the market is considered the most efficient form of resource allocation because it provides a quasi-cognitive function in a distributed way: it sets prices via the interplay between supply and demand. The price for an item in a market thus is an emergent property that takes into account the value perceptions of every participant in the system. Search engines and systems like Google Books mostly operate on the basis of similar mechanisms: the choices of Internet users, their navigational paths, their assessments and queries come together in setting the 'value' of each unit of information and, just like a price, this value can fluctuate with the ebbs and flows of shifting interests. The result is a level of visibility for each unit of information and a very practical 'cost' expressed by how easily it can be found. 'Cheaper' books, the most popular titles, float on the top while others require a much higher investment of time and skill: one can only reach them at the price of coming up with an advanced query. At the 'right' price, the choice of 'good' books stems from a complex interplay between the book itself and its 'demand' as expressed by the number of citations, references, requests, visits, and so on. By transferring techniques from Web search to the world of books, the services offered by Google are able to provide not only *access* to knowledge, but also an *evaluation* of the knowledge it mediates, an evaluation that is *epistemic* in its own right. The rules by which this market-based ecology of knowledge operates are made operational through algorithms that are, in keep with tradition, unavailable to the public. Its *normative thrust* is therefore only available to critique on a very general level.

The choice of ranking techniques that are similar to market mechanisms mobilises many of the objections put forward by political economists: that the basic assumptions of rational choice and equal access to information defended by neoclassicists are fundamentally unrealistic; that markets therefore are prone to bubbles, disequilibria, inequality, exclusion, and herd behaviour; that powerful actors can largely skew things in their favour. The choice to organise visibility and access through market mechanisms is therefore very much disputable; it is a value choice that implies winners and losers. But aren't systems of knowledge always (also) value systems? Certainly. What makes the Google model remarkable is the sheer amount of data it takes into account, its algorithmic production method, and its radical, market-based *empiricism*. What makes it significant is the fact that it is based on the everyday practices of information search and knowledge production of a very large number of people.

## Conclusions

The transformation of the book into a digital document is set to have important repercussions. For the publishing world, the transition to digital distribution promises to have implications as large as those already experienced by other sectors of the cultural industries. For the rest of us, the convenience of access, the advanced search features, and the different forms of transtextual navigation provided by services like Google Books have the potential to affect significantly how we find and make use of books. Thanks to its dominant market position and its immense financial and technical capabilities, the company from Mountain View plays a central role in these transformations. On these pages, I have concentrated on the computational aspect of the Google Books project, in particular the question of how new orderings of knowledge result from the coming together – so characteristic of our time – of content, database, algorithm, interface, and the capturing of user interactions and practices.

How do we evaluate all these changes around the book? As an epochal disruption? As a change of civilisation? I would propose, with Foucault, that what we are currently witnessing, 'is a day like any other, or rather, it is a day that is never quite like the others' (Foucault 2001a, 1267). Technological changes, both *causes* and *consequences*, accompany changes in the economic, social, cultural, and political domains and interact in complex and contradictory ways with them. It would be a shame to hide these complex dynamics behind the oversimplified assessment that we are moving from one 'age' to another. But among the forces that make our days not 'quite like the others' is the transformation of our knowledge practices and the emergence, in gestation since at least the 1940s, of knowledge techniques that are intimately related, on one side, to a dense network of concepts organised around a very particular understanding of information as a resource and, on the other, to a machine that can give these concepts a mechanical performativity. Google Books has provoked so many strong reactions because the project is placed precisely at the intersection between conflicting conceptions of how knowledge can and *should* be organised and mediated. The digitisation of the book transforms its status as both a commodity and as an object of knowledge, and companies like Google and Amazon.com are central actors on both levels.

The database and the algorithm frame *govern* the search for books and the way we read in a way that is fundamentally different from those that drive libraries or school curricula. I would suggest however that we not yield to the temptation of attributing intrinsic value to either set of mechanisms. Both imply situated configurations of power relations and both produce their own vectors of emancipation and dominance. The question is rather how we can develop the intellectual tools we need to analyze and criticise the computational perspectives offered by the omnipresent interfaces and to develop well-informed practices. How should we debate the values that go into the design of information and how should we develop regulatory frameworks that ensure a balance between democratic government and 'algorithmic governance' (Berns and Rouvroy 2009)?

In this text, I have tried to show how the Google Books service can derive significant, and potentially valuable, informational 'intelligence' from the algorithmic exploration of both a very large collection of books and a very large database of captured user interactions. The project should therefore not only be seen as a book distribution platform but, more importantly, as a manifestation of a much larger, and somewhat fantastical, attempt to redefine *knowledge* as *information* and thereby make it amenable to software procedures. This redefinition implies significant changes in modes of access and use, as well as a substantial rearrangement of the power structures than run through the anatomy of knowledge. The book as a data object thus sits directly at a cultural fault line that goes much deeper than the question of whether we read on paper or on a screen. The intellectual and political challenges are considerable.

## Notes

1   http://www.google.com/about/corporate/company/, accessed October 21, 2011.
2   http://books.google.com/.
3   According to its own affirmations, Google had scanned 15 million books out of an estimated 130 million in October 2010 (http://booksearch.blogspot.com/2010/10/on-future-of-books.html, accessed October 21, 2011).
4   Note that these measures of relevance make use of the statistical distribution of a word or word combination throughout the entire corpus. Put simply, a word is considered significant when frequent in a certain title and rare in the entire corpus. The quality and size of the corpus therefore influences how well an individual title can be analyzed.
5   This increasing 'detachment' of information, first from its physical and then from classificatory constraints, has prompted David Weinberger to declare that 'everything is miscellaneous', in the sense that a piece of information can 'hang on many branches [of a classificatory system], it can hang on different branches for different people, and it can change branches for the same person if she decides to look at the subject differently' (2007, 83).
6   Like many other companies, Google distinguishes between 'class A' (one vote per share) and 'class B' (ten votes per share) shares. This structure allows the founders and top-level executives to keep full control over the strategic direction of the company while extensively tapping the markets for capital.
7   http://books.google.com/ebooks.
8   According to Darnton (2011), this attempt to create a bookstore rather that a pure search tool is one of the reasons why the collective settlement between Google, the Authors Guild, and the Association of American Publishers was not approved by the courts in March 2011.
9   There are important limits due to polysemy, the difficulty to establish context, and the general complexity and situatedness of language and meaning. My point is, however, that even relatively unsophisticated techniques can deliver very interesting results if applied to large volumes of high quality data.
10  http://ngrams.googlelabs.com.
11  http://www.culturomics.org.
12  A 'gram' can be one ('1-gram') or several words ('n-gram'). The culturomics project fully counts *all* grams from one to five over the 5.2 million books.
13  http://www.google.com/support/websearch/bin/answer.py?answer=106230.
14  http://www.google.org/flutrends/.

# Bound to be a book

*Towards print as multimedia and e-books as paperbacks*

Florian Cramer

By the nineties, artists' and scholars' visions of 'unbound' books had shifted to the new medium of screen-based electronic literature. This seemed to be the consequent next step from concrete poetry and experimental artists' books towards a more comprehensive new culture of nonlinear writing and reading. Today, 20 years later, the relation of the old and the new medium seems to have flipped. There is now a mainstream, in graphic design and contemporary art, of print books with experimental and 'unbound' characteristics all the while e-books have settled on highly conventional linear formats. In this article, I will attempt to reconstruct why this might be more than a momentary freak accident of book history.

'When you open the book unbound, you will change it' (Cayley 2011). This premise was not just a promise. Published in a 1995 hypertext special issue of *Postmodern culture* – one of the very first online arts and humanities journals and discussion forums – John Cayley's *Book unbound* was a programmed, generative electronic text. It was technically based on Apple's HyperCard, an early hypertext, multimedia, and visual programming environment. HyperCard was freely bundled with every Macintosh from 1987 to 1991, saw its last update in 1992, and was ultimately abandoned in 2000 (Wikipedia 2004). 'HyperCard stacks' were black-and-white, ran on non-networked personal computers, and operated with mouse and keyboard. Otherwise, they were 'apps' according to contemporary terminology, i.e. small multimedia-centric computer programs.

Around the same time, electronic literature became a thriving academic field. It anticipated net art and even the World Wide Web itself by a couple of years, had its own conferences and festivals, specialized literature departments in the u.s. and Europe, and an extensive body of research literature on hyperfiction and e-literature. Still today, regardless of the fact that the field has shrunk dramatically, this strand of electronic literature has its own academic body, the Electronic Literature Organization (elo), whose research continues to be focused on a very small canon of works written for the most part in the academic world of American creative writing programs. More or often than not, these were the same literature departments – and even the same writers – that also produced its theory and criticism.

In the early nineties, HyperCard provided not only the foundation for most experimental computer poetry like that of Cayley and, for example, the French computer literature pioneer Jean-Pierre Balpe. The more mainstream 'expanded books' published by Bob Stein's company Voyager in 1992 were HyperCard stacks as well. One of Voyager's showcase products was 'Annotated Alice', an electronic version of the *Alice in Wonderland* edition with the annotations of Martin Gardner. Voyager's expanded books had taken inspiration from the release of Apple's first PowerBook notebook computers in 1991. In 2010, history repeated itself when Apple released the first iPad and 'Alice for the iPad' was developed by the London-based software and electronic book company Atomic Antelope. Similarly, the conference that preceded this book, The Unbound Book, took place in 2011 without the organizers having been aware of Cayley's *Book unbound*. Were the unbound books of nineties electronic literature just premature products because the hardware technology hadn't been there yet? Will 2012 technology solve the obstacles and finally establish the paradigm of unbound hypermedia books?

Even if the above *déjà-vus* of Apple buzz products and unbound books should be coincidental, it is striking how the debate on electronic literature seems to have stalled. In his famous 1991 essay *The end of books*, the American novelist Robert Coover wrote that

> In the real world nowadays, that is to say, in the world of video transmissions, cellular phones, fax machines, computer networks, and in particular out in the humming digitalized precincts of avant-garde computer hackers, cyberpunks and hyperspace freaks, you will often hear it said that the print medium is a doomed and outdated technology, a mere curiosity of bygone days destined soon to be consigned forever to those dusty unattended museums we now call libraries (Coover 1994).

Not much seems to have changed in electronic literature criticism in the 20 years since then. It appears as if it is the only field of new media studies that hasn't been updated and revised. The multimedia school of electronic literature has become *Alice in Wonderland* caught in an endless-pointless loop like at the hatter's tea party.

One year after Coover's article, his fellow Brown University literature professor George Landow for the first time linked electronic literature to poststructuralist literary and media theory. Drawing on Jacques Derrida and Roland Barthes as much as on Ted Nelson and Andries van Dam, he wrote on the first page of his book *Hypertext*:

> All four, like many others who write on hypertext or literary theory, argue that we must abandon conceptual systems founded upon ideas of center, margin, hierarchy, and linearity and replace them with ones of multilinearity, nodes, links, and networks. Almost all parties to this paradigm shift, which marks a revolution in human thought, see electronic writing as a direct response to the strengths and weaknesses of the printed book (Landow 1992, 2-3).

Landow still wrote this without any reference to the Internet and one year before the release of the first graphical web browser. Nevertheless, he did not advocate unbound electronic books. Unlike other electronic literature critics, his point was not a shift from print books to digital hyperbooks in a narrow sense, but more generally a shift from printed matter to networked writing – to the medium, in other words, that ultimately became the World Wide Web. What Landow envisioned as a 'revolution in human thought' became, in the everyday reality of the Internet, something much more down to earth. It was not Derrida and Barthes who became the paradigms of contemporary electronic writing culture but bloggers and the Anonymous movement, for example. Hypertext became a lesser paradigm for Internet writing than predicted, and where it still rules, for example in Wikipedia, it is used in a pragmatic manner that hardly matches the initial speculative visions of a hypertext 'docuverse'.

These shifts from initial utopias and expectations to later usage culture very much corresponded to those in audiovisual media. In the early nineties, it was commonly assumed that film and television would become interactive and turn into 'virtual reality'. They remained linear. Immersive interactive 3D audiovisuals nevertheless became a reality and mass product, but in its own proper medium of computer games. Games and films sometimes compete, sometimes even converge, but for the most part remain separate genres with their own particular aesthetic qualities, technical constraints, audiences, and cultures. Correspondingly, books and the web now coexist as two competing, sometimes converging yet for the most part independent forms of publishing. The web has largely discarded books for periodically updated reference works, such as telephone books, bibliographies and encyclopedias. Conversely, the book is still the preferred medium for large quantities of text that are read in its entirety or at least in long parts, and for works that are collected and archived long-term. Both media compete in areas of midsize publications that are neither dependent on periodic updates, nor necessarily on long-term archiving. Conference proceedings and comic strips fall under this category, for example. In none of these cases did the form of the publication change as radically as predicted in the nineties. And just as the transition of films and TV to digital files and streams was a symbolic form transitioning into a new medium that did not fundamentally change the symbolic form of film from the symbolic form of computer games, the transition of books into digital files does not imply fundamental changes of the symbolic form of books.[1]

Books, in this sense, do not mean printed matter by definition. In the last few years, electronic books finally have emerged as mass media, but since they retain the characteristics of books versus the web, they differ from the hypermedia electronic book culture envisioned in the nineties (and, under the banner of electronic books as game-like iPad apps, still today). Contemporary electronic book culture is best exemplified by the two commercial and anti-commercial extremes of Amazon's Kindle e-book store and the underground critical theory text repository aaaaarg.[2] Despite their opposite politics, both are based on the same concept of symbolic form and medium: the electronic book as a straightforward, no-frills downloadable text file offered for a multitude of reading devices. The Kindle e-book store has been modeled, in design, technology, and business model, after Apple's iTunes store for paid music file downloads; aaaaarg conversely is the text-cultural equivalent of underground mp3 file sharing.

Digital audio thus provides an important history lesson for electronic books. Just as electronic literature had been mostly synonymous with experimental hypermedia writing in the nineties, electronic music had been synonymous with computer-generative algorithmic music since Lejaren Hiller composed the *Iliac suite* in 1956. It was the music expected for the year 2001, in Stanley Kubrick's film and elsewhere. Since the nineties, electronic composition has also involved interactive interface controls like the ones provided by the programming environments Max/MSP and Pure Data. But the notion of electronic music had already shifted by the seventies and eighties when it became pop. In 2001, digital audio did not travel in space, but stayed firmly on the ground where people shared mp3 files.

Just like mp3 files, electronic books only became popular when they remained technically simple and universally playable while providing – unlike Project Gutenberg – attractive contemporary material. The popularity of textfiles.com and aaaaarg.org is neither dependent on any particular electronic reader hardware nor a particular e-book file format. Even Amazon's Kindle is no longer intrinsically linked to the e-ink reader of the same name, but can alternatively be run as a software app on various devices (including iPhones and Android phones).

Particularly in the ASCII and ePub formats, electronic text files mean the second historical transformation of the way books are bound: after having morphed from pre-medieval scrolls to codices, electronics have transformed them into a medium in between a scroll – with text having no static pagination – and a codex, since the physical limits of the display still amount to a de-facto page.

And how important is it really for the electronic book to be a networked medium? The conference panel for which this paper was written had the following abstract:

> Online the book becomes part of a vast, interactive network of footnotes, endnotes, hyperlinks, social tags, geo-location search capabilities, animations, video and sound. It becomes an occasion for social annotations and collaborative communities of readers and authors.

This sums up Bob Stein's contemporary effort, two decades after the Voyager expanded books, of redesigning electronic books as social media. Aside from that, it is a description of the World Wide Web rather than the book. What is the sense of making electronic books like the World Wide Web when there already is a World Wide Web? If conversely the World Wide Web would be an e-book, readers would likely not be able to read it a few years later because of broken links, spammed social tags, depreciated geo-location programming interfaces, and obsolete video and sound codecs. So far, interlinked networked media have only remained stable in closed systems such as the JSTOR database of humanities papers or in the Digital Object Identification System (DOI).

Just like the HyperCard stacks of the early nineties, the multimedia CD-ROMs and Macromedia Shockwave projects of the late nineties, Flash applets of the early 2000s, and the iPad apps of the 2010s, a contemporary multimedia e-book would likely not work on the hardware, operating system, and screen of an electronic device in the year 2020. 'Alice in Wonderland' would have to be reprogrammed from scratch again, an initiation rite for every new e-book-startup and every new generation of hardware and software on the market. On top of its sheer absurdity, this brings the consumerist nightmare of endless recycling, remaking, and reselling throwaway media from the film and music to the publishing industries.

It is likely no coincidence that Carroll's novel became the recurring showcase item of electronic literature since it is perhaps the only best-selling, all-popular piece of literary avant-garde and experimental writing in the Western world, a text lending itself to media experiments while still having the sufficient mass market to recuperate the software development costs.[3] The gamification of books, in other words, is possible, but limited to niches, and comes at the price of complex, unstable file formats.

Unbound books existed much earlier than electronic computers, as artists' experiments with the medium of the paper codex. With forerunners in classical and medieval visual poetry and Victorian children's books, the twentieth century was a 'Century of Artists' Books', to quote the title of Johanna Drucker's seminal book on the subject. (Drucker 2004) One of Drucker's examples is the book 'Boundless' by the American artist and graphic designer David Stairs. (Ibid, 177) Consisting of circular pages that are spiral-bound throughout their entire circumference (and therefore cannot be opened), and the letters 'Boundless' on their cover, it is the perfect emblem of the dialectics of the bound and the unbound book. By virtue of its circularity, the book's binding has a boundless surface. Binding and unbinding thus exists in a paradox. Despite this paradox, Stairs' object of reflection still leaves binding as the lowest common denominator of a book, something that can't be escaped even when it is subverted.

A book, it follows, is almost anything bound together or unbound in negative reference to the former. True boundlessness is never achieved, and being unbound does not mean to be boundless.

While this sums up the spatial, synchronic dimension of a book's binding, there also is a temporal, diachronic one. A book is a bunch of stuff bound together so that it does not fall apart. The motivation for not having a book fall apart is its future readability – one, ten, or 100 years later. There are exceptions to this; telephone books (that are being phased out for the more apt unstable medium of Internet databases) and less common ones like an auto-destructive book by the contemporary artist Jan Voss whose pages are slowly being perforated by two worms living inside the corpus.[4] But just like Stairs' work, this book is a negative extrapolation, an exception of instability proving the rule of stability all the more by the virtue of its several hundred, heavy, oversize pages. Even within print culture, the book has typically been thought of as a more stable and durable medium than a short-lived newspaper or flyer. The same is happening in electronic publishing. Just because of their relative simplicity, straightforwardness and collectability, text files have become the electronic books of our time. ASCII has been stable since 1963; the Project Gutenberg and textfiles.com as the oldest electronic literature repositories (with files dating back to the early seventies) have outlived, in their pure technical readability, all hypermedia literature. Based on ASCII and simplified XHTML in a zip file, ePub will remain accessible for the same reasons.

No definition of the book, however, is set in stone. The creation of the World Wide Web as a dynamic, up-to-date, ephemeral and unstable medium of writing has not necessarily pushed the notion of the book towards similar unstable attributes, as expected in the nineties, but on the contrary helped to solidify its notion of a comparatively stable, long-term medium. Short-lived information, from news journalism to telephone registers and city maps, has migrated from print to the web for the opposite reasons. The chances to still find a research paper published online ten years later are dim – in the worst case, it has vanished, in the second worst case, it still is online but its URL has changed. The ubiquity of content management systems with their automatically assigned URLs, prone to breaking with every software upgrade, has worsened this situation, but print is not the only solution. The book as a more stable medium than the web is not at all an issue of print or electronics. Electronic text files, just like print books, can survive longer than a web site on a server as its single point of failure – because their storage is distributed, with as many backups as there are readers of a book.

There are parallels to this new appreciation of low-tech simplicity in the contemporary visual arts. In the 1990s, many experimental artists who had previously worked with unstable do-it-yourself media such as video, performance, and small press print publications happily moved to the web as an efficient and inexpensive community medium of artistic production and communication. 20 years later, there is a contrary resurgence of non-electronic media in the contemporary arts, particularly of self-published books and zines. These media have become a counterculture to the Internet with its corporate, data-mined social networking and throwaway information culture. The binding of these books and zines has also become social and cultural glue. Just like structural experimental 16mm filmmaking began in the 1960s as an act of resistance against cinema's glamour and dream factory, but turned into an act of love for the endangered medium of celluloid by the 2000s, the poetics of artists' books have shifted from de(con)structions of the codex – in its double sense of binding and book of law – to a celebration and expansion of its tangible materiality.

Johanna Drucker points out how even in their most unstable forms, books never do away with their material unity or binding: 'In examining the way artists have interrogated the structure of the book, it is important to begin with the obvious but also profound realization that a book should be thought of as a whole. A book is an entity, to be reckoned with in its entirety' (Ibid, 122).

Looking at two classical examples of unbound literary books, Marc Saporta's card stack novel 'Composition no. 1' and Raymond Queneau's sonnet 'One hundred thousand billion poems' whose lines are slit so that every single one may be chosen from 12 alternatives, it is obvious how both works explode the codex. Queneau's still retains its spine; Saporta's, though arguably the most radically nonlinear novel of all times, is still bound by virtue of the envelope that holds its pages and the finite number of pages of which it consists. In both examples, binding becomes even more accentuated. The books thus prove what Drucker writes in the same chapter:

> To remain artists' books, rather than book-like objects or sculptural works with a book reference to them, these works have to maintain a connection to the idea of the book – to its basic form and function as the presentation of material in relation to a fixed sequence which provides access to its contents (or ideas) through some stable arrangement. Such a definition stretches elastically to reach around books which are card stacks, books which are solid pieces of bound material, and other books whose nature defies easy characterization (Ibid, 122f).[5]

If the notion of the book is tied to a 'stable arrangement' of material in one item or unit, then it becomes all the more obvious why the notion of electronic literature became problematic after the early nineties. In its American schools, it did not mean literary writing on the web, but most of all the creation of standalone, one-entity works in analogy to the book: HyperCard stacks, Storyspace hypertexts, Macromedia director presentations, Multimedia CD-ROMs, Flash applets. Each technological crisis and obsolescence of those file formats therefore amounted to an aesthetic and literary crisis of this genre as well.[6] Other schools of electronic literature, for example in Germany and Russia, that simply understood their practice as writing online, moved to blogging, and eventually converged with op-ed journalism.

Perhaps surprisingly, Drucker's notion of the book as 'the presentation of material in relation to a fixed sequence which provides access to its contents (or ideas) through some stable arrangement' is very close to the technical specification of ePub, the open standard file format for electronic books:

> EPUB Publications are not limited to the linear ordering of their contents, nor do they preclude linking in arbitrary ways – just like the Web, EPUB Publications are built on hypertext – but the basic consumption and navigation can be reliably accomplished in a way that is not true for a set of HTML pages.[7]

The codex, as a binding of diverse stuff within one whole, migrates into a data navigation structure: 'A key concept of EPUB is that a Publication consists of multiple resources that may be completely navigated and consumed by a person or program in some specific order'. In other words, e-books as defined here are not unbound books at all. As opposed to web sites, they

- are offline media, self-contained documents without external links or embedding, based on a subset of HTML and CSS that does not require network connections;
- are based on static text, with audio, video, and scripting as purely optional and non-essential features. The ePub specification specifies that every e-book must remain readable and usable on readers that do not support any of them;[8]
- are read-only documents, with no internal support for input forms, annotations, or alterations of the text;
- do not prescribe a particular visual look or layout, but are supposed to look differently on different reading devices.[9]

Since e-books, in the above sense, follow the mp3 file paradigm of the lowest common technological denominators of portability instead of audiovisuality, predictable behavior instead of complexity, they are far more restricted in their media richness and artistic design possibilities than print books. A project on e-book-design at the Piet Zwart Institute Rotterdam confirmed these observations. One of the students, graphic designer Megan Hoogenboom, adapted Paul van Ostaijen's 1920s visual poem 'boem paukenslag' – a classic of Dutch avant-garde literature – to ePub, with the result that the visual poetry of the text could only be adapted using the crudest hacks in the technical syntax of the ePub file. The resulting file only properly displayed on one particular model of the Sony Reader since other devices destroyed the (essential) pagination or could not render the poem's large font letters. While some of these compatibility issues were a déjà vu of browser incompatibility in the early years of the World Wide Web, most of them were intrinsic to the very concept of ePub. Since the format is designed to be independent from display size (from mobile phones to high definition screens) and display technology (whether e-ink, color LCDs or braille) and have no predefined pagination, it has rendered the graphic design paradigm of the page and even the screen unworkable.

Consequently, media richness, visuality and tactility have become the domain of print. Artists' books and periodicals have turned into a graphic design genre for which in particular the publications of Dexter Sinister/dotdotdot have set a contemporary art trend. Along with this trend, print as a whole is moving from mass media to a boutique niche, not unlike calligraphy did after the invention of the printing press. In what could metaphorically be called heat death of print, all printed matter strives to become coffee table books, with 'warm' materiality and 'unbound' characteristics, privileging collector's value over everyday use value. What Drucker investigates in the fifth chapter of her book, 'The Artist's Book as a Rare and/or Auratic Object' (Drucker 2006, 93), is rapidly becoming the business model for the whole print industry, the print book as a fetishized collector's item like vinyl LPs. Many if not most print books today are subsidized – by academia, institutions, non-profits, and companies – because of the desire for a long-term readable publication, but also because of the long history and resulting prestige of the book. Because of these factors, the crisis of paper book publishing has not yet been as visible, at least in Europe, as for example the foreclosure of record stores.[10]

With print becoming boutique publishing, electronic books are striving away from the 1990s hypermedia coffeetable. They are conversely turning into today's equivalent of paperbacks, cheap (or even pirated) books with the added convenience of folding book and library into a single reading device. Although applications like Apple's iBook Store visually simulate bookshelves, complete with fake wood, on iPhone and iPad screens, e-book libraries in the end can't be shown off like in the Great Gatsby. If e-books will be the no-frills books for no-frills reading, running keyword searches over, carrying around, and illegally sharing with friends, then e-books will unbind the book in the same way that mp3 has unbound audio recordings. It is, however, not the kind of unbinding imagined in 1990s interactive hypermedia visions.

## Notes

1   The term 'symbolic form' is used here according to Ernst Cassirer's *Philosophy of symbolic forms*.
2   http://aaaaarg.org. Though the site, in order to dodge takedown notices, is constantly adding and contracting the number of 'a's in its domain name.
3   Kolja Bedürftig voices a similar concern in a 2011 article for the professional organization of German book traders: "Ich sehe eine Analogie zwischen den 'Multimedia-CD-ROM-Projekten', die in den späten 90ern gehypt wurden und den 'enhanced' E-Books. Problematisch sind heute wie damals die Produktionskosten, die schnell den Rahmen sprengen können", http://www.boersenblatt.net/442555, accessed October 2011.
4   Voss is also discussed by Drucker (1996), pp.171-172, 204-208.
5   Her statement that 'All books are visual'', p. 197, needs to be contested though in a time of audiobooks and e-books that can alternatively read as braille or via text-to-speech software.
6   http://idpf.org/epub/30/spec/epub30-overview.html.
7   http://idpf.org/epub/30/spec/epub30-overview.html. This is why the Electronic Literature Organization initiated the 'Acid-Free Bits' and 'Born-Again Bits' initiatives, with no success yet (Electronic Literature Organization 2003 and 2005).
8   'Scripting consequently should be used only when essential to the User experience, since it greatly increases the likelihood that content will not be portable across all Reading Systems and creates barriers to accessibility and content reusability', http://idpf.org/epub/30/spec/epub30-overview.html.
9   Bedürftig: "Schon bei einfachen EPUB-Dateien, die einen gewissen Anspruch an das Layout erfüllen sollen, besteht aktuell das Problem, dass für verschiedene Plattformen optimiert werden muss. Alternativ suche man vergnügt nach dem kleinsten gemeinsamen Nenner...".
10  Although in the Netherlands, printers are foreclosing on a large scale at the time of this writing (late 2011). Even the variety of paper available for book production is massively declining, according to print designers. (My thanks to Nienke Terpsma for this information.) On the book as a carrier of prestige, see Giesecke (1998), and Van der Weel (2011a), chapter three.

# Digital readers' responsibilities

Alain Giffard

In the last chapter of the *History of reading in the West*, Armando Petrucci (1999) discusses 'a future for reading'. In this essay from 1995, he points out that the questions to ask are not so much about the future of the act of reading per se, but rather about the nature of the reading activity and the place devoted to reading in our culture. He observes the fast diffusion of reading practices that he associates with the figure of the 'anarchist reader': simply reading in order to read. According to Petrucci, the anarchist reader – the reader of the future whom we could perhaps call the 'consumer reader' – wants no responsibility, and takes none. This reader refuses the constraints of the canon – the order of texts – and refuses the constraints of the order of books. Instead, through his practices, he is an agent of the dissolution of the traditional 'order of reading' in the West.

Many commentators consider the digital reader a worthy successor of the anarchist reader. But whether he is regarded as an anarchist or as a consumer, the portrait of the digital reader I will draw here suggests that he actually has a lot of work to do: he carries the burden of several responsibilities.

## Responsibility for the text

The first responsibility of the digital reader is that towards the text itself and towards its medium. The digital online reader assumes, up to a certain point, a part of the work of the author and publisher. He puts himself in the author's place by performing *la clôture du texte*, the closure of the text. He selects, collects, and binds together different fragments of texts. His reading may be highly purposeful and determined, or full of swerves and lapses. In any case, he faces what Milad Doueihi (2011) calls the anthological nature of the web: fragments of writing, some of them connected in small networks of text.[1] No one reads beyond the first ten results presented by a search engine. And everyone follows a double path, a mixture of systematic 'beacons' provided by the search engine and hyperlinks provided within the text. The product of this process is not a book, nor the equivalent of a book, but only a sort of provisional corpus, a personal fair copy, so to speak.

But in order to produce a text that is ready for reading, each chunk of it must first be assessed. The fragmentation of the digital text as a provisional corpus or personal anthology requires it to be bound into a coherent whole, and its diversity and multiplicity requires editing. The reader, like an editor, has to differentiate original texts from information, original information from duplicates. And, of course, he has to judge not only the genre or category of the text but also its special value. So the reader confers a sort of fluid authority on text, by selecting and extracting its constitutive fragments, not from the whole web, but from the specific smaller networks of texts they are part of.

Browsing is the name given to this activity of editing and binding the digital text. It is a typical performance of digital reading, widespread and as yet rather mysterious, since little research has been done on this kind of reading.

This practice of browsing I have suggested could be referred to as 'pre-reading', a notion that derives from the Roman *praelectio*. Various situations have occurred in the history of reading when such preparation for reading was regarded as essential, for example to read a scroll, or a text without word spacing. In fact, pre-reading appears necessary each time the distance between the reader and the text – or its medium  is too great.

Mostly it is the technology of the medium that stands in the way of a direct reading. But sometimes a particular public is too far from the text or the medium for cultural reasons. For example, the Irish monks of the seventh century, as they were non-native speakers of Latin, faced particular difficulties with unseparated words, the *scriptio continua*. The Jesuit *praelectio*, probably the most famous example of an exercise of preparation for reading, was a sort of first-level interpretation of the text.

In the digital environment, pre-reading is probably a transitional activity: the digital text is not yet stabilised (if it ever will stabilise), and digital literacy is only beginning to be formalised. Also, it would appear that browsing, as a preparation for effective digital reading, is mostly aimed at allowing the reader to master the medium rather than the text (the 'content'). Browsing is a mediatic performance. Here, in the midst of the act of reading, the beginning of an economy can be observed: the approach to the text makes the actual reading easier.

An analogy with the author and the publisher is useful – though it should not hide the specific responsibility of the digital reader. Unlike in the case of writing and publishing, the reader's 'anthological gesture' of binding and editing does not lead to the circulation of the resulting text. On the contrary, it separates texts from the network that is the Web. The readings may be shared later, as recommendations, tags, and commentaries, but the act of browsing and constituting the provisional corpus or anthology itself is not shared. 'One author, one text, one book' – the principle of the classic book – is replaced by 'Many authors, many texts, one anthology'.

The reader's responsibility here is about the quality of the anthology – the selection of each fragment and the consistency of the whole – but mainly it is about the quality of reading itself: is it well prepared for? Calling this an 'ethics of browsing' is perhaps going a little too far. More precisely it is a responsibility for the knowledge and know-how involved in pre-reading.

## Responsibility for one's reading

It is not without reason that the question of attention has recently become important in public debate, becoming one of the main bones of contention with regards to digital reading. Reading is an act of attention. The different reading methods have always been based in some way on conceptions and practices of attention that the Latins named *catena* (chain of ideas or images). And reading has become a major form of attention training.

Pediatricians, psychiatrists, and neuroscientists have all pointed out different factors that variously stand in the way of attention when engaged in digital reading.[2] The notion of cognitive overload is a good summary of these obstacles.

Some obstacles are in the domain of legibility, reminding us of all the efforts of typography to overcome them when making printed books. More significant are the obstacles in the domain of readability. Cognitive overload appears in time as well as in space. Hyperlinks – not the original principle of hyperlinks as devised by Ted Nelson and others, but their actual functionality and appearance on the Web[3] – are a good illustration of this necessity to solve reading problems external to the text. Hyperlinks have to be evaluated a priori by the reader so he can make up his mind whether to activate them or not. The reader must project himself mentally to the end of the link and decide between the security of a text with which he is beginning to be familiar and the uncertainty of opening a new, maybe richer one. All of these considerations weigh on the principal task of reading, and the consequence of this overload is tantamount to the classical risk of breaking off the thread of reading. Similarly, multimedia and the multi-tasking interface are another cause of cognitive overload.

So it seems that the digital environment as a whole – text, medium, interfaces, as well as the hardware itself – produces a range of serious obstacles to the attention needed for reading. Sometimes digital reading presents itself as just a bunch of distractions.

Nevertheless this notion of distraction needs to be investigated. In the example of Cassian as a young monk unable to pray because his mind is besieged by the memories of the frivolous fables of Ovid (a traditional case of conflicts between *catenas*), or in the popular poem by Jacques Prévert, 'The dunce', distraction is an exit out of a world of representations towards a second one, clearly exterior. Is distraction in digital reading the same? Or is it, more likely, the product of a conflict between two kinds of attention inside the process of reading: a 'text-driven attention' and a 'medium-driven attention'? The printed book is a splendid medium with a great capacity to be easily forgotten and refound during the act of reading. In comparison, the digital medium is noisy and uncertain. However, a minimal dose of medium-driven attention is not a bad thing. The digital reader is actually threatened less by the attention the medium demands than by the confusion between the two attentions. I am suggesting that browsing conceived as pre-reading could be one way to coordinate the two attentions.

Attention is not only a foundation for the psychology of reading. Rather it is the bridge between the cognitive and the cultural side of reading. The digital reader has a responsibility for his attention because he has a responsibility for the type of reading he engages in. Deep and sustained attention is directly connected with deep and sustained reading, that is to say, in all the cases where reading and reflection are strongly associated. Cognitive overload and the confusion of the two types of attention are not only a problem for readability, or strict efficiency of reading. They are also a threat to the association between reading and reflection.[4]

The association between reading and reflection is not at all natural. On the contrary, it is a historical and cultural construction. It was first conceived by Augustine as an association of *lectio* and *meditatio* and systematised in the twelfth century by Hugh of Saint Victor (1939) in his *Didascalicon*.[5] It is mainly characteristic of the studying type of reading, of reading as an intellectual exercise, or a 'technology of the self'.[6] But as a general method, including a certain type of attention and memory, reflective reading is present as an object of education, training, and transmission in larger fields of the cultural practice of reading.

Maybe the best example of this conception of reading which insists on the link with reflection can be found in the preface that Marcel Proust wrote for his translation of John Ruskin's book *Sesame and lilies* (Proust and Ruskin 2011). In the first lecture in this book, Ruskin supports the programme of public libraries in England. He challenges utilitarianism and the conception of knowledge as a means of individual and material progress and argues that reading is entering the life of the spirit. In opposition to this argument, Proust develops the theory that reading by itself does not allow one to enter the life of the spirit. Reading is a beginning, and literacy a knowledge of the beginnings. Its true value lies in the power of the preparation for reflection or meditation, which are specific activities of intellectual life. In another passage of the text, Proust criticises the confusion between reading and what we now call 'information access'. After all, Proust appears as an heir to the tradition of reading as a spiritual exercise and a practice of the self, mostly of the combination of reading, reflection, and memory.

Recently, the American psychologist Maryanne Wolf (2007) published a book about the reading brain entitled *Proust and the squid*. Wolf's general thesis is that psychologists' research meets the point of view of the author of *Remembrance of things past*. The convergence point is the association of reading and reflection, the power of reading as a preparation for reflection. It is an astonishing and maybe bitter lesson for humanities scholars that the great texts of the philosophy of reading nowadays need to be confirmed and legitimised by the neurosciences and cognitive sciences.

As the debate between Proust and Ruskin shows, the question of the reader's responsibility for his own reading and particularly the choice between different types of reading, including the link with reflection, is neither new nor confined to digital reading. But the peculiarity of digital reading is the real difficulty to distinguish and recombine these two types of attention. It is always possible to print the page and undertake a deep reading on paper – research has shown this to be a common practice – but such a practice is not exactly a demonstration in favour of digital reading (Liu 2006). It is one of the primary effects of the use of digital technology in the process of reading that so much attention is claimed by the medium and that it presents so many obstacles to readability and reflection.

## Responsibility for the technology

Traditionally the technology of reading can be found in two main places: in the medium (book and paper) and in the reader himself, as a method, or art of reading.

Historians of reading have insisted on the fact that readers do not access the text directly, but that they do so in the material form of a book.[7] And they consider that reading is autonomous, not only in regard to the text, as in literary studies, but also in regard to the medium. In this perspective, technologies are seen as devices supporting the reading, inside the medium, or accompanying the reader's practices.

Computing has brought a new category of technologies in the form of equipment: a reading machine. In fact, the history of the computer is mixed with the history of the reading machine. The tandem e-reader/e-book (device and medium) is one instance of this mechanisation of reading through computing.

For a long period the technology of digital reading merged with the design of hypertext. Vannevar Bush, Douglas Engelbart, Ted Nelson, and Tim Berners-Lee are the canonic representatives of this orientation.[8] The destiny of digital reading seemed to be hypertextual readings, and hypertext is still the one and only collective reading project that has emerged from the computer science community.[9]

But, in spite of the success of hyperlinks, and the reference to hypertext in different formats, the new trend in digital reading is very different. In the classical hypertext ('Memex' or 'Xanadu'), producing hyperlinks was a method for the reader to create his own path for reading. This is no longer the case with the web: web technologies consist in reading hypertext, and not hypertextual reading.

A second difference, maybe more important for our subject, must be emphasised: a major objective since Vannevar Bush was to produce a reading device (machine and techniques) with the aim of aiding the human reader. The new trend is for devices that read for themselves, robots, for example. These new devices are industrial; they produce what I have called 'industrial readings'.[10]

The abandonment of the project of computer-assisted hypertextual reading has created a new situation of technology by default.[11] There is not a lack of elementary techniques; techniques are in the text, the medium, the devices, and on the side of the reader; in fact the digital reading environment is bursting with techniques. But they are not organised, nor integrated in a general design for the human reader.

The responsibility of the reader is to make this technology become effective by default. He performs a sort of one-off and local technical process. This process is the rebellious shadow of the act of reading. It may be described as a sequence of decisions: choosing hardware, software, formats, functionalities, and operations, and laying them out in a way adapted to a certain type of reading. For example, the reader must choose between computer, tablet, e-reader, or a mix. He must decide to stick to the screen or to print the text. He has to choose the format to archive the text, and where to place any annotations.

But this technological work of the reader comes up against a huge difficulty. The various means of digital reading are produced by industries. These industries digitise the means of reading and digitise the texts. They trade in readings and readers. They may be called reading industries, to emphasise the difference with book publishers, those classical figures of the cultural industry. They do not belong to the 'content industry' but to the 'access economy'.

Above all, reading industries, such as Google, are one of the principal vectors of the 'attention economy', which presents two sides: the production of attention, and the trading of attention. All the activities and all the techniques of the reading industries, as attention industries, are turned towards the trading of reading and the trading of readers. The technological orientations and the business models of Google, Amazon, and Apple are quite different, but the general scheme is that of the access economy and attention economy.

So the technological work of the reader will not only involve the difficulties of a technology by default. The reader of the twenty-first century encounters a lot of extraordinary novelties. Not only the act or the activity of reading is being changed by technology; the life of the reader is utterly transformed. Reading robots have appeared in the last twenty years, and they are now present in all domains of life, and all day long. Many users of the web are so fascinated by technology that they look at the texts produced by robots as if they were written by people. These texts are more and more customised, fit to everyone's personalised profile, and many readers do not even suspect it. Recommendation engines, for example, are very promising. Contextual advertising is another example. Looking for an interview with Vannevar Bush in *Life* magazine, it was splendid to discover all the digitised old issues on Google Books. There was some original advertising around the article about Bush. But there was also a lot of modern advertising linked to the old advertising. Attention industries succeed in performing this miracle: to transform dead marketing of dead products into a new raw material for present-day marketing.

These few examples show that as far as technology is concerned, the first responsibility of the reader is to criticise it. He must distinguish good or mediocre techniques that can accompany him in his reading from others that are only means to trade readings and readers. The digital reading space is no longer a personal place but has become a public and commercial place. Personalised technology resembles personal technology, but it has the opposite effect.

## Responsibility about training and creation of a public

Since Armando Petrucci published his essay 'Reading to read: A future for reading' in 1995, reading has gone through profound changes. In many countries, the number of books and newspapers being read has significantly decreased. Of late, the number of books – and especially the number of newspapers – sold has also begun to fall. The performance of reading, after decades of progress, has begun to diminish, slowly but regularly, for twenty years. The development of digital reading, though it is neither the origin nor the cause of these various decreases, is of course another major shift in reading.

Something else has changed since 1995. Petrucci contrasts the 'dominant culture' – reading as it is taught in school, the order of reading answering to the canon, the order of texts – with the new 'anarchist reader' who refuses the canon and adopts individual ways of reading.

Today, to stick with the expression 'the dominant culture', we must put it in the plural: *the dominant cultures*. The first one is the classical one transmitted through education; the second one is industrial and organised around the attention economy. Public authorities continue to provide school education, but they also sustain the attention economy, in the same way as they have encouraged audiovisual media. In 1995, the competition between television and books took place outside the question of reading, and its influence, examined by Petrucci, was exterior. Today the competition between digital reading and classical reading is about the very practice of reading. Accordingly, the making and the learning of digital literacy, as well as its connection with general literacy, have become crucial. The digital reader is responsible for digital literacy, and he acquires and practises it almost without any help from the public authorities.

Digital literacy is specific but clearly dependent on classical literacy. It may be conceived as a branch of general literacy, not as a parallel road. The different activities and knowledges corresponding to the reader's responsibilities for the text, the type of reading, and the technology: all of them need general literacy. And literacy is not only knowledge; it is also exercise. Reading not only consists in a series of reading operations. Reading is an activity, a practice. In fact, the reading exercise is at the centre of literacy.

In *The shallows*, Nicholas Carr (2010) distinguishes classical and digital reading and considers them as two different 'ways our mind works'. This part of his demonstration is based on the theory of neuroplasticity. If the notion of a profound cognitive difference between the two readings is to be verified, the theory of neuroplasticity will confirm the necessity to preserve the exercise of classical (deep and sustained) reading, and the connection with reflection. On the other hand, I do not see why the theory of neuroplasticity should demonstrate the impossibility of conceiving and combining two types of exercises for the two types of reading.

Anyway, digital literacy and training for digital reading cannot only be individual activities. Maybe the most important responsibility of digital readers is to become a public, a general public, or different reading communities.

Very quickly, the Web has given an important place to the reader and to something that may be called 'published reading'. Blogs often present journals of reading on the Web. The practices of commentary, annotation, tags, and posting on social networks have extended this trend. There are some specific communities of readers, but mostly communities of collaborative writing and reading, on the model of Wikipedia. Being trusted with selecting, writing, and browsing as well, the reader's status has grown in the digital environment. But, on the other hand, there is nothing like the general public as Immanuel Kant, for example, imagined it, around the principle of publication: Öffentlichkeit.

The public of digital readers is divided into many different groups, according to heterogeneous logics.

In 'Explorations in the libroverse', Adriaan van der Weel (2011c) writes:

> And if we have any doubt whether we are capable of willingly destroying our carefully constructed knowledge machinery, let's face it, the new generation is already doing it. They appear very happy to forego the guidance of their elders and betters, and to be comfortable in finding their own way through the jungle.

This may be an optimistic prospect that illustrates the differences between 'readers of the book' and 'digital native readers'. I should like to call to mind another division line: gender.

In the last period, in many western societies, the attitudes of women and men towards reading have diverged. Women read more books. Among the young, the gender gap is impressive, both in terms of the number of books read and in terms of the quality of reading. Girls are better readers and perform better at school. Professionals of the book, teachers, librarians, and even publishers, are mostly women. The boys say goodbye to the book when they become teenagers. A large minority has great difficulties with attention. They seem to prefer computer and videogames; but for most of them classical literacy is not sufficient for the practice of digital reading.

Gender has always been a 'significant variable' of the order of reading. Did you say, 'the order of reading'?

## Notes

1   About the anthological nature of the web, see also: Milad Doueihi, *L'Humanisme numérique* (2011).
2   A selection by an amateur, among many books and articles: Gary Small and Gigi Vorgan, *iBrain: Surviving the technological alteration of the modern mind* (2008); Thierry Baccino, *La lecture électronique* (2004); David S. Miall and Teresa Dobson, 'Reading hypertext and the experience of literature' (2001); Diana DeStephano and Jo-Anne LeFevre, 'Cognitive load in hypertext reading: A review' (2007); Eyal Ophir, Clifford Nass, and Anthony D. Wagner, 'Cognitive control in media multitaskers' (2009); Ziming Liu, 'Reading behavior in the digital environment' (2006).
3   See also Kircz and Den Boef in this collection.
4   The merit of Nicholas Carr, with his article 'Is Google making us stupid?', 2009, is to have introduced for the general public the question of digital reading and its link with reflection. See: Nicholas Carr, *The shallows: What the Internet is doing to our brains* (2010). I have presented a commentary of this book in: Alain Giffard, 'Critique de la lecture numérique: *The shallows* de Nicholas Carr' (2011).
5   About Augustine: Brian Stock, *Augustine the reader: Meditation, self-knowledge, and the ethics of interpretation* (1996). The *Didascalicon* of Hugh of Saint Victor has been edited by Charles B. Buttimer (1939). Hugh is one the chief authors studied by Mary Carruthers in *The book of memory* (1990).
6   Michel Foucault introduced the idea of reading as a 'technology of the self', or a 'practice of the self' in *L'Herméneutique du sujet* (2001b). See: L.H. Martin et al: *Technologies of the self. A seminar with Michel Foucault* (1988).
7   See the introduction by Guglielmo Cavallo and Roger Chartier to *A history of reading in the West* (1999), and Roger Chartier: *The order of books: Readers, authors, and libraries in Europe between the fourteenth and eighteenth centuries* (1994).
8   The two classics of hypertext are: Vannevar Bush, 'As we may think' (1945), and Ted Nelson, *Literary machines* (1980). See also: James M. Nyce and Paul Kahn, *From memex to hypertext* (1991).
9   'Hypertextual Derrida, Poststructuralist Nelson?' In *Hypertext: The convergence of contemporary critical theory and technology* (1992), George P. Landow tries to establish the convergence of critical theory and hypertext technology. From Derrida's notion of 'De-Centering', he assigns a new place to the reader of hypertext: 'All hypertext systems permit the individual reader to choose his or her own center of investigation and experience'. In *Writing space: The computer, hypertext and the history of writing* (1991) Jay David Bolter is still more radical about the convergence and the new role of the reader. In a passage titled 'The reader's response', he writes: 'It is sometimes uncanny how well the post-modern theorists seem to be anticipating electronic writing...The new medium reifies the metaphor of reader response, for the reader participates in the making of the text as a sequence of words.' About the particular atmosphere of this convergence period, before the web appeared, see also the books edited by Edward Barrett: *Text, context and hypertext* (1988), *The society of text* (1989), and *Sociomedia* (1992). For a commentary on this question: Alain Giffard, 'Petites introductions à l'hypertexte' (1997).
10  For a more complete presentation of industrial readings: Alain Giffard, 'Des lectures industrielles' (2009). An English summary: Alain Giffard, 'Digital readings, industrial readings', in *Going digital: Evolutionary and revolutionary aspects of digitization* (2011).
11  An old example of such a device is the Computer Assisted Reading Environment ('CARE'). I prepared this software, together with the philosopher Bernard Stiegler, when I was in charge of the design of the information system of the Bibliothèque Nationale de France, in the 1990s. See: Jacques Virbel, 'Reading and managing texts on the BNF station' (1993), Bernard Stiegler, 'Machines à écrire et matières à penser' (1994), Alain Giffard, 'La lecture numérique à la Bibliothèque de France' (2008).

# The digitisation of narrative reading

*Theoretical considerations and empirical evidence*

ANNE MANGEN

Reading is a neuronally and intellectually circuitous act, enriched as much by the unpredictable indirections of a reader's inferences and thoughts, as by the direct message to the eye from the text. This unique aspect of reading has begun to trouble me considerably as I consider the Google universe of my children. Will the constructive component at the heart of reading begin to change and potentially atrophy as we shift to computer-presented text, in which massive amounts of information appear instantaneously? [...] [I]s there either sufficient time or sufficient motivation to process the information more inferentially, analytically, critically? (Wolf 2007, 16)

## 'To read or not to read' should not be the question

In 2007 the National Endowment for the Arts (NEA, an independent agency of the United States federal government offering support and funding for art projects) published a report that caused quite a stir. The report was titled *To Read or not to read: A question of national consequence* (Iyengar 2007), and succeeded an almost equally disturbing NEA research report published three years earlier, titled *Reading at risk: A survey of literary reading in America* (Bradshaw and Nichols 2004). Summarised in brief, these two reports presented a gloomy picture of the status of reading in general, and literary and recreational reading in particular, among Americans – primarily young Americans. Literary reading was shown to be in sharp decline, and the authors expressed serious concerns about the far-reaching and long-term societal, cultural, and intellectual implications of this decline for the entire nation. Government-funded literary reading programs were launched in schools and libraries, and major efforts were made in an attempt to counter the ominous downward spiral. Judging from the findings in the most recent research report from the NEA, the efforts have been successful. The report published in 2009 is titled *Reading on the rise: A new chapter in American literacy* (NEA 2009) and conveys, by and large, a positive message: for the first time since the NEA began surveying American reading habits in 1982, the percentage of Americans who report reading literature (defined as novels, short stories, poems or plays online or in print) has risen rather than declined, going from 46.7 per cent in 2002 to 50.2 per cent in 2008 (NEA 2009).

The NEA publications were criticised – by some members of the community of digital arts and electronic literature in particular – for promoting a narrow conceptualisation of (literary) reading. Literary scholar at University of Maryland, Matthew Kirschenbaum (2007), contends that the NEA reports fail to acknowledge the ways in which reading is being remade in light of digital technologies. E-books, Google's large-scale digitisation of books, and online book catalogs show how 'reading is being both re-imagined and re-engineered, made over creatively as well as technologically' (Kirschenbaum 2007).

The act of reading, narrative and literary as well as non-narrative, has dispersed onto a wealth of digital screen technologies, such as e-books, surf pads, reading tablets, and even smart phones. This allows proponents of digital technologies to claim that children and young adults have never been reading (and writing) as much as they do today – after all, much if not most of what they do with their laptops, iPods and mobile phones is, arguably, reading (and writing).[1] Digital technologies, therefore, should rather be considered major facilitators of crucial communication and literacy skills in the twenty-first century.

Is there really any legitimate reason for concern that our, and our children's, modes, habits, and skills of reading have changed and even possibly atrophied as a consequence of the quite comprehensive changes in media and technology use and preferences? Is it the case that children read more and not less these days and that this is due to the increasing use of digital technologies in and outside of schools? If so, why do studies on the PIRLS data find that reading ability falls as leisure use of computers increases (Gustafsson and Rosén 2005)?[2] And why is it not the case that countries with the highest percentage of computers in and outside of schools do not score significantly higher on reading skills as measured in the PISA Digital Reading Assessment (OECD 2011)? These are important and pertinent questions. However, adequately answering them requires that we pose the questions with warranted precision, at the appropriate level of distinction. Every time we intend to discuss whether children or teenagers – or, anyone else – read more or less, we should make explicit what kinds of reading, what kinds of texts and literature, in what medium, under which circumstances and in which situations, and with what purpose, we are talking about. The complexity of the issue requires more fine-grained and distinct conceptualisations of the act of reading, the reader, and the material that is being read. The theoretical and phenomenological implications of the ongoing and increasing digitisation for the reading process and experience are complex and multifaceted and are only beginning to be fathomed. The depth and range of the problem complex represents a considerable challenge, requiring that we pose our questions at levels of considerably finer granularity than a polarised either-or debate.

The focus in this article is on *the changing interfaces of reading* and what this might entail for the cognitive-perceptual-sensorimotor processes involved in (primarily narrative, linear) reading – an aspect which is regretfully undertheorised in today's field of reading and literacy research. 'Interface' is understood in a broad sense, as including audiovisual and ergonomic affordances of the technological device with which the reader interacts (e.g., the binding, pages, and spine as well as the print text of the book, compared with the keyboard, computer mouse, and the audiovisuals of the screen of the desktop computer, the buttons on a Kindle or the audiovisually provided navigability options on the iPad touch screen). There is quite a lot of research addressing the impact of features such as hypertext navigation on cognitive load (for a review, see DeStefano and LeFevre 2007), the challenges pertaining to multitasking (e.g., the cognitive costs associated with switching between tasks) (Bowman, Levine, Waite, and Gendron 2010; Fox, Rosen, and Crawford 2009; Hembrooke and Gay 2003; Jacobsen and Forste 2011; Judd and Kennedy 2011; Lin 2009; Lin, Robertson, and Lee 2009; Ophir, Nass, and Wagner 2009), and the new challenges and possibilities for creative production and distribution inherent in educational multimedia design (Kirschner, Kester, and Corbalan 2011; Mayer 2001; Moreno and Mayer 2007). Considering the fact that children and young adults spend much of their time playing games, chatting, sending emails, and updating their Facebook profiles while (occasionally or frequently) at the same time doing their math homework, these are important topics of study. However, they do not necessarily tell us much about the effects of the affordances of digital technologies on certain aspects of reading, such as comprehension of long-form linear texts. For this reason, I will be focusing on the potential impact of the digital interfaces of computers, e-books, and smart phones, on so-called long-hand, sustained reading of linear texts that are composed, structured, and intended to be read linearly and sequentially, such as narratives (whether literary/fiction or prose/non-fiction). It might be argued that most of the reading performed digitally is of the 'opposite' kind, that is, ad-hoc, non-sequential, fragmented reading of interactive, multimedia hypertexts. However, e-books based on electronic paper (such as the Kindle) are designed for long-form reading,[3] and high schools, universities, and public libraries are increasingly providing e-books, implying that all kinds of reading might as well take place on screen. The questions beg themselves: How and to what extent might our comprehension and experience of linear, narrative (or non-narrative) texts differ when they appear on electronic paper on an e-book as compared to being printed on paper? Does it matter whether the text of, say, Stieg Larsson's *Girl with the dragon tattoo*, is printed on sheets of paper and bound in cloth, or is displayed in electronic ink on a Kindle? Do students perceive, recall, and comprehend the content differently when they read and annotate their geology study texts on an iPad or in the print text book? The skill of reading and comprehending narrative, linear texts is a major part of the skill of reading in general. Teaching children and young adults to develop and use appropriate and efficient reading strategies for narrative comprehension is a vital and fundamental part of reading instruction methods and programs at both beginning and advanced or continuing levels (Cain and

Oakhill 2004; Duffy and Israel 2009; Graesser and Bower 1990; Graesser, Millis, and Zwaan 1997; Kintsch 1998; McNamara 2007; Sweet and Snow 2003; Zwaan 1993, 1996). Reading and listening to narratives hold a prominent position in the human development of literacy, from the reading of children's picture books to stimulating and cultivating reflective thought and intellectual growth. Assessing literary/narrative reading comprehension is a main task in large-scale, international comparative reading and literacy assessments, such as PISA,[4] PIRLS[5] and ALL.[6] Hence, the ongoing, large-scale digitisation of narrative reading by increasingly replacing the print book with screen displays (whether electronic ink or LCD touch screens) warrants closer and thoroughly theoretically informed scrutiny, as it will supplement our broader understanding of the ongoing changes in reading as a skill and experience overall.

## Multisensory, embodied reading and ergonomic affordances

Intellectual activities such as reading and writing imply the human body, the human mind, and some material object or device on and by means of which we read and write. By corollary, they are highly device-dependent. This further implies that, rather than being exclusively cognitive and intellectual enterprises, reading and writing are inherently multisensory and embodied (Mangen 2008; Mangen and Schilhab 2012; Mangen and Velay 2010). We do not read only with our eyes and in our heads (not even in the most rigorous experimental settings). Neither do we write merely with our fingers and hands, even though it may certainly seem as if we do. Experimental studies of the writing process show interesting differences in patterns of crossmodal connections and sensorimotor integration of the eyes and the hands during handwriting (Alamargot, Chesnet, Dansac, and Ros 2006; Caporossi, Alamargot, and Chesnet 2004) and typewriting (Inhoff and Gordon 1997; Wengelin et al. 2009).

Different technologies require, address, and engage our corporeal, sensory, phenomenological being-in-the-world in highly particular and specialised ways. Whether we read in books or on computer screens, or write with keyboards or by putting pen to paper, we interact with a specific physical, technical, and ergonomic interface, as implemented in a technology or device (e.g., a print book, e-book, or computer) (Haas 1996; Mangen 2008; Mangen and Velay 2010). These interfaces yield different technical and material features. They present us with a wide range of *affordances* (Gibson 1979) – i.e., opportunities for perceptual and sensorimotor interaction – which will impact the reading and writing process and experience, in subtle and more obvious ways. The interface of print, for instance, requires that we turn pages by taking one page and leafing through a pre-ordered stack of papers. This yields distinctly different ergonomic affordances than those found in digital reading devices, in which we 'turn pages' by clicking with a computer mouse located somewhere on a table, by pressing keys on a keyboard, or by lightly sweeping a finger across the iPad touch screen (Liesaputra, Witten, and Bainbridge 2009a, 2009b; Marshall and Bly 2005).

The haptics of reading, however, is not well covered in reading research literature (Mangen, 2008).[7] Nevertheless, recent findings in the theoretical paradigm called 'embodied cognition' suggest that our manual interaction with the reading device during reading might be more intrinsically connected with the perceptual and cognitive processes entailed in reading than is usually assumed. Embodied cognition is a cross-disciplinary paradigm emerging from psychology, neuroscience, biology, philosophy, evolutionary theory, and anthropology. The central concept is that all acts of cognition are fundamentally embodied; there are strong links between motor actions and visual perception, and sensorimotor acts play a central role in cognitive processes on several levels (see, e.g., Shapiro 2010; Thompson 2007; Varela, Thompson, and Rosch 1991). In reading research, the physicality and ergonomics of the technical interface with which we interact is rarely addressed. There are by now a large number of theoretical, empirical, and experimental studies on perceptual and cognitive aspects of digital reading (e.g., the gaze patterns of on-screen and on-paper reading and the cognitive load of hypertext reading), compared to print reading. However, few pursue to any depth the important questions pertaining to the volatility, or lack of fixity, of the digital text on the reading process. Unlike print texts, digital texts – whether they are displayed on a computer screen or on a reading tablet, e-book, or surf pad – are ontologically intangible and detached from the physical and mechanical properties of their material support (Z. Liu 2008; Mangen 2008, 2010; Morineau, Blanche, Tobin, and Gueguen 2005). A more phenomenological way to say this is that the digital text displayed on a screen (and this applies to any kind of screen technology, whether we talk about an LCD touch screen on an iPad, or the electronic ink technology of a Kindle, etc.) is not part of the perceptual object of the computer, e-book, surf pad, or smart phone in the same way as the print text is part of the perceptual object of the print book. When reading digital texts, our sensorimotor (haptic and tactile) interaction with the reading device is experienced as taking place at an indeterminate distance from the actual text, whereas when reading print text we are physically and phenomenologically in touch with the material substrate supporting the text (on which the text is imprinted) itself (Mangen 2008). In digital technologies the connection between the text content (document) and the material support is split up, allowing the technological device to display a multitude of content that can be altered with a click. The book, by contrast, is a physically and functionally unitary object in which the content cannot be distinguished from the material platform or substrate. Such a detachment might plausibly have important implications for the reading experience, and it calls for a substantial understanding of the role of the physicality and tangibility of the document and, as a corollary, the fixity of the text, during reading. According to Liu (2008), the tangibility of the printed document is one of the main reasons why digital technologies will not be replacing paper documents any time soon:

The simple tangibility of the printed document is another reason for its continued popularity, despite the existence of electronic equivalents. People are generally comfortable with information only when they can 'feel it' in their hands and can make sure whether the important information is recorded properly. Why are all the important messages and agreements (e.g., diplomas, certificates, and contracts) put on paper? One reason is that paper documents embrace credibility of information. The saying 'put it on paper' conveys the importance of this tangible document medium (Z. Liu 2008, 144).

Paper will not disappear, concludes Liu, simply because 'there are too many reasons for its existence and a practical substitute has not been found' (Z. Liu 2008). Microsoft research scientist C.C. Marshall (2005) comes to similar conclusions:

The changes in reading and reading technologies don't imply that there's a single way the future of reading will play out. In practice, reading is a heterogeneous activity and reading technologies are better for some things than they are for others. Choosing a single platform to support reading and critical thinking is not only unnecessary, it seems unlikely (Marshall 2005, 144).

Rather than waiting in vain for the universal reading device replacing them all, we might fare better acknowledging that the different technologies have defined and distinct features rendering each one of them more appropriate in certain settings and for certain purposes than for others. The still unrealised myth of the paperless office might be taken as evidence of this fact (Sellen and Harper 2002).

## A redefinition of reading

In her book *Writing technology: studies on the materiality of literacy*, Christina Haas (1996) explores the implications of the changing materiality of reading and writing technologies on how writers read, perceive, experience, and engage with their own texts during writing. Pointing out how writing researchers typically neglect the potential role of the materiality of the writing technology, Haas warns about what she calls 'the transparent technology myth':

The 'technology is transparent' myth sees writing as writing, its essential nature unaffected by the mode of production and presentation. The most serious drawback to the transparent technology assumption is that it encourages an overly positive, whole-hearted acceptance of computer technology without any consideration of possible negative effects of that technology. Viewing technology as transparent encourages a belief that writers can use computer technology without being shaped by it, and therefore discourages any examination of how technology shapes discourse and how it, in turn, is shaped by discourse (1996, 22).

The parallels to reading research are quite obvious. In order to address the question of technology in reading adequately, perhaps a redefinition of reading is in order. Due to the diffusion of reading onto a plethora of different devices and platforms, I suggest we redefine reading in order to capture properly the differences between whatever reading entails in these very varied circumstances. Reading, I contend, can be defined as embodied, multisensory engagement with a display of static and/or dynamic configurations (i.e., types and kinds of information; signs and semiotic representations) implemented in a technical, physical device which has particular sensorimotor, ergonomic affordances (Mangen and Schilhab 2012). The ways in which these affordances interact with sensorimotor-perceptuo-cognitive processes during reading present themselves as pertinent and vital research questions for empirical studies of reading.

Of particular interest is the ways in which we use our fingers and hands when handling and navigating in a document while reading (Mackey 2007, 2011; Mangen 2008). It is certainly no coincidence that the most lasting reading technology has been the one we can comfortably hold in our hands and where the human hand-eye coordination is taken into consideration in optimal ways (Manguel 1996, 2004; Sellen and Harper 2002). Pointing at pictures, flipping paper pages back and forth, bookmarking and dog-earing, annotating in the margins etc., readers use their fingers and hands extensively during reading. Perhaps even more interesting, the reader's haptic and tactile interaction with reading material is not necessarily of a conscious and deliberate, goal-directed kind. Cathy Marshall and Sara Bly (2005) have found that readers frequently engage in what they call lightweight navigation, i.e., unselfconscious acts of haptic manipulation of reading material. Studying self-recorded sessions of subjects reading the print version of *The New Yorker*, Marshall and Bly observed two particular phenomena that, arguably, have no digital equivalent: the lightweight navigation that readers use unselfconsciously when they are reading a particular article, and the approximate navigation readers engage in when they flip multiple pages at a time. More specifically, this lightweight, unconscious navigation on paper included: (1) Narrowing or broadening focus by manipulating the physical magazine; (2) letting one's eyes stray to a page element out of the textual flow; (3) looking ahead in the text to preview or anticipate; and (4) looking back to re-read for content. Pondering why these apparently important kinds of navigation are absent in digital reading, Marshall and Bly conjecture about lightweight navigation:

> Perhaps it is possible, but like other kinds of digital interaction (e.g., annotation), this type of navigation becomes interruptive rather than unselfconscious and integrated into the flow of regular activities. Page turning has shown itself to be a prime example; the lightweight navigation that is an important, yet invisible, part of reading on paper is not easily reclaimed in digital page turning (Marshall and Bly 2005).

Obviously, whether or not the reader has a need for extensive back-and-forth navigation in a text, as well as the kinds and degrees of possible and/or preferred navigation acts, will depend on several factors – among which the type of text being read. Due to their linear structure, long, narrative texts may quite plausibly be one type of text accentuating the issue of navigation and, by implication, be a good test bed for comparing the ergonomic affordances of screen and paper interfaces.

### The prison house of print and the tyranny of linearity; the role of linearity, coherence, and fixity in reading comprehension

In much of the popular debate on the new (and cool) versus the old (and boring) technologies, seemingly unspectacular and at the same time quite fundamental features of textual communication, such as linearity and fixity, are under vigorous attack. In a book evocatively titled *Everything bad is good for you* (Johnson 2005), popular culture pundit Steven Johnson presents an interesting thought experiment. He asks the reader to imagine a parallel world identical to the real world of today, but for the fact that video games had been invented long before books. In this other world, kids have been playing video games for a long time – and then, all of a sudden, this thing called 'a book' comes along. What would teachers, parents, and the cultural elite be inclined to say about this new medium? Perhaps, ponders Johnson, something along the following lines:

> Reading chronically understimulates the senses. Unlike the longstanding tradition of gameplaying – which engages the child in a vivid, three-dimensional world filled with moving images and musical soundscapes, navigated and controlled with complex muscular movement – books are simply a barren string of words on the page. [...] Books are also tragically isolating. While games have for many years engaged the young in complex social relationships with their peers, books force the child to sequester him- or herself in a quiet space, shut off from interaction with other children. [...] *But perhaps the most dangerous property of these books is the fact that they follow a fixed linear path.* You can't control their narratives in any fashion – you simply sit back and have the story dictated to you (Johnson 2005, 25; italics mine).

Barring the fact that Johnson himself admits to slight exaggeration and the fallacy of claiming that reading is intellectually flawed due to lack of sensory stimulation (a point pursued to some length by N. Carr (2010)), the above quote warrants more serious attention than perhaps Johnson originally intended. Despite being hyperbolic, Johnson's denunciation of the fixed linearity of the print text is not a singular case. With the emergence of hypermedia, social networking systems, collaborative technologies, and the overall tendency in contemporary media ecology to go from the logics of the print page to the logics of the screen (Kress 2003), claims about the alleged superiority of simultaneity, flexibility, and network structures rather than sequentiality, fixity, and temporal order abound. Open network structure, for instance, is simply assumed and claimed to be superior to conventional characteristics of the written text, such as sequentiality. Possibly the most flamboyant proponents of such ideology-based assertions are found in the early generation of hypertext theory in the 1990s, conspicuously colored by poststructuralist theory. For these theorists, hypertext represented the liberation of the reader from the tyranny of the linear (print) text, a liberation implying the conflation of reader and author (Cohen 1996; Kendrick 2001; Landow 1997, 2003; Saint-Gelais and Audet, 2003). This feature, claim these theorists, adds an aesthetic and seductive dimension to the reading experience far surpassing that gained from print reading. The fact that hypertext literature (as well as research on hypertext literature)[8] has largely remained an obscure curiosity largely unknown to mainstream readers with an interest in literature and literary reading, however, casts serious doubts on its alleged superiority over print literature.

Despite repeated and convincing disclosures of major flaws of reasoning in such arguments, the bashing of linearity and linear (print) text persists. Courtesy of an unfortunate laziness in research communities that allows unevidenced assertions to continue to thrive and circulate, influential actors in the book and reading industry can asseverate that 'Everybody is trying to think about how books and information will best be put together in the 21st century. *You can't just be linear anymore with your text*' (Simon & Schuster executive); 'E-books should not just be print books delivered electronically; we need to take advantage of the medium and *create something dynamic to enhance the experience*. I want links and behind the scenes extras and narration and videos and conversation' (senior vice president of HarperStudio, an imprint of the publisher HarperCollins). Or Google Book Search manager Adam Mathes: 'Books often live a vibrant life offline, but they'll be able to live an even more exciting life online.' Nicholas Carr (2010), who collated these pronouncements, posits the inevitable question: what does it mean for a book to live an exciting life? Does such an exciting life, whatever it entails, support and facilitate the comprehension of the text? Where is the empirical evidence supporting such claims?

Rather than relying on unsupported claims and uncorroborated assertions, the research community would benefit from paying more attention to empirical evidence from research supported by scientifically established paradigms and based on solid theoretical conceptualisations and methodological procedures. As a matter of fact, theoretical knowledge on the process of narrative reading comprehension and empirical evidence from reading research on narrative text comprehension undermine many of the claims being made about the alleged added value of a digitised text for the reading experience. When we read a text, whether a detective novel of the page-turner kind, an experimental piece of avant-garde poetry, or a piece of non-fiction prose on climate change, we engage in mental reconstructions at many levels and forms (Goldman, Graesser, and Van den Broek 1999; Graesser and Bower 1990; Graesser, Singer, and Trabasso 1994; Tapiero 2007;

Zwaan, Langston, and Graesser 1995; Zwaan and Radvansky 1998). For a start, we mentally reconstruct the text as we read, based on the gist or the meaning (content-based reconstruction). Moreover, we build a mental reconstruction of the structure, physical layout, and disposition of the text. The longer the text is, the more important this reconstruction of the layout or structure can be assumed to be. Several experiments in reading and writing research have shown that spatial mental representation is useful for reading comprehension (Cataldo and Oakhill 2000; Eklundh 1992, 1994; Haas 1996; Le Bigot, Passerault, and Olive 2009; Piolat, Olive, and Kellogg 2005; Piolat, Roussey, and Thunin 1997; Therriault and Raney 2002). Writers and readers develop a 'global perspective' (Eklundh 1992) or a 'sense of the text' (Haas 1996) as they progress through it. This perspective is based on both the core meaning(s) conveyed in the text, but equally importantly, on the text's compositional structure. When reading and writing on a computer, scrolling disrupts the user's sense of this physical structure and consequently such lack of fixity could embody significant disruptions to ongoing mental reconstruction. Hence, difficulties in reading from computers may be due to disrupted mental maps of the text, which may be reflected in poorer understanding and ultimately poorer recall of presented text (Piolat et al. 1997).[9]

A recent study in experimental psychology is particularly interesting in this regard. Ackerman and Goldsmith (2011) examined subjective and objective differences between on-screen learning (OSL) and on-paper learning (OPL). The subjects were undergraduate students of social sciences and humanities; the study material was expository texts (1000-1200 words, containing graphics and illustrations; the format and number of pages were identical on screen and on paper). The authors measured subjects' recall of information and comprehension of the text, their self-regulation of learning (e.g., allocation of time for task); as well as their prediction of performance (e.g., how well do they think they will perform on the subsequent tests?). Experiment one tested the subjects under fixed study time; in experiment two, time was self-regulated. The results showed that under fixed time constraints, test performance (multiple choice) did not differ significantly. However, when study time was self-regulated (experiment two), poorer performance was observed on screen than on paper. These results suggest that the primary differences between screen and paper are not cognitive but rather metacognitive; subjects made less accurate predictions of performance and demonstrated more erratic study-time regulation on screen than on paper. Furthermore, the lower test performance of on-screen learning was accompanied by significant overconfidence with regard to predicted performance (shorter study time and lower level of actual learning), whereas on-paper participants monitored their performance more accurately. These findings led Ackerman and Goldsmith to conclude:

> People appear to perceive the printed-paper medium as best suited for effortful learning, whereas the electronic medium is better suited for fast and shallow reading of short texts such as news, emails, and forum notes […]. The common percep-

tion of screen presentation as an information source intended for shallow messages may reduce the mobilization of cognitive resources that is needed for effective self regulation (Ackerman and Goldsmith 2011, 29).

Hence, empirical evidence from psychological research casts serious doubts on claims about the tyranny of print and the superiority of digital technologies for supporting reading comprehension, especially for more complex and challenging reading processes.

## How social can the act of reading be?

Popular discourse and, more seriously, scholarly papers on reading and learning with digital technologies have come to ascribe unwarranted, and unevidenced, positive value to certain terms to the exclusion of others. In the wake of such value-laden rhetoric, dichotomies abound where the terms on the one side of the line are privileged and, implicitly, the terms on the other side are considered old-fashioned and outdated. Some of the most prevalent dichotomies in the discourse on digital technologies and reading and, by implication, learning, are the following:

| | | |
|---|---|---|
| social | *vs* | solitary |
| network structure (i.e., non-linearity) | *vs* | sequentiality and linearity |
| openness (i.e., unfinished, in progress) | *vs* | closure, something finished |
| immediacy; simultaneity | *vs* | temporal order |
| flux (i.e., flexibility, dynamics) | *vs* | fixity |

Needless to say, in today's cultural and rhetorical climate the concepts on the left side represent the 'cool' ones, whereas the right hand side partners are often ridiculed or marginalised as 'outdated' and out of touch with contemporary reality. Commenting on this phenomenon, Nicholas Spice, publisher of the *London Review of Books* (LRB) has made some pertinent observations:

> We overestimate, romanticize, and fetishize certain things: the openness of form over completed things, fragmentation over linearity, the draft over what is finished, the spontaneous over what is considered. [...] There is a fetishization of real-time over artificial time. What happens spontaneously is supposed to be better than long form and contemplation. [...] Do these things add value to the text, the richness of the text? Is the real conflation to be found between information and the information chain and what we do with that information? (Adema 2011)

The fetishisation of the social over the solitary is perhaps particularly evident in current discourse. Bob Stein, founder of The Institute for the Future of the Book, presents his credo that 'social reading is no longer an oxymoron' and 'the age of the individual is coming to an end' elsewhere in this volume.[10] In other words, the 'I' is in trouble again – and this time around, we cannot primarily blame the poststructuralists.[11] According to Stein, we must stop conceptualising the book as a medium for solitary pursuit of reading; the book must be reconceptualised and re-made as a platform for communal, networked activity – e.g., social reading.

Stein and his colleagues at the Institute for the Future of the Book are not alone in viewing reading as a social act. The 'new literacies' paradigm and sociocultural approaches to reading and literacy research appearing with the so-called 'social turn' (Pearson 2009) define reading and literacy as socially situated practices that arc historically, socially, and culturally relative and idiosyncratic and which must be studied as such. The insistence of the social character of reading continues to dominate the field to such an extent that it occasionally appears dogmatic; one could also, with G. Salomon, term it 'situational determinism' (Salomon 1993). The problem, however, is that such a view of reading flies in the face of both common-place experiences, as well as psychological theories of reading. In the article 'The new literacy: Caveat emptor', Philip B. Gough takes issue with the view stemming from anthropologist Brian V. Street et al. that literacy (and, by implication, reading) is social. Gough's clear and logical argumentation deserves to be quoted at length:

> Is literacy social? [...] Let us grant that Literacy is 'socially embedded'. Congresses, parliaments, and school boards discuss it; the meaning and import of literacy is surely a matter to be socially negotiated. But I would argue that the act of reading, that is, literacy itself, is one of the least social of human activities. When I think of social activities, I think of conversations, of football games, of parliamentary debates. Reading may be involved in these activities. We converse about what we have read, we read the program or the score at the game, a speaker may even read a statement to the House. But to call these 'literacy activities' is like calling an aspirin bottle 'Discourse-bound' (Gee [...] has done just this[12]); they are social activities because they directly involve other people, and they only incidentally involve reading. Ordinary reading, in contrast, strikes me as one of the most private, unsocial things which people do. We often do it alone, and if we do it in the presence of others (as in libraries or aeroplanes), we interact with others only at the cost – the interruption – of our reading. I think that reading is most naturally construed as an act which is primarily not social, and it distorts our ordinary language to call it so (Gough 1995, 81).

More than fifteen years after its publication (in a special issue on 'New Literacies' in *Journal of research in reading*), Gough's article warrants renewed attention. The largely ideology-driven conceptualisation of both reading and literacy as social practices continues to permeate the theoretical as well as political and educational discourse. This seems to me to be a most unfortunate conflation of two different levels of conceptualisation.[13] Obviously, the psychological, phenomenological act of reading – from low-level processes of attentional mechanisms and visual perception, to higher-level cognitive processes of anaphoric referencing and inference-based comprehension – is arguably individual. Applied to writing, Spice clarifies the conflation as follows:

> We shouldn't make the mistake of conflating two sorts of benefit and value. One of the best things of new media is the way it has facilitated contact between people, not only in virtual space but also in physical space, for instance with the LRB bookshop. This was impossible in the old system; you could not reach the people economically. But this is a benefit that has to do with social organization; it has nothing to do with the content and the value of the content and the things that are discussed. I think here solitude is very important. People can write books together but obviously they don't do it. As any psychologist would tell us, you cannot produce interesting, deep and complex thoughts [or texts; A.M.] quickly; you need time to think them out. More than simple blogosphere blatter, we are talking about solitude and time. The evidence is not very strong that the content and value of what is being said is very high (Adema 2011).

As evidenced by both empirical studies on multitasking and cognitive load, as well as by theories of human (neuro)psychology and neurobiology, it is an inevitable consequence of the human cognitive architecture that the processes involved in, and required for, reading necessarily preclude extensive socialising carried out simultaneously. Such an incompatibility holds, whether we read short news blurbs in the morning paper, or we try to make our way through Rowling's *Harry Potter*-series – perhaps even more so for the latter. The deep, sustained focus required to read a long, linear text is simply irreconcilable with social activity, whether online or offline. The fact that reading the *Harry Potter* novels has prompted massive social events (online and offline) and experiences shared by millions of young people, does not counter the fact that each one of these children and teenagers (and adults) have read the letters, words, sentences, and paragraphs in solitude.

## Concluding remarks: On hypes and hopes

We could do away with much poor theorizing, ideology-ridden assertions, and uncorroborated claims in the field of reading and literacy studies if our common discourse, research questions, and innovation projects were better informed by proper knowledge about the basics of human information processing. Unevidenced claims, derision of dissenters, and ignorance of empirical evidence spoil the scientific discourse and make the field prone to reproducing and circulating a number of hypes. The 'digital natives' hype is a case in point. Coined by digital technology guru Marc Prensky (2001), the digital natives are said to be different from all generations before them because they think, learn, behave, and communicate differently simply due to the fact that they have grown up with and been exposed to and immersed in digital technologies. Claims about this new generation (whether they are called the Net Generation (Tapscott 1998, 2009), the Google generation (Rowlands et al. 2008), e-learners (C.-C. Liu and Chen 2005; Macdonald 2004), New Millennial Learners (Pedró 2007), or Homo Zappiens (Veen and Vrakking 2006) are being put forth without empirical evidence, couched in sensationalist language, and followed by urgent claims about the need for radical change in education systems and teaching methods. 'The single biggest problem facing education today is that our Digital Immigrant instructors, who speak an outdated language (that of the pre-digital age), are struggling to teach a population that speaks an entirely new language' (Prensky 2001). Echoing claims such as Bob Stein's that the age of the individual is coming to an end (and, hence, requiring urgent and fundamental changes in education systems and programs, for one thing) are astounding assertions that have been appropriately described as 'academic moral panics' (Bennett and Maton 2010; Bennett et al. 2008) in which arguments are often couched in dramatic language, proclaim a profound change in the world, and pronounce stark generational differences:

> Such claims coupled with appeals to common sense and recognizable anecdotes are used to declare an emergency situation, and call for urgent and fundamental change. Another feature of this 'academic moral panic' is its structure as a series of strongly bounded divides: between a new generation and all previous generations; between the technically adept and those who are not; and between learners and teachers. A further divide is then created between those who believe in the digital native phenomenon and those who question it. [...] Those who refuse to recognize what is described as an inevitable change are said to be in denial, resistant and out of touch, and are portrayed as being without legitimate concerns [...]. Teachers, administrators and policymakers have every right to demand evidence and to expect that calls for change be based on well-founded and supported arguments. [...] [M]any of the arguments made to date about digital natives currently lack that support (Bennett et al. 2008, 782-783).

Obviously, for a field aspiring to scientific legitimacy, this is not a sustainable course. It is my contention that a more viable route to scientific legitimacy and cross-disciplinary relevance goes via knowledge about the ways in which human beings perceive, engage with, process, and learn from representations displayed on an interface implemented in a technology with certain ergonomic and cognitive affordances. Obtaining such knowledge requires a change of perspective. We should ask ourselves what questions we will make our starting points and guiding lights for exploration and debate. As observed by multimedia theorist Richard Mayer (2001), when we ask, 'what can we do with these technologies?' and when our goal is to 'provide access to technology', we are taking a technology-centered approach with a 100-year history of failure:

although different technologies underlie film, radio, television, and computer-assisted instruction, they all produced the same cycle. First, they began with grand promises about how the technology would revolutionise education. Second, there was an initial rush to implement the cutting-edge technology in schools. Third, from the perspective of a few decades later, it became clear that the hopes and expectations were largely unmet. What went wrong with these technologies that seemed poised to tap the potential of visual and world-wide learning? I attribute the disappointing results to the technology-centered approach taken by the promoters. Instead of adapting technology to fit the needs of human learners, humans were forced to adapt to the demands of cutting-edge technologies. The driving force behind the implementation was the power of the technology rather than an interest in promoting human cognition (Mayer 2001, 9-10).

Obviously, promoting human cognition demands knowledge about human cognition. Might we dare to hope for a more balanced future in which hypes and sensational but unevidenced claims are being marginalised by rational insights originating from sound theoretical and empirical research?

## Notes

1   Claiming that the printed book is soon-to-be obsolete, British author of children's books, Terry Deary, has announced that he will be writing for mobile phones as it is the preferred device of his young audience ('Woman's hour', BBC 4, 7 October 2011).

2   The Swedish study shows 'that the entry of computers into the home has contributed to changing children's habits in such a manner that their reading does not develop to the same extent as previously. By comparing countries over time we can see a negative correlation between change in reading achievement and change in spare time computer habits which indicates that reading ability falls as leisure use of computers increases' (http://www.ufn.gu.se/english/News/newsdetail/poorer-reading-skills-following-changed-computer-habits-of-children.cid991610).

3   http://www.amazon.com/gp/product/B0051QVESA/ref=famstripe_k.

4   OECD Programme for International Student Assessment (http://www.pisa.oecd.org/).

5   Progress in International Reading Literacy Study (http://www.pirls.org/).

6   The Adult Literacy and Lifeskills Survey (http://nces.ed.gov/surveys/all/).

7   Haptic perception involves both the tactile perception through our skin and the perception of the position and movement of our joints and muscles (commonly referred to as the kinaesthetic sense modality). For example, when we click with the computer mouse, we sense the mouse click both through the receptors on the skin on our fingers, as well as through the position and movement of our hand and fingers.

8   For a succinct criticism of the preposterous rhetoric of poststructuralist hypertext theory, see Miall (1999).

9   Some might argue that the superiority of print in supporting reading comprehension of linear texts observed thus far might be explained by age or generational differences; that children growing up with digital texts as their primary reading material rather than print texts will naturally develop reading comprehension abilities better suited for digital reading than print reading. These claims remain unsubstantiated by research literature; empirical studies cast serious doubts on the alleged differences in cognitive abilities and reading or

learning performance of the so-called 'digital natives' (S. Bennett and Maton 2010; Sue Bennett, Maton, and Kervin 2008; Burhanna, Seeholzer, and Salem Jr 2009; Helsper and Eynon 2010; Jones, Ramanau, Cross, and Healing 2010).

10 Also see http://e-boekenstad.nl/unbound/.

11 The dispersal of the subject was one hallmark of post-structuralist theory and of all theoretical strands springing out of it. Literary theorist Norman Holland wittily pointed out the absurdity of many of the claims from the burgeoning era of deconstruction in the 1980s: 'Not so long ago, I attended a conference with a typical 1980s title: Self and Other. There I heard about the disappearing self, the vanishing self, the deconstructed self, the self on the edge, the self within the self (presumably some kind of indigestion), the marginal self, and so on. I got worried, having just published a book called *The I*, having therefore a certain vested interest in the self above and beyond one's usual concern for oneself. My worries, alas, proved correct. The I is in big trouble. The best literary theorists of today seem to have declared war on the I or the self, and *you's* and *I's* are vanishing wherever you (if you still allow me that pronoun) look' (Holland 1992, 107).

12 I.e., Gee, James Paul. 1988. 'Discourse systems and aspirin bottles: On literacy'. *Journal of education* 170(1): 27-40.

13 Reading obviously has implications on societal, political, and cultural levels. However, the discourse on reading and literacy would benefit from a clearer and more consistent distinction between what is entailed in the individual process of reading and what is meant when referring to literacy as a concept of broader reference. An alternative could be to have 'literacy' refer to social levels, and 'reading' to refer to the individual level (A. van der Weel, personal communication).

# E-reading essentials in a time of change and unfixity[1]

Ray Siemens and Corina Koolen, with the INKE Research Group

**Notes from a talk given at *The Unbound Book: Reading and Publishing in the Digital Age***

Measured in part by a dizzying array of conferences and papers on digital reading and e-books, the significant interest at the moment in issues related to e-reading suggests that we are looking in the face of our reading culture's unprecedented change. For centuries we have grown comfortable with the staple of our reading culture being transmitted through the medium of print, and the advent of the digital medium has uprooted practices that have long been familiar. Indeed, the current situation in e-reading is uncertain and unstable, especially so if the basis for our understanding of e-reading is device-oriented and technologically-focused; a multitude of new devices like dedicated e-readers and the enhanced e-book and formats related to these devices are embraced by the consumer-driven marketplace they race toward, while minutely-iterated versions of the same are hailed first as the future of digital reading and, seemingly a moment later, declared obsolete. Such a lack of fixity makes it difficult to assess the state of e-reading from an academic perspective, especially so if we tie our intellectual engagement of e-reading to such technological action, reaction, and turmoil. But if not tied *there*, where should we focus our attention? In this contribution we suggest a new theoretical foundation via which we might begin to understand a future for e-reading beyond the context provided to us by currently unstable instances of digital e-reading devices and the materials they rely upon. By re-conceiving current textual models from different perspectives, such as historical and material perspectives on reading, we can begin to understand the full system of reading and achieve the full benefit that electronic textuality can deliver.

**Beyond mimicry: An exciting future for e-reading, but an inconvenient present**

A staple of our reading culture is the book, an object often (mis)taken to stand for a multitude of reading objects we frequently use and, perhaps not surprisingly, one that has become a touchstone in consideration of e-reading modelling. This touchstone, however, is not necessarily a convenient one; modelling the book in electronic form is problematic. In addition to its status as a physical object, the

**Figure 1: The New York Times on the Kindle**

book is a comprehensive metaphor for textual forms of communication. Phrases such as 'book history' or 'book culture' point to a condensation of a range of materials through which we consume information, including earlier configurations of the book, such as scrolls, or artefacts such as newspapers and archival documents (Siemens et al. 2011a, 49). The book then remains 'an abstract, generalized idea that emphasizes common features over historical particularities' (ibid).

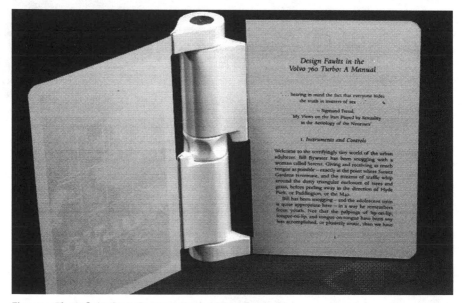

**Figure 2: The Infinite Page Turnover Device (Timothy Yeoh)**

Reading has, of course, always been done through a device of some kind. The book is every bit as much a technology as is the e-reader – a fact sometimes overlooked in any survey today of reading devices, which would typically focus on the digital objects we take less for granted than we do their print counterparts. The Kindle (Figure 1) is just one example of the many dedicated e-reading platforms available and familiar to us; much e-reading takes place also on non-dedicated devices, such as smartphones, PDAs, tablets, and laptops. Equally important for the purpose of understanding elements of e-reading, though less familiar to us because they have never seen commercial production, are devices such as seen in Figure 2, the Infinite Page Turnover Device, an experiment from several years ago made of two e-reading device 'sheets' that allowed the reader to enjoy the literal physical act of turning from one page to the next.

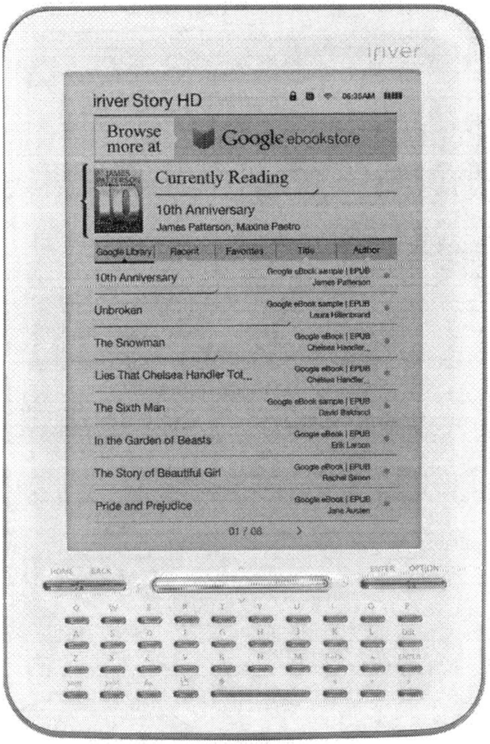

Figure 3: Google's iriver Story HD

The multitude of such devices suggests, truly, that there is a very exciting future ahead for e-reading. That said, at the moment we are experiencing what might best be described as an inconvenient present. The very best such devices seem to be able to do is attempt to mimic some basic elements of functionality found in print media (such as annotating in the Kindle) and the book form (such as with the

Infinite Page Turnover Device) and, further, as in the case with the marketing initially associated with Google's iriver Story HD e-reader (Figure 3), to draw on nostalgic associations with the print medium: the rounded edges and the rim colour were intended 'to inspire the familiar nostalgia of your favorite book'.[2] Further, the best examples of these devices and the documents they house do not yet meet the standards of quality, content, and functionality that have evolved over centuries of (print) publications. Devices such as the Kindle have proven to be adequate (for many) to perform a specific kind of reading, but they also lack critical features and functions of more complex reading processes, such as reading for studying or doing academic research (Aaltonen et al. 2011, Lam et al. 1999; see also the next chapter in this volume). Such devices are, still, pale reflections of the models they attempt to mimic, and the content they provide does not yet afford the basic functionality, versatility, and utility of the printed page.

Figure 4: A student using TouchBookmark, which emulates finger bookmarking (Yoon et al. 2011)

Even so, we strive forward. Much academic research into the development and practical use of digital reading devices necessarily has its roots in the recent and current print-based practices of information transmission, with a focus on emulating paper-like affordances. As a result of this, a number of devices that have been developed (or additions to existing devices that have been made) use mimicry of paper affordances as a goal rather than a means to an end. These for instance support navigation through paper-related haptics, such as flipping and page holding (Yoon et al. 2011). One of the conceptual limitations in this type of research is the failure to recognise that the device – or its interface for that matter – is only a small part of the ecosystem related to reading and communication. Without intervention, this type of modelling the book as an imitation will continue to prevail and result in e-reading environments that fail to live up to their potential.

As we imagine a future for e-reading and the devices that support it, we need to look beyond the devices themselves, beyond the natural mimicry of the book form that is their staple, and toward device-independent systems and practices associated with reading that, while manifest in reading devices across numerous iterations in specific media (e.g. clay tablet, scroll, printed book), have evolved across media-specific iterations. We should be focusing less on mimicking the look and feel of the book and page and, rather, be more concerned with modelling function and use and, further, the full system of reading.

## A research approach to e-reading

Fuelling e-reading research and development at the moment is a strong and positive convergence of hardware developers, content providers, and readers. Hardware developers are building devices that are intended for certain types of reading engagement; content providers are increasing their delivery of electronic materials to us, among them materials in 'open' form, and readers are, themselves, becoming increasingly technologically sophisticated and computationally empowered. But few involved in this convergence understand the theory and pragmatics associated with traditions of knowledge conveyance related to the medium that lies at the heart of implementing e-reading – something that has been a focus of those practising the humanities for centuries. Such understanding is a crucial contribution to this convergence.

The first fruit of such understanding is perspective. The advent of the e-book has made the book visible to us as an object of study in new ways that have, in turn, metaphorically and analogically fertilised and fomented our understanding of new forms of e-reader book-ishness and e-reading. Not only does this suggest that there is still much to be learned about books and reading in the context of their electronic counterparts but, further, it also points us to the fact that there are a great number of domains that inform our understanding of the book (Siemens et al. 2011a, 36). To explore this, a research cluster was formed in 2005-6 (entitled Implementing New Knowledge Machine: Human Computer Interaction and the Electronic Book) that included broad-based expertise in its composition of researchers and representative stakeholding research partners from a large number of disciplines, ranging from literary studies to bibliography and book history, computer science, philosophy, visual communication design, robotics, and beyond. This group concluded that to achieve fully all the benefits of computation in electronic books and documents, research in this area must begin with a (re) conception of core critical and textual models from the following perspectives: the evolution of reading and writing technologies from antiquity to the present; the mechanics and pragmatics associated with written forms of knowledge; strategies of reading and organisation within those forms; and the computational possibilities latent in written forms and manifest in emerging technology.

The key areas of disciplinary convergence to answer these questions, which eventually took shape in the Implementing New Knowledge Environments (INKE) group, were determined to be the following four disciplines, each with their own perspective (as per Siemens et al 2008, 2009b) and research team:

## 1. Textual Studies (TS)

To understand how digital textuality is affecting practices associated with the engagement of materials in new media, TS documents the features of past textual forms and practices to provide the vocabulary and theoretical framework for implementing new knowledge environments. The emerging field of Digital Textual Scholarship conceives of its materials in broad terms that encompass artefacts like scrolls, newspapers, transcriptions of oral folktales, photographs, small-press periodicals, poems, and plays in manuscript, electronic literature, video games, multiple versions of films, and unpublished archival materials. TS brings several approaches to bear upon all manner of human artefacts, digital and analogue. These include book history's interest in books as primary mediators of human relationships and in the book as 'the text' on a human scale, bibliography's focus on print material as physical, machine-produced vehicles of abstract texts; and literary theory's sensitivity to the complexities of form, content, and materiality in all linguistic mediation. Digital textual scholarship also involves an anthropological understanding of texts as the universal human work of weaving or fabricating with words, as well as a psychological understanding of texts as artefacts embedded in cognitive networks of attention and memory.

## 2. Reader Studies/User Experience (UX)

UX studies the complex processes involved in engaging with materials in print and digital environments. This team conducts studies with individuals engaging with humanities artefacts in a variety of contexts and for various purposes. These artefacts may include different types of content, including alphabetic language, icons, sound, or images; they may be straightforward or complex in structure and may contain marginalia or annotations, as each of these variables might modify cognitive and affective response as demonstrated by empirical user studies in digital environments. We read in many different ways, adopting different physical stances and mental attitudes dependent on the formal properties of the text and the object of the reading enterprise (e.g., whether it is for pleasure or study), and taking into account factors beyond. Study of individuals engaging with such materials must take into account the complexity of the reading enterprise.

## 3. Interface Design (ID)

ID's focus is founded on the assumption that theoretical models for representing textual material are in their early stages and do not fully accommodate the visual and logical dimensions of texts. The process of reading involves understanding not only the logical structure of content, as the Text Encoding Initiative (TEI) structure emphasises, but also the integration of visual information provided by typography and the disposition of text; the layout of the text may help reading and visual memory, as one's ability to retrieve information depends in part on spatial cues consistent from one act of reading to another. Further, rapid advances in computer hardware and software provide opportunities not possible even five years ago in the complex environments in which we work: consider larger screens, faster microchips, increased bandwidth, and electronic paper as well as new sensory modes of interaction. Given the emerging possibilities offered by new media, it remains vital to develop methods and models that rethink conventions of print material and examine emerging born-digital genres, such as e-literature, and to consider how reading culture is affected by the rise of 'social' computing environments, such as the popular Web 2.0 applications and the semantic web environments.

*4. Information Management (IM)*
A key problem that the electronic medium poses is that of facilitating ways that allow readers of digital materials to store, retrieve, share, annotate, and navigate information more efficiently than in the past. Traditional approaches dominate even the most current search resources but are proving insufficient for several reasons, namely that digital information is unstable, its volume is increasing rapidly, and there is a profusion of data formats. Strategies for addressing these issues do exist: the chief research challenge for archives or large corpora of texts is to provide a means of organisation and access to a radically expanding and heterogeneously formatted body of materials. The chief research challenge for individual artefacts is to provide contextual information for producers and consumers of dynamic reading environments. Our research is a combination of the best of several knowledge management strategies, which consist of the speed and power of the search engine, deep textual-analysis methods used by the scholarly community, consistently encoded corpora in specific knowledge domains, and emerging opportunities provided by the social networking technologies. Moving towards the goal of providing ways to organise and access the expanding and diversely formatted body of digital material in ways that best serve the needs of users, IM's goal is to facilitate the informational underpinnings pertinent to robust e-reading environments.[3]

## Larger questions related to understanding reading in the electronic medium

The full system of reading comprises more than the materiality of the object or the mechanical practice of reading, and the book itself is something more than a physical artefact: it is a knowledge object that requires a systemic approach in order to be adequately analysed. The work of INKE's groups builds upon four questions to address this full system (as per Siemens et al. 2008, 2009b):

*1. How has reading changed since the rise of digital media, and how can the history of textual practices inform the future?*
To answer this question we must understand the human presence in any recorded text, combining close study of material artefacts with interpretive inquiry into human activities. The same techniques of close reading and rigorous material study, long applied to print and manuscript, need to be extended to digital arte-facts and online knowledge environments in all their multimedia forms. INKE bridges the study of print and digital texts in order to develop a technical vocabu-lary for describing the salient features of digital texts – where *text* is understood to include *any* recorded text, in consideration of aspects of the full spectrum of mul-timedia. This vocabulary and its theoretical underpinning inform the work of the entire project, such that our prototyping activities take into account the material transmission of all such artefacts (manuscript, print, and digital).

*2. How has our experience of information changed since the rise of digital technologies and the Internet?*
Although reading is the key intellectual and cultural foundation of literate soci-eties and the fundamental activity of scholars, we have little knowledge of how reading and the way we experience information is modified and extended in new media environments. In the early- to mid-nineties, humanities scholars expressed excitement about the possibilities of digital text, predicting that the experience of reading and information access would change fundamentally as a result of digi-tal delivery and the integration of media such as sound, images, and video. How-ever, such prophetic writings were not based on systematic research with users. Although there have been a number of studies with users from the perspective of interface design and software engineering and several with readers of scientific literature, little progress has been made in understanding how digital media may affect readers' experience of literature and multimedia artefacts, both printed and digital.

*3. What new features can we design to improve digital information environments and their interfaces, based on our knowledge of user needs, behaviours, and cultural contexts?*
Given the emerging possibilities offered by new media, we are still left to under-stand and develop methods and models to: (1) extend reader control of digital texts; (2) develop and test prototypes that address issues raised by the printed page met-aphor and give readers and researchers better control of their activities. We can do this by revisiting the notion of page boundaries, devising experimental visual tools related to navigation, designing advanced means of bookmarking and anno-tating, implementing new digital metaphors that may derive, for instance, from

sculpture or visualisation rather than from the codex book, and exploring possibilities for parallel displays and related tools; (3) create tools that merge reading culture with prototypes of social software; and (4) design prototypes that rethink and re-present genres of print material as well as examine some of the emerging born-digital genres.

*4. How can we better design or process the data underlying and serving the needs of those using digital information environments?*
A key problem posed by the electronic medium is that of finding ways to allow readers of digital materials to store, retrieve, share, annotate, and navigate information more efficiently than in the past. Traditional approaches dominate even the most current search resources, but they are proving insufficient for several reasons: digital information is unstable, its volume doubles approximately every three years, and there is a profusion of data formats. Key strategies for addressing these issues do exist: the chief research challenge for archives or large corpora of texts is to provide means of organisation and access to a radically expanding and heterogeneously formatted body of materials; the chief research challenge for individual artefacts is to provide contextual information for producers and consumers of dynamic reading environments. Forward-thinking work here combines the best of several knowledge management strategies: the speed and power of the search engine, deep textual-analysis methods used by the scholarly community, consistently encoded corpora in specific knowledge domains, and detailed user-recorded results provided by the social networking technologies of what are now known as Web 2.0 tools.

## Next steps

This work deliberately moves away from the mimicry that dominates device-oriented e-reading research, development, and production at present and, rather, situates research inquiry relating to e-reading concerns within a fuller system of *reading* activity that draws on a full, interdisciplinary understanding of pertinent intellectual traditions and understood practices and situates it within the context of contemporary computational possibility and current e-reading concerns, working to anticipate and address future concerns as well. Such a project is by no means static and requires continual engagement with a body of work that spans disciplines and sectors. To this end, an annotated bibliography of current work is included as an essential context for such concerns today.

## Notes

1  This paper was presented by Ray Siemens at The Unbound Book: Reading and Publishing in the Digital Age (2011). The talk's video presentation is available at http://vimeo.com/channels/203095.
2  http://www.iriverinc.com/product/productOverview.asp?pn=storyhd, August 2011. The page that contained the quoted phrase no longer exists.
3  Recently, in the INKE team structure, IM, and UX researchers were incorporated wholly into TS and ID groups, and work has begun on creating a new group the focus of which will be on modelling and prototyping exclusively.

# Electronic environments for reading

## A select annotated bibliography of pertinent hardware and software (2011)

Corina Koolen, Alex Garnett, Ray Siemens, and the INKE, ETCL, and PKP Research Groups

### Introduction

Print technology and especially the codex are powerful metaphors that resonate in the construction of new, digital reading environments. To transcend the limits of the bound book, the full system of reading needs to be taken into account. This bibliography, which is an exploration of pertinent hard- and software in digital (scholarly) reading, has the aim to inform such an endeavour, and thus includes articles from several disciplines concerning reading, conceived in a broad sense. The articles have been selected for the insight they give into the current state-of-the-art in research on reading hard- and software and developing (digital) reading paradigms.

### Hardware

*Physicality and user experience*
Aaltonen, Mari, Petri Mannonen, Saija Nieminen, and Marko Nieminen. 2011. 'Usability and compatibility of e-book readers in an academic environment: A collaborative study'. *IFLA journal* 37: 1, 16-27.
A trial that combines e-readers and electronic library material at the Aalto University School of Science and Technology, from the autumn of 2009 until the summer of 2010. E-reading devices are discussed from the viewpoint of the library collection: is it possible to read academic journal articles on an e-reading device? Due to DRM restrictions and file format restrictions such as PDF, which cannot be read on Kindles, it is a cumbersome process to transfer articles to the readers tested. In addition the usefulness and usability of the e-readers is tested by a small group of students. They report several problems for academic work. For instance 'students and researchers [...] use multiple resources and need the ability to jump from one document to another, making use of links and cross references. This is not yet possible on most e-reader devices' (25).

Cull, Barry W. 2011. 'Reading revolutions: Online digital text and implications for reading in academe'. *First monday* 16: 6. http://firstmonday.org/htbin/cgiwrap/bin/ojs/index.php/fm/article/view/3340/2985

This article, written from the perspective of an academic librarian, surveys many recent developments in social and cognitive reading behaviour with respect to the technological circumstances that enabled them. His argument is a generally focused one, but his conclusion is aimed at librarians: reading will change, and any librarian that does not change with it can only be called unhelpful.

Gradmann, Stefan, and Jan Meister. 2008. 'Digital document and interpretation: Re-thinking 'text' and scholarship in electronic settings'. *Poiesis & praxis* 5: 2, 139-153.

The authors note that while electronic document publishing has greatly simplified the indexing and delivery process, the relatively linear scholarly workflow of previous years remains unchanged, except that we are now producing PDFs rather than printed journals. A truly new paradigm – which they appear to assume will somehow involve XML – will instead allow for branching paths, with inline annotations and version identifiers providing new ways of interacting with documents. Here they clearly anticipate the 'Beyond the PDF' movement that arose more recently. Gradmann and Meister go on to theorise about the problems of 'born digital' workflows for the humanities – namely, that the idea of reducing the world to measurable chunks is almost directly opposite the traditional goal of humanists – and conclude with reasonable apprehension that 'the core issue [of digital adaptation] seems to be discreteness'.

Hillesund, Terje. 2010. 'Digital reading spaces: How expert readers handle books, the web and electronic paper'. *First monday* 15: 4. http://firstmonday.org/htbin/cgiwrap/bin/ojs/index.php/fm/article/view/2762

The author points to the fact that most research on digital reading has focused on cognitive aspects, while the body is as important in the reading act itself. Based on research by Anne Mangen (2008, also in this bibliography) and Sellen and Harper (2002) he conducted qualitative interviews among a group of humanist and social science scholars in 2009. This article provides a number of interesting clues in the cognitive and physical aspects of academic reading.

Mangen, Anne. 2008. 'Hypertext fiction reading: Haptics and immersion'. *Journal of research in reading* 31: 4, 404-419.

The author stresses the importance of sensorimotor affordances in the act of reading fiction. By providing a predominantly phenomenological framework through which she analyses hypertext fiction, she argues that the computer does not lend itself to phenomenological immersion (cf. Marie-Laure Ryan) like a book (her choice of wording) does. The main strengths of this article are 1) its argument for conducting empirical research concerning haptics and different sensorimotor affordances in handling codices and digital devices (most paper-emulating prototyping, as can be found in the next section of this bibliography, is based on cognitive research); 2) the framework it provides for analysing such affordances. Mangen's article can serve as a base for empirical research; see for instance Hillesund (2010) in this bibliography.

Marshall, Catherine. 2003. 'Reading and interactivity in the digital library: Creating an experience that transcends paper'. *Proceedings of the CLIR/Kanazawa Institute of Technology roundtable*, 1-20. http://csdl.tamu.edu/~marshall/KIT-CLIR-revised.pdf
A clear overview of what reading entails and what paper affordances need to be taken into account in designing digital reading devices and how these can be transcended. Properties discussed are (local) mobility; materiality – where the author warns that physical form factor of the reading device should not be matched to the physicality of reading; interactivity – by which she means gathering, clipping, annotating, and sharing, on all of which she expands. The author then relates the affordances of digital reading, by discussing the notion of the portable personal digital library and some situation-specific capabilities, such as shared annotation. To conclude, she stresses the importance of transcending paper in innovation and the necessity of recognizing that people need more than one platform for reading and critical thinking.

*Hardware design*
Hinckley, Ken, Morgan Dixon, Raman Sarin, Francois Guimbretiere, and Ravin Balakrishnan. 2009. 'Codex: A dual screen tablet computer'. In *Proceedings of the 27th international conference on human factors in computing systems*, 1933-1942. Boston, MA: ACM.
A dual screen tablet computer that has a couple of advantages over other prototypes: the addition of implicit background sensing through sensors and collaboration support. The sensors detect a number of different positions (p. 1935) and act accordingly. The screens are not used as a dual page metaphor as in the codex (but still called 'page', interestingly enough) but as split pages. The software is based on note-taking software InkSeine, which is included in the list on e-reading software. The Codex allows for wireless connection to a desktop computer, so it can be used as a scrapbook for instance. This prototype and experiment is one example of print codex mimicry (the name of course attests to this) while incorporating some digital affordances that might be promising.

Hwang, Jane, Jaehoon Jung, and Gerard Jounghyun Kim. 2006. 'Hand-held virtual reality: A feasibility study'. In *Proceedings of the ACM symposium on Virtual reality software and technology*, 356-363. Limassol, Cyprus: ACM.
This might be a promising perspective in navigating digital libraries as related to hardware. Many researches on virtual reality (VR) assert the benefit of large

displays.[1] This article however, suggests that in combining motion-based interaction and a handheld display, the user's perceived field of view can be better than in a large, visual-only display. The study compares three interfaces: motion-based (hand-held with two hands), button-based (hand-held with two hands), and three keyboard and mouse interfaces with different screen sizes, from small to large screen (non-handhelds).

Yoon, Dongwook, Yongjun Cho, Kiwon Yeom, and Ji-Hyung Park. 2011. 'Touchbookmark: A lightweight navigation and bookmarking technique for e-books'. In *Proceedings of the 2011 annual conference extended abstracts on Human factors in computing systems*, 1189-1194. Vancouver, BC: ACM.

A paper presented at the Computer-Human Interaction conference 2011 (CHI 2011). It presents a prototype that again mimics behaviour in codex use: finger bookmarking. This we have seen in other research, but the difference in this case is that it uses the touchscreen instead of (as yet non-existent) e-paper affordances. By holding a touch point on a touch screen, a reader can 'remember' a page, like keeping a finger in a book. The reader can then continue to other pages. Flicking the touch will return the reader to the touch point page. A couple of test users enjoyed the similarity to paper affordances.

## Software

*Interfacing (digital) reading*
Baumer, Eric, Mark Sueyoshi, and Bill Tomlinson. 2008. 'Exploring the role of the reader in the activity of blogging'. In *Proceeding of the twenty-sixth annual SIGCHI conference on human factors in computing systems*, 1111-1120. Florence, Italy: ACM.

This article, while not about a reading tool or tools *per se*, provides an excellent thinking-through of the affordances of reader discourse in electronic documents. The authors begin by noting that the shift in literary theory of the 1960s and 70s toward analysing the reader's response to literature has not quite been carried through to our study of digital media. In order to understand the behaviour and expectations of blog readers, they conducted an ethnographic study of 15 participants, which revealed that blog reading is a deeply habitual process – simultaneously productive and time wasting – and that blogs unsurprisingly command a great degree of authenticity relative to other written media. The study also suggests that while blog entries may be posted in a particular sequence, this is the only sense in which blogs can be said to have temporality; they are characterised by 'non-chronicity'.

Cockburn, Andy, Amy Karlson, and Benjamin B. Bederson. 2009. 'A review of overview+detail, zooming, and focus+context interfaces'. ACM *computing surveys* 41: 1, 1-31.
An elaborate overview of four types of interface (the fourth interface, cue-based systems, is not mentioned in the title) that allow a user to view part of a screen in more detail, either based on graphical or semantic properties. Different types of applications are discussed, such as navigating though documents and texts (7.2.4) or computer program navigation (7.2.5). The conclusion is that although empirical research indicates that none of the systems is ideal, the benefits eventually often outweigh the costs. A combination of focused and contextual views outweighs constrained single-view. The *goal* of the interaction is crucial in finding the right combination, however. An example can be found in Hornbæk et al. (2002) where comprehension is better aided by overview+detail (thus deep reading), but reading is faster with fisheye, an example of a focus+context interface (thus search).[2]

Loizides, Fernando, and George R. Buchanan. 2008. 'The myth of find: User behaviour and attitudes towards the basic search feature'. In *Proceedings of the 8th ACM/IEEE-CS joint conference on Digital libraries*, 48-51. Pittsburgh, Pennsylvania: ACM.
This article discusses one of the most powerful features, and one most often taken for granted in any electronic document reader: the Control+F search shortcut. Although the authors write extensively on the results of a user study, the essential conclusion is this: many people do not use Ctrl+F, and those that do are typically disinclined to use a more sophisticated search system (e.g. with features such as spelling correction) because it is not as lightweight as Ctrl+F.

Milne, David, and Ian H. Witten. 2008. 'Learning to link with Wikipedia'. In *Proceeding of the 17th ACM conference on Information and knowledge management*, 5090518. Napa Valley, CA: ACM.
This paper reports on an ongoing project in automatically parsing and embedding noun-phrase links in Web pages, using Wikipedia as a reference. Linking with Wikipedia – or, as the authors say, 'wikifying' pages – has so far succeeded where similar projects have failed, thanks to Wikipedia's breadth and (supposed) impartiality. For example, where similar lookup engines might require a great deal of editorial effort to create a functional 'dictionary' and attempt to use the long-standing WordNet lexical database for disambiguating word meanings, Wikification is based on statistical relevance judgments, using one of the largest such databases in existence (dwarfing WordNet's coverage of noun phrases). In this paper, the authors explain in detail their method for making these relevance judgments, noting that the overall machine-derived statistical relevance for their results is somehow identical to that of the aggregate relevance judgment of their user study participants – 79 per cent.

Qayyum, Muhammad Asim. 2008. 'Capturing the online academic reading process'. *Information processing & management* 44: 2, 581-595.

This article, an extension of the author's dissertation work, reports on the electronic document reading, sharing, and interaction habits of graduate students. He found that the vast majority of annotations fall into just two categories – underlined or highlighted text and anchor points for some marginalia. Either selection of text (in the first case, the original author's, in the second, the reader's) could be indexed by a sufficiently powerful reading environment and presented to the reader or readers as a table of contents of notes. One finding from this study that subverts a key assumption of open online annotation systems is that many individuals do *not* want to inherit an already-annotated document, even less so if the prior annotator is anonymous. While we can learn much from the wisdom of crowds, we seldom set out to read a self-contained document with these crowds in mind, as doing so can be confusing or overwhelming. It is thus a sensible assumption that the annotation layer should be secondary to the original text in a well-designed reading environment – and worth considering when this assumption may *not* hold true.

Weel, Adriaan van der. 2010b. 'New mediums: New perspectives on knowledge production'. In *Text comparison and digital creativity*, edited by Wido Th. van Peursen, Ernst Thoutenhoofd, and Adriaan van der Weel, 253-268. Leiden: Brill. http://www.let.leidenuniv.nl/wgbw/research/Weel_Articles/15_knaw_Weel_rev_Aug09.pdf

A conceptual perspective on knowledge production. The author stresses the problematic aspect of using not only familiar technological features, but also traditional *concepts* in the production of new digital environments. He analyses the history of medium transition and the specific socio-technical nature of the digital medium to prove his point. This article gives a meta-perspective on the transition of knowledge from the paper to the digital medium. Four models show what the affordances of the computer as a 'Universal Machine' are, leading from mark-up to a collaborative model, and provide a basis for a more profound use of the digital medium.

*Personal e-reading software and interface design*
Bier, Eric, Lance Good, Kris Popat, and Alan Newberger. 2004. 'A document corpus browser for in-depth reading'. In *Proceedings of the 4th ACM/IEEE-CS joint conference on Digital libraries*, 87-96. Tuscon, Arizona: ACM.

This is one of few approaches that tries to integrate document finding/reference search, storing, and reading. Five still important desiderata are described on which the system is based. For example, '[v]isualizations of a bookplex should reveal information at several levels of granularity, from individual documents to all documents in the bookplex' (90). A bookplex is the environment in which documents are stored and retrieved. Three tools were implemented: a reference extraction tool, a document finding tool, and a corpus browser (with a Zoomable User Interface (ZUI)). The tools offer a combination of automated extraction and search, and user input.

Bottini, Thomas, Pierre Morizet-Mahoudeaux, and Bruno Bachimont. 2011. 'A model and environment for improving multimedia scholarly reading practices'. *Journal of intelligent information systems* 37: 1, 39-63.
The authors present a document model and experimental software tool for academic analysis of multi-medial 'documents', such as audio recordings of lectures and sheet music, with the intention of leading up to some form of publication. Whereas in other systems in this bibliography multi-medial content is treated as a unity, if it is included at all, this model allows for within-document spatial and/ or temporal annotation of several types of non-text documents. It also allows for linking between (parts) of the documents. The model is described comprehensively. The authors have also implemented the model by making a generic module and two software tools implemented for specific groups: an audio recording annotation tool and a musicological annotation tool. The former was used as an educational tool where students could build a structure for and annotate an audio recording of a lecture. By giving the teacher access, the analysis process leading up to the presentation students were required to give (the construction of which was also facilitated by the tool) could be judged. The generic tool offers an interesting mix of detailed and overview presentation of information, annotation, and linking of information, which could possibly also be applied to a combination of textual and non-textual documents. The users of the interface did find it too crowded however.

Siemens, Ray, Cara Leitch, Analisa Blake, Karin Armstrong, and John Willinsky. 2009. 'It may change my understanding of the field: Understanding reading tools for scholars and professional readers'. *Digital humanities quarterly* 3: 4. http://digitalhumanities.org/dhq/vol/3/4/000075/000075.html
Report on a user opinion study among digital humanists and graduate students on using the scholarly article reading tools embedded within the Public Knowledge Project's Open Journal Systems. The authors have embedded the actual research process in the study, not focusing on single document reading, but on how readers position texts in a field and the wider context. According to the authors, the single most interesting finding from this research was that the reading tools were overwhelmingly found to be better at locating articles within their respective scholarly context than actually assisting with individual readings. The most likely reason volunteered for this is that there are simply not many productive ways that software can intervene in readers' variously idiosyncratic means of interacting with isolated documents (with the exception of annotation, which was not well-supported by Open Journal Systems at the time of the study). Indeed, their think-aloud protocol evinced almost as many descriptions of individual reading

processes as commentaries on the tools themselves. The results are organised in several themes that can be used for informed design of new interfaces concerned not only with usability and speed of navigation, but also with the quality of the information that is accessed – a primary concern for academics.

Tashman, Craig S., and W. Keith Edwards. 2011. 'LiquidText: A flexible, multi-touch environment to support active reading'. In *Proceedings of the 2011 annual conference on Human factors in computing systems*, 3285.3294. Vancouver, BC, Canada: ACM.

LiquidText is prototype tablet software that offers various within-document manipulations for active reading that are not found in software on touchscreen devices today. LiquidText is based on the assumption that paper affordances are not necessary and can even impair the reading experience by trying to copy them. The authors detail a user study which was designed with the express purpose of determining which components of active reading (annotation being the long-standing example) are still better supported by pen and paper than they are in electronic reading environments. One of the findings: the least organised and most valuable insights are usually located in a cross-document context, not in a single PDF or Word file but in the margins of Powerpoints and email threads, and this type of annotation is supported in the software. A video on its workings is available on YouTube: http://youtu.be/gpA_bGUm3Wo.

*Social e-reading software and collaboration tools*
de la Flor, Grace, Marina Jirotka, Paul Luff, John Pybus, and Ruth Kirkham. 2010. 'Transforming scholarly practice: Embedding technological interventions to support the collaborative analysis of ancient texts'. *Computer supported coope-rative work (CSCW)* 19: 3, 309-334.

This is a thorough research project, involving a different type of 'humanities reading' than the other texts in this bibliography. The authors have studied the natural collaborative practice of researchers in a Classics department, who were trying to decipher text from (images of) an ancient tablet. Subsequently, a Virtual Research Environment (VRE) was developed for supporting this analysis, based on the features the researchers would want – which turned out to be different than envisioned by the authors beforehand. The authors conclude that rather than sup-porting intricate automated digital processes, the focus should be on facilitating interpretative practices and discussion among researchers.

Eklundh, Kerstin Severinson, and Henrry Rodriguez. 2004. 'Coherence and interactivity in text-based group discussions around web documents'. In *Pro-ceedings of the 37th Annual Hawaii international conference on system sciences* 4. Washington, DC: IEEE Computer Society.

This paper begins from a discussion of linguistic turn-taking to present a novel system prototype intended to aid with contextualizing multi-threaded electronic discussions across time and space. The authors discuss some of the shortcomings of traditional email and give particular attention to supporting informal 'citations', even if these are only simple hyperlinks in part of a larger discussion. The defining feature of the system interface they present is the ability (i.e. the requirement) for each new discussion entry to refer to one or more of several others, with corresponding timestamps and navigational aids. They note that this system appeared to encourage the use of implicit reference by deictic terms such as 'you', which is not traditionally common in electronic discussion. However, perhaps more interesting than the system itself are the visualisations that the authors present in the article's final pages; they provide a substantially more intricate network graph than ordinary threaded discussion trace data – which is, of course, still being actively mined today.

Erickson, Thomas. 2008. "Social' systems: Designing digital systems that support social intelligence'. *AI and society* 23: 2, 147-166.
This article is a cogent and intelligent summary of the best practices for designing social electronic collaboration spaces, which are sufficiently transparent to their users with respect to social interaction. Erickson focuses on how we silently and effectively communicate the rules of engagement for any particular scenario and revisits some prototypes that he has created over the past decade for helping to guide the rules of *online* interactions, without under- or over-communicating. In closing, he lists six points for effective social representation, each of which builds on the idea of making each participant's action visible to everyone in the same manner, but leaves the interpretation of this action to the user.

Fitzpatrick, Kathleen. 2007. 'CommentPress: New (social) structures for new (networked) texts'. *Journal of electronic publishing* 10: 3. http://quod.lib.umich. edu/j/jep/3336451.0010.305?rgn=main;view=fulltext
The author discusses a different model for digital publishing. The argument is built up from the perspective that experiments have relied too often on the metaphor of the codex and the incorrect notion of the single, isolated academic author and reader. Instead, the author states, the metaphor of the network, allowing for dialogue, is more efficient, with the blog as a good starting point. This has materialised in CommentPress, an open source Wordpress theme and plugin, now Digress.it (http: //www.digress.it).

Hoadley, Christopher M., and Peter G. Kilner. 2005. 'Using technology to transform communities of practice into knowledge-building communities'. *SIGGROUP bulletin* 25: 1, 31-40.
This paper brings together the perspectives of learning, knowledge building, communities of practice, and online communities; it presents two theoretical frameworks to support the design of online communities for knowledge building: one on learning in communities of practice (CoPs) called C4P (content, conversation,

connections, (information) context, and purpose) and one on learning through technology, Design for Distributed Cognition (DDC). Together these frameworks provide a general base for online knowledge community building, which the authors demonstrate with two examples. For more research on scholarly online collaboration and a converged perspective see Leitch (2009).

Leitch, Cara. 2009. 'Social networking tools for professional readers in the humanities'. Whitepaper.
The author identifies three key strategies for social media use in the humanities: evaluating (concerning identity), communicating, and managing. An overview of social networking sites and tools is provided, and a bibliography of articles in the area of collaboration is presented, concerning: the background of social media and collaboration; approaches to collaboration through social networks, including a number of expert(ise) retrieval methods (see McDonald 2003, Marlow et al. 2006, and Hoadley and Kilner 2005 in this bibliography); and issues of identity, privacy and trust. This whitepaper was published as an appendix in Siemens et al. 2012.

McDonald, David W. 2003. 'Recommending collaboration with social networks: A comparative evaluation'. In *Proceedings of the SIGCHI conference on Human factors in computing systems*, 593-600. Ft. Lauderdale, FL: ACM.
This article identifies user issues in recommending experts using social networks, which are important to consider before integrating social networks into groupware. The authors used quantitative and qualitative methods to describe two existing social networks in a middle-sized company: a work context structure and a more personal social structure, which, not surprisingly, have a reasonable overlap. This information is used to build and test the Expertise Recommender system, that recommends experts in less familiar parts of the company, based on either of the two networks, or a 'no matching' principle, where the networks are not used and only expertise is considered. The authors summarize the outcome in a useful list of recommendations for designers, that include for instance the need for user control and perceived trade-off. For a broader base in research on scholarly online collaboration and a converged perspective see Leitch (2009), also in this bibliography.

McGann, Jerome. 2004. 'Marking texts of many dimensions'. In *A companion to Digital Humanities*, edited by Susan Schreibman, Ray Siemens, and John Unsworth. Oxford: Blackwell. http://www.digitalhumanities.org/companion/
A careful and deep conceptual analysis of what 'text' actually is and how knowledge of its autopoetic nature can inform our computational processing of it. The author offers a framework to parallel print and digital technology from a systemic angle, pointing to the multidimensionality of text. He thereby provides a release from the codex metaphor and opens up the concept of 'reading' to a more social approach.

Marlow, Cameron, Mor Naaman, Danah Boyd, and Marc Davis. 2006. 'HT06, tagging paper, taxonomy, Flickr, academic article, to read'. In *Proceedings of the seventeenth conference on Hypertext and hypermedia*, 31-40. Odense, Denmark: ACM.
This article presents a framework for tagging systems. A conceptual model integrates resources, users, and tags, laying a base for a holistic approach to social tagging. Two organisational taxonomies for social tagging systems are then presented that describe 'system design and attributes' and 'user incentives', which the authors believe to have a substantial effect on the tags and the users. These are then applied to Flickr, a social image annotation website, and Del.icio.us (now delicious), a URL tagging website. Although one should note that Yahoo! Research Berkeley employees have conducted this research, the framework provides a decent basis to consider when building a tagging system. It shows how the design model of the tagging system has great influence on the shape of the output. For a broader base in research on scholarly online collaboration and a converged perspective see Leitch (2009).

Marshall, Catherine, and A.J. Bernheim Brush. 2004. 'Exploring the relationship between personal and public annotations'. In *Proceedings of the 4th ACM/IEEE-CS joint conference on Digital libraries*, 349-357. Tuscon, AZ: ACM.
This study, in equal parts about annotation and collaboration, looks at the way that personal annotations are transformed for public sharing and discussion. Chief among its findings is the fact that annotators seem be very conscientious about what it is they share: relatively little private annotation material is eventually shared online (25 per cent) or used as the basis of online discussion (8 per cent), and when it is, it is usually transformed with no small effort to be made intelligible to a broader audience. Also important is that the annotations that most commonly formed the basis of a future discussion were simple marginal notes with anchors in the text.

Ribière, Myriam, Jérôme Picault, and Sylvain Squedin. 2010. 'The sBook: Towards social and personalized learning experiences'. In *Proceedings of the third workshop on Research advances in large digital book repositories and complementary media*, 3-8. Toronto, ON, Canada: ACM.
A position paper on the need for e-books to become more social, especially when it concerns students' learning needs. The authors first explain the model they would suggest: within-textbook annotation, with the book itself being the social community, instead of asking readers to sign into one (this should give rise to some privacy questions). To find annotations that are of use to a reader, the authors propose several features. The interesting aspect of this paper, however, is that it also suggests using learning paths, steps readers take (i.e. the books they read) to learn something, thus also not only treating reading as social, but also widening the idea of the book itself as a standalone item. The suggestions are being addressed in a

collaborative research project (until 2013), in which Alcatel-Lucent, Abilene Christian University, and Cambridge University Press are involved.

Schreibman, Susan. 2002. 'Computer-mediated texts and textuality: Theory and practice'. *Computers and the humanities* 36: 3, 283-293.
A discussion of several theories that can inform electronic research in literature. The author argues that the digital scholarly edition is freed from the limitations of the codex and discusses several theories (including Versioning and Reception Theory) that help envision a broader conception of what a scholarly edition can entail and that rather than creating a digital library, the result will be more like an enhanced monograph.

Siemens, Ray, Mike Elkink, Alastair McColl, Karin Armstrong, James Dixon, Angelsea Saby, Brett D. Hirsch, and Cara Leitch. 2010. 'Underpinnings of the social edition? A narrative, 2004-9, for the Renaissance English Knowledgebase (REKn) and Professional Reading Environment (PReE)'. In *Online humanities scholarship: The shape of things to come*, edited by Jerome McGann, 401-460. Houston: Rice Unversity Press. Accessed December 16, 2011. http://shape-ofthings.org/papers/RSiemens/RSiemens.doc
In developing an electronic scholarly edition, a group of researchers, including Implementing New Knowledge Environments (INKE) and the Public Knowledge Project (PKP), has built a proof-of-concept Professional Reading Environment (PReE) to facilitate a more flexible use of the Renaissance English Knowledgebase (REKn). The publication discusses the challenges, successes, and consecutive considerations for future implementations in detail, which entails moving from desktop to a Web application and a personal environment to one enriched with social media.

Siemens, Ray, Meagan Timney, Cara Leitch, Corina Koolen, and Alex Garnett, with the ETCL, INKE, and PKP Research Groups. 2012. 'Toward modeling the social edition: An approach to understanding the electronic scholarly edition in the context of new and emerging social media'. *Literary and Linguistic Computing* 27: 4, 445-461. http://web.uvic.ca/~siemens/pub/2011-SocialEdition.pdf.
A framework that provides groundwork for the social edition, a scholarly edition that combines the dynamic edition (where the text is structured as a database and can be transgressed hypertextually) with the possibilities of social media – positioning the text as a process rather than a product. In two appendices, one of which is the whitepaper by Leitch (2009, also in this bibliography), the parameters for this work are explored.

Skaf-Molli, Hala, Claudia Ignat, Charbel Rahhal, and Pascal Molli. 2007. 'New work modes for collaborative writing'. In *International conference on Enterprise information systems and web technologies*, edited by Narayana Swamy Kutti and Bobby Granville, 176-182. ISRST.

This conference paper employs the popular (although this popularity is declining) Computer-Supported Cooperative Work (CSCW) matrix to categorise and describe new techniques for collaborative writing and editing. Using Google Docs as a referent, the authors explain that while it supports both synchronous and asynchronous modes of writing (as you can use Google Docs perfectly well when working alone), it does not allow you to work in a bubble, that is to say, to work collaboratively without being confronted with real-time changes made by other contributors. The authors also draw distinctions between when collaboration systems *send* and *receive* data; in the Google Docs model, this is system-initiated and thus effectively automatic (and unhelpful for version control), whereas in a Wiki or traditional version control system (VCS), it is user-initiated. They rate several systems according to their performance on what they call the SRI, or *send-retrieve-initiate* model, and note that Google Docs performs relatively poorly on this model, sacrificing control in favour of perceived ease of use. However, training non-developers to use a traditional VCS is not easy.

### Notes

1   See for instance Ni, Tao, Doug A. Bowman, and Jian Chen. 2006. 'Increased display size and resolution improve task performance in information-rich virtual environments'. *Proceedings of graphics interface 2006*. Quebec, Canada: Canadian Information Processing Society. 139-146. Print.

2   Hornbæk, Kasper, Benjamin B. Bederson, and Catherine Plaisant. 2002. 'Navigation patterns and usability of zoomable user interfaces with and without an overview'. *ACM transactions on computer-human interaction*, 362-389. Print.

# Writing differently in the digital era

## Hamlet in Hyperborg

Joost Kircz and August Hans den Boef

In this paper we argue that the inherent potential of digital technology enables us to write scholarly and educational texts more effectively. In narrative prose fiction, the author strictly determines the reading path.[1] In scholarly and educational writing about literary texts, the author tends to wish to cater to a variety of different readers. Hence, it is desirable to provide the opportunity for readers to follow many different reading paths, in order to facilitate various purposes such as exploration, learning, and research. In print, we are already familiar with books with dual reading tracks, one for general understanding and another for more in-depth knowledge. A famous example is the textbook *Gravitation* by Misner et al. (1973), which Kaiser extensively discusses (2012). But in a digital environment we can easily enable a plurality of reading paths in educational and scholarly texts. In order to accommodate these, we will stress the importance of enabling a structural change in discursivity in the transition from paper to electronic substrates. It goes without saying that such a development demands new sets of tools to be developed.

By a structural change in discursivity we mean the way in which the intrinsic capabilities of the medium allow narrative elements to be disposed. This is more than adding embellishments, such as the addition of the rattle of the dying or the primal scream of the new born, by way of an 'audio-illustration'. Textual and non-textual components alike may actively add to the argument, depending on their value. Are we content with the metaphor of a scream in the form of a picture, or do we need the very scream itself? The new technologies extend the discursive capability of the human author.

This issue is becoming more and more important as, at present, we see the transfer of traditional paper-based books to a great variety of electronic books. These electronic books or e-books can be displayed on two very different kinds of screens: the stable and very readable but not very dynamic e-ink based readers, and the dynamic but less comfortable LCD screens on laptops, tablet computers, and smartphones. These differences impose limits on what multimedia components can be used by the author. As technology continues to develop, comparative in-depth studies have been performed in order to draw general conclusions. However, many studies of only a few years ago on the technological and ergonomical aspects of e-readers are already obsolete due to this rapid development. In general we can say that though linear reading of fiction or non-fiction literature is possible on an e-ink reader such as the Amazon Kindle or Kobo Touch, in the case of educational and scholarly texts, paper versions are still widely preferred for study, whilst their electronic representations are well accepted for reference and look-up (e.g. Ackerman and Goldsmith 2011, Siegenthaler et al. 2011, Cull 2011, Woody 2010). The question remains, under what conditions can a book incorporate multimedia components in such a way that the reader enjoys and prefers the electronic form above a printed version?

Historically 'the Book' has been considered a convenient object composed of bound printed paper pages. At present we are in the process of redefining the notion of the book, and we see a discussion on what we understand by e-books (e.g., Cramer, Kovač, this volume). In 2008, Vassiliou and Rowley already catalogued and analysed 37 definitions of e-books to conclude that: 1) 'An e-book is a digital object with textual and/or other content, which arises as a result of integrating the familiar concept of a book with features that can be provided in an electronic environment', and 2) 'E-books, typically have in-use features such as search and cross reference functions, hypertext links, bookmarks, annotations, highlights, multimedia objects and interactive tools'. They pose that: 'A two-part definition is required to capture both the persistent characteristics of e-books, and their dynamic nature, driven largely by the changing technologies through which they are delivered and read'. Hence, the new issue at stake is not only to what extent the representation of book content in e-versions equals paper in its ease of use but also what more the author can do, using the inherent properties (Van der Weel 2011a) of electronic-based methods for conveying the author's message and meaning to the reader.

The main thrust of this contribution is that, contrary to post-structuralist thinking, in an electronic environment we need a well-structured practice to enable the environment's essential property: its capacity to connect any element in its network to any other element. Below, we investigate what tools are required for creating new educational and scholarly works. In doing so we hark back to the original fundamentals of a proper hypertext system that enables the author to create a new way of structuring his or her narration while at the same time enabling the reader to follow various reading paths.[2] The key issue is that hyperlinks – the bidirectional linking of two or more text or media 'chunks' – should have a rhetorical meaning and are not just unidirectional 'see also' indicators as we know them at present.

In this article we mainly deal with educational and academic texts. It goes without saying that literary works can perfectly follow the methods we propose, but the essence of a literary work is that it is primarily the author in his or her time and context that takes the narrative and structural lead, leaving it to the reader, most often in quite another context and time, to make sense of it. In educational and academic texts, the primary purpose is to elucidate issues to others (colleagues, students), and to present insights or conclusions, which does not necessarily imply following the author's reading path – page by page, exactly as the book or paper is written. Kircz (1991) makes the following distinctions between different types of readers of educational and academic writing: a) the non-reader – the university administrators and others who count and archive output; b) the informed reader, who is a colleague in the same field, knows what he or she is looking for, and therefore reads very selectively; c) the partially informed reader, who might be a novice in the field and skims the work for possible clues to the issues discussed, and finally d) the uninformed reader, who is the person that wants to learn something new and hence reads the work conscientiously from beginning to end. It goes without saying that, in a real-life academic environment, one and the same person may play one or more of the roles thus described. Hence, an important implication of these distinctions is the necessity for the structure of an electronic publication to be such that each type of reader can select his or her own (reading) path. This dovetails with extensive research in reading and information retrieval (IR) practices on the way in which readers look for components in research papers and how for that purpose journal articles, for instance, can be *disaggregated* into their components – abstract, underlying data, conclusions, bibliography, and so on. Researchers then reaggregate the components into new structures (see Sandusky and Tenopir 2008 and references therein for a fine overview).

## 1 The historical context

While it may seem as if digital media facilitate a straightforward conversation between a multimedia author and his or her reader, we feel the need to review certain aspects of such an assumption. This is necessary because new technologies change the way in which we express our reasoning and feelings, but they do not necessarily change the goal or directions of that reasoning.

In the development of writing, there have been clear structural changes arising as a consequence of the interplay between a new medium (stone, clay, paper) and its attendant technologies and a new, often larger, audience emerging as a result of the ever growing number of copies involved. In considering these changes, it is important to make a strict distinction between the copying of an existing text into a new medium and the development of qualitatively new ways of presentation suited to a new medium (see also chapter 3 of Van der Weel 2011a). As many books have already described the evolution from clay tablets to the printing press and the consequences for the structure of the narrative,[3] in this section we will only touch on select aspects by way of examples and metaphors for our argument.

Ong (1982) and Eisenstein (1979) have extensively treated the development of the book and textual fixity.[4] The problem of fixity is often addressed in new media discussions. Unfortunately, in many of these discussions, three different issues are often mixed up. One pertains to the very existence of the content; the second to the reliability, or continued integrity of the content (or parts of it) in a medium that is often regarded as ethereal, and the third to the very different ways a reader may move through the text.

Thus firstly, we have the text (or other media components) as published the first time. This version is simply there and will only vanish if deliberately all copies, including all backups and – in the case of an Internet publication – also on all servers, are erased on the level of the file itself. The whole field of digital forensics is built on this fact (Kirschenbaum 2007).

Secondly, the pristine version can be easily 'improved' or added to or otherwise changed, by deliberate editing by the author or by others. However, unlike in the old days, when unknown scribes changed and improved or corrupted copies, every digital change has a retrievable digital signature: for instance, the date-and-time stamp and the IP number of the connection of the collaborator who added to or even changed the material in the original version. Hence, in the digital environment a work may exist in a plurality of versions. However, the author(s) of the original content can declare a particular version the right or definitive one, at a certain moment. For academic papers, this is normally the version that has been accepted and published by a scholarly journal. In the same vein, Van der Weel (2003) makes a distinction between the instability of form and content, on the one hand, and 'existential' instability on the other. The formal aspect is related to layout and representational media (from paper size to browser technology) and it demands, if we want the form to remain fixed, the integration of form and content in one file, such as a PDF file. Existential instability is a new phenomenon: an example is rendering a web page built up from various external databases that could be as ephemeral as spoken words. Nevertheless, just as the spoken word has been captured by the tape recorder, so are websites – temporarily – stored in the cache memory of the computer used or on the big servers of data stores and warehouses.

The third issue is that of the various ways a reader may move through hyperlinked text. This has the effect that no two readers will necessarily read the chunks of which it consists in the same order, or read the same amount of text: the text is 'fluid' from one reader to the next.

The cultural consequences of fixed text have been listed well by Eisenstein (1979; mainly chapters 2, 6, and 8):
– the reusability of old works or parts thereof;
– an enormous growth in the dissemination of identical information;
– the emergence of standardization of presentation and judgement;
– the development of typography;
– new forms of data handling;
– the possibility of error correction.

As discussed in detail by De Waard and Kircz (1998) in scientific articles, a distinction should be made between functions that are related to the technology used (general presentation – typography, page numbers, etc. – and registration and indexing systems) and functions used in order to enhance communication per se (see below in section 3). In the digital world, all of the six points made by Eisenstein continue to be relevant. At the same time, there is in the new medium a proliferation of versions, comments, pastiches, analyses, and re-creations that can be edited, changed, and reused, without – in principle – much ado, on a scale and with an ease that are quite unique to the new environment. So, in the afterlife of a once-published digital treatise, a multitude of new texts and other media expressions emerges around the original content that could be represented by a tight web, or better graph, with vertices and edges of different quality, certification, and value. In order to extract those elements that are useful for a particular reader, a whole novel set of tools is needed. Defining those tools goes hand in hand with defining how best to publish a digital text.[5]

The history of written text is rife with examples of the development of reading aids such as word separation, spacing, punctuation, page numbers, easily readable type fonts, and other features that we now regard as 'normal' (Cavallo 1999; Parkes 1999; Saenger 1999). New tools will likely look like old ones, but unless we cast the work into a fixed unity of content and form, such as in a PDF file, some aids, such as page numbers, may disappear altogether. *Digital humanities quarterly* (http://digitalhumanities.org/dhq/) has solved the lack of page numbers by counting paragraphs. This way of avoiding page numbers harks back to the practice of numbering verses in the Bible, but it need not be seen as an instance of technology forcing us into 'going backward'. After all, in most cases paragraph numbering gives a greater granularity than page numbering for looking up parts of text and communal reading.

There are other aspects of text production in which the past can be instructive for our view of the present and our expectations for the future.[6] As has been stated many times, commencing with the printing revolution itself, too much information will only drive people mad. Freedom of the word is essential, but it cannot be equated with drowning in bit streams. In the present, just as in the past, making sense of cultural developments means systematizing, structuring, and comparing experiences, information, and knowledge. In the digital era, we are only now taking the first steps in an attempt to do so, as all instances of human utterances are now on one unique – digital – platform available for structuring, indexing, and deep analyses. In exploring *digital born* writing, we explore at the same time the pros and cons of replicas of old forms of expression in a new environment, as well as the need to determine common ground by mutually agreed structuring.[7]

At present we witness two not fully antagonistic developments in such structuring. On the one hand, we have massive research endeavours that use probabilistic methods to sieve through and filter information chunks, on the basis of their context, from the enormous flood of web documents. On the other hand, we have the development of the semantic web (http://www.w3.org/2001/sw/), in which the emphasis lies on properly naming information objects and their relationships. Below, we discuss what new structuring tools can and should be created within the general philosophy of the semantic web.

## 2 The challenge of Hypertext

In the 1960s, Ted Nelson had already founded the Xanadu project, the principal insight of which was that 'if text and other media are maintained as referential structures, the resulting structure will have powerful advantages over merely moving the contents around' (http://www.xanadu.com/tech/). Nelson became a keen critic of the World Wide Web, as he considered it too 'chaotic':

> Its one-way breaking links glorified and fetishized as 'websites' those very hierarchical directories from which we sought to free users, and discarded the ideas of stable publishing, annotation, two-way connection and trackable changes (Nelson 1999).

Mainstream web development followed a pragmatic path, and Nelson's critique is still valid. Hypertext – the system of linking parts of text to other parts of text in an ineradicable way (in the sense, described above, that later versions can always divert from the original) – has been around since the late 1980s (Conklin 1987) and became a fertile ground for web development and index and ontology studies.

However, its expression as web over the pre-curser of Internet changed the world. This is the hypertext success story of Tim Berners-Lee (Berners-Lee and Cailliau 1990) using HTML (HyperText Markup Language). This language followed the hierarchical model provided by SGML (Standard Generalized Markup Language, ISO 8879).[8] While being a great step in the process of international standardization of machine-readable documents, SGML was complicated and in many ways a restrictive model, based on the notion of independent files in a hierarchical file management system. The watered down version HTML also considers objects as independent bricks linked together with untyped hyperlinks between them, excluding the possibility of overlaps and it became the engine for the hypertext web explosion. While the Web as such is non-hierarchical, all individual HTML and XML documents that make up the 'docuverse' are hierarchically structured.[9]

The central issue for educational and scholarly materials is that we want a free and certified, that is to say authoritative and validated vis-à-vis quality, roaming through large numbers of texts, pictures, and various versions thereof on the one hand, and, on the other hand, scaffolding, railing, indexing, and signposts. In cultural studies, hypertext is often seen as the model and tool for fluid, unfettered communications (see, e.g. Landow 2006). A critique of the over-enthusiastic acceptance of hypermedia by post-structuralist thinkers is given by Cramer (this book).

In educational publications, we find many examples of hypertext in the form of various pieces or chunks of text, pictures, graphs, and video and audio files tied together through the usually blue-coloured clickable standard hyperlink. However, the question remains whether that is enough, and the immediate answer is 'No'. The navigational technology is still too primitive. First and foremost, the fact that present-day hyperlinks are still not bidirectional means that reading a book with four fingers between the pages is just as easy as, if not easier than, reading the same book in e-form and using the 'go back one page' button in a browser. The advance of 'bookmarks' in modern e-books is a fix to make up for the lack of bi-directionality. Present day e-ink readers allow for links within a document but not yet between documents. The page, be it a book page or a web page, which is only a geometric container of content, remains the prime logistic aid, despite the odd experiment with other kinds of markers, such as the above-mentioned numbered paragraphs in the *Digital humanities quarterly*. The fundamental problem is that we 'link' from a position in a text to another file or page and not to another position in a text. This is also the essence of Nelson's critique. We are not able to have a patchwork of 'cuttings', 'clippings', or loose pages in front of us as raw material for a new work, because we miss the appropriate tools to put these chunks of material at our fingertips. Despite all fantastic advances of the last years, in storing complete libraries and complete journal editions from issue one in retrievable repositories, we still have to address this fundamental problem.[10]

The second, equally severe problem, whose impact is especially strong in the context of academic publications, is that links are not typed: a link is a link is a link. For the sake of clarity, we discuss here only links between documents. Links are also possible and widely used within documents. Many a discussion has taken place and attempts have been made to address this deficiency, but, in practice, no publications exist yet in which links also have a well-defined meaning. We just click from one place to another, without any indication of why, other than the knowledge that the author has felt some need to point us in a certain direction. In that sense, the hyperlink is like the footnote – it can prove and claim anything, but it is often broken, which is similar to a reference mentioned in a footnote that is not available to the reader (for a nice overview of the various roles of footnotes, see in particular chapter 1 of Grafton 1997).

A third issue is the need to take into account the argumentative nature of a scholarly or educational text. The author of such a text wants to convey knowledge and meaning based on theory and facts, which is very different from the conveyance of meanings and emotions in literary texts. Given the fact that the Web allows all types of discussions and interactions, research on structures to facilitate comprehension by the reader within this *mer à boire* is plentiful (see Schneider et al. 2012 for a recent extensive overview). In the research field of scientific communication, some work has been done to try and develop argumentation schemes as a limited structure for 'typed' hyperlinks (De Waard and Kircz 2008, Kircz and Harmsze 2000, Harmsze 2000). In those works, which are a continuation of earlier work done by, for instance, Trigg and DeRose in the 1980s (reviewed by Harmsze 2000), a clear division is made between links that organise the structure of the text and links that indicate reasoning such as explication, elaboration, or worked-out example.

In the current essay, it is suggested that distinct textual modules should be defined in an attempt to *disaggregate* the standard presentational form. The organisational relations, materialised in typed hyperlinks, are those that are the basic 'road signs' in the modular structure and deal with the whole module and not parts thereof. Think about the 'administrative/bibliographic' module – the bibliographic references – and the sequence of modules such as introduction, methods, experiments, results, and discussion. Relations in the so-called scientific discourse call for a different kind of typed link. Here the links deal with understanding the underlying reasoning. For these types of relations, a taxonomy based on the Pragma-dialectical method was developed. This method has as its goal the organisation of discourse activity in the real world, when people are trying to convince one another (Van Eemeren and Grootendorst 1992; for a short discussion, see http://en.wikipedia.org/wiki/Pragma-dialectics). These links are composed of two groups: a) relations explicating communicative intent, such as elucidation and argumentation, and b) content relations, such as similarity, synthesis, causality, and elaboration.[11]

Dancing from hyperlink to hyperlink does provide us, in principle, with much more information than we ever were able to access with the help of a good library, as we now have the content of all libraries available to us online, but this does not necessarily deepen our understanding, as long as the reason for the linking is not clear-cut. Typed hyperlinking is essential in order to cut one's way through the jungle of the World Wide Web, but given the limits of present-day technology, we are forced to rescue integrity through writing a well-reasoned explanation before we suggest a link for the reader to follow. This reasoning 'around', for instance, a bibliographic reference is the subject of computational methods for identifying the meaning of a part of text (Angrosh 2012). In other words, in a digital environment, authors should not be allowed any longer to just enter a hyperlink to some other entity without explicitly saying why. In scholarly communication, this should become an imperative. No bibliographic reference should be accepted without a strict reason of why it is cited. (Such a practice would, incidentally, also immensely improve the whole field of citation studies, as it will immediately provide the significance of a citation, instead of the actual non-discriminatory counting and normalising. After all, a reference in the introduction of a paper has a completely different significance than one in the methodology section.) We suggest that a formal typology of hyperlinks as a method of pre-coordinating should be much simpler than deriving the meaning later on through parsing techniques, such as information extraction and summarisation methods. Obviously, a typed link can have multiple indicators or metadata, such as date, author, meaning one (agree with), meaning two (elaboration), and so on.

In conclusion, this means that in order to allow authors (and commentators or annotators) to use hyperlinks as argumentative navigation a tool, a formal technology has to be developed. If we have such tools, working with them is a matter of metadata management. The various types of links that are considered desirable within a specific work will depend on its genre and level of scholarly depth. Within an application, it should be possible to switch such a tool on or off, so that the text is not littered with links, allowing a reader to remain at the level of complexity that fits the demands of the moment.

Typed hyperlinks, apart from being bidirectional, are not symmetric at all. If a reference is made to another author, the significance of this reference is only symmetric in the simplest cases of, for instance, mutual agreement, mutual disagreement, or the catchall 'see also' symmetry. In all other cases, a hyperlink is asymmetric. This means that if, say, I refer to another person's work and cite a sentence from it, I do this for a specific reason. However, the author being cited or simply referred to has, in most cases, neither knowledge of nor a qualified opinion about my writing.

As long as hypertext tools are still defined within the paradigm of office automation and disallow proper argumentative reasoning, a real breakthrough will be difficult. In that sense, we can refer to Shillingsburg's outcry that for scholarly editions, we simply miss the tools to make them convenient for readers and textual scholars alike (Shillingsburg 2009). The task upon both authors and editors to define these tools is now pressing.

## 3 Structure as glue between author and multiple readers

Text that has been put to paper as the author created it is the basis for various ways of reading. Though most people read novels without a pen or pencil in hand, this is different for scholarly and educational texts, as dealt with in this paper. Here, the text is a point of departure or an ingredient for further study and understanding. Humanists made a clear break with the scholastic past in the late fifteenth century, when the book began to be used for annotations and for abstraction and reformulation of the content by the reader (a new way of reading well described by Grafton 1999). It is important to keep a keen eye on this, as present technology struggles with the capacity to add notes, scribbles, and annotations to electronic versions of books and articles. These obstacles have to be removed before a fully electronic writing and reading environment will flourish.

A second fact stressed by Grafton is that people in the past diligently copied large parts of texts, and even whole texts, not only from manuscripts but also from printed books, a technique that was used until the advance of the photocopier. Copying a cherished fragment of text, among other reasons, served an important purpose of internalising its content. Of course, this has much to do with the ancient craft of memorising. In the electronic environment, where 'cut-and-paste' is now possible, the question arises as to what extent the loss of this internalisation by reiteration, be it by uttering a memorised text or by manually copying it, might signify a change in the depth of understanding. Further research on electronic learning environments must solve this issue. An important implication of the above is that in the creation of new structures for text presentation, not only the level of information coupling but also the coupling of understanding is at stake.

## 4 The Darnton model

At this point, it is useful to compare our reasoning with that of Darnton in his often-quoted pyramidal layer model (Darnton 1999). Darnton contrasts the use of hyperlinks with a 'layered cake' model of book publishing:

> The top layer could be a concise account of the subject, available perhaps in paper-back. The next layer could contain expanded versions of different aspects of the argument, not arranged sequentially as in a narrative, but rather as self-contained units that feed into the topmost story. The third layer could be composed of docu-mentation, possibly of different kinds, each set off by interpretative essays. A fourth layer might be theoretical or historiographical, with selections from previous schol-arship and discussions of them. A fifth layer could be pedagogic, consisting of sug-gestions for classroom discussion and a model syllabus. And a sixth layer could contain readers' reports, exchanges between the author and the editor, and letters from readers, who could provide a growing corpus of commentary as the book made its way through different groups of readers.

In this model, Darnton misses the essence of hypertext by sticking to a hierarchi-cal model of different – isolated – reading modes. The issue here is that hyperlinks are not just footnotes but, in our opinion, refer, with a reason, to various relevant texts, which Darnton puts in his fourth layer. A properly structured hypertext work comprises all the aspects mentioned in Darnton's list. The quintessential point is that the hypertext version, which can change in time due to continuously added new materials, discussions, and edits, is the new e-book. The next question is then: which reading path does a particular reader want to follow? Darnton's six layers are places where the author can address and therefore in fact enable cer-tain – horizontal – reading paths. Our point of view is not a conflation of all these paths but an argument that, while reading, one should be able to make shortcuts or diversions and thereby enter the various Darntonian layers. At some points in the texts and at some moments of digesting the material, a reader might be interested in some further details. For instance the family relations of the leading character in a scientific biography who is a descendant of famous scientists and married into another famous scholarly family, whilst the same reader may want to skip all elaborations on geographical aspects and related discussions and com-ments. Hence, a structured typed-hyperlink typology needs to be flexible enough to allow comprehensive reading and at the same time prevent the reader from going too far astray in the embarrassment of richness. A publication model on the basis of modules, as described in the next section, may provide a more suitable alternative for publication in this respect.

Harmsze (2000) worked out in the greatest detail a 'modular' model for a text enriched with typed hyperlinks, to be applied in the field of Physics. The model allows various reading paths in addition to its reliance on a completely different kind of summary or abstract. A summary is most often a contracted version of the full text. But that is not always the case. An abstract of a seventeenth-century treatise on natural philosophy written for engineers can be completely different from an abstract written for philosophers. The first category of readers is likely to be more interested in the mechanics of the reported experiments, whilst the second category of readers may be more drawn by the interpretation and general context of the work. For the different types of abstracts of a scientific hypertext paper, we refer to Van der Tol (1998). His conclusion is the following:

> In a modular electronic environment, the abstract has primarily an orientation function. It fulfils this function best when it provides a balanced representation that refers explicitly, in the informative mode, to the various stages in the problem-solving process. It also has to contain labelled links that connect phrases of the abstract to the related modules of the article. At least each main module of the source text should be linked to the abstract.

Part of Van der Tol's work was an attempt to determine the extent to which the strict modular structure enables a coherent new form of scholarly discourse. After all, a scholarly article is an argumentative – often problem-solving – story that is characterised by many repetitions and iterations. In that sense, strict modularisation that is simply disaggregating a work into its constitutive elements might be too strong a demand. The conclusion that can be made is that it is possible to apply modularisation to standardised publication formats, such as academic journals in material sciences and biomedicine. This method might prove to be problematic, however, if we extend it to include the modularisation of school courses in an electronic learning environment, because here it is often the case that students of different background need different presentations of the same material.

In the actual example given below of the use of hypertext to create parallel and overlapping discourses, we have to constantly keep in mind what the balance is between form and content. The necessary technology is a consequence of that. So, we don't argue what can be done with the present-day technology, but what ought to be done given the implicit capabilities of these techniques. In this example, we try to illustrate how the ideas of asymmetric bi-directionality of links and rhetorically structured modules can become guidelines to writing in the field of the humanities.

## 5 *Hamlet* in Hypertext: An Example

Shakespeare's *Hamlet* is a well known, highly popular, and often-studied piece of literature, and as such it is a good basis for the discussion of our model and its pertinence for humanities scholarship. We take two examples of writing about *Hamlet*, both of which accord with the standard rhetorical scheme of an argumentative text, such as an academic paper. In the problem-solving process that academic papers try to reflect, the steps involved are as follows:
- introduction of the investigation;
- outline of the research process;
- description of the environment, tradition, and context in which the research takes place;
- development of own novel research activities;
- conclusions made on the basis of the research;
- reviewing other authors' results and ideas on the same subject;
  thoughts on further/future research.

In what follows we conceptualise a structure for more-or-less closed and comprehensive short pieces of texts that fit within each slot of the above scheme. A relatively independent but self-sufficient piece of text, which fits this Lego-brick paradigm, we call a module, in accordance with previous work mentioned above. Modules, in other words, must be self-contained and comprehensive chunks of text. Note that the length of these texts is not a factor at all. In that sense, the restriction is more rigid than the idea of 'lexia' – the somewhat arbitrarily delimited excerpts of a few words to a number of sentences that capture and convey meaning in the 'best possible' way – proposed by Roland Barthes as the smallest narrative unit.

With the modular scheme thus in place, we next propose two types of authors that may be associated with a scholarly inquiry: in our concrete case, we consider a Shakespeare scholar and an educational author to be pertinent examples. While these types of authors would each adapt their writing to their intended reading public, both narratives will be part of one hypertext network, comparable with George P. Landow's Victorian Web (www.victorianweb.org), a large and comprehensive repository on 'the literature, history, & culture in the age of Victoria'. Though, based on a clear hierarchical structure, and including many illustrations, the Victorian web lacks the important characteristics of typed, asymmetric links discussed above, and, hence, remains within the limits of the present commercially available tools.

As a third way of writing, we can envision a transformation of the play itself, according to the above argumentation scheme, which would make it a newly structured literary hypertext work. As a result, we will end up with another version of the same play, which can be juxtaposed with the original one. Below we expand on two examples; one a scientific article and the other an educational one.

*First module: Introduction*
In our rhetorical scheme, we start by introducing the scholarly inquiry. This stage-setting phase can be manifold. For the sake of this example, we take on the task of examining the sources on which the story of Hamlet is based. For the educational version, we may skip the too-obvious overview of Early Modern English or the study of the structure of a Shakespearian play; instead, we may concentrate on a more contemporary aspect: what were parent-children relations like in the past? Note that we are talking about two new digitally born texts, about, but independent of, the original one: Shakespeare's *Hamlet* and obviously with links to the digitised full-length text of Shakespeare's *Hamlet*, as well as to other relevant texts.

What will emerge therefore are two different discourses that are parallel to each other. This means that in the introductory part or module, we will find two different introductions on why and how *Hamlet* is used as starting point, with reference to the original text where pertinent. To do that, we will need a standard version of *Hamlet* to which all references in the texts will point. In certain cases, versions of the source text of the play, which act as bases for the educational or scholarly work, might differ. This means that our resource can be linked to a scholarly edition that has all annotated versions of the various editions of *Hamlet*.[12]

In this introductory module, we also refer, with due credits, to all relevant authors who have already published on the subject and discuss these works briefly in order to explain the importance of our own work and the contribution that it makes to the field. The hyperlinks to these other works will indicate if we are in agreement with, feel neutral about, or are critical of these works.

*Second module: The research process*
In the second module, we deal with the articulation of the purpose of the article that the scientist or the educational author is writing. For the scholarly study, the search for relevant material might cover any topic connected to or treated in the play – from the psychological problems of a boyhood deprived from fatherly care to the religious undertones pervading the play, but, as mentioned above, for our purpose here we choose to concentrate on finding the literary-historical sources of the story and the influences of other authors on the composition of the play. For instance, we know from studies on Shakespeare (Bevington 2011) that he had knowledge of ancient as well as contemporary literature, as well as a keen feeling for the fashion of his period. Shakespeare in his plays paraphrased parts of Thomas North's translation of Plutarch's selected *Lives*, and occasionally quoted from the *Gesta Danorum*. He had read English writers such as Geoffrey Chaucer, Edmund Spenser, and Philip Sidney as well as translations of classical drama. At the same time, he was up to date with the new school of drama writing as exemplified by his contemporaries Thomas Kyd and Christopher Marlowe. So, in discussing the possible influences, links to the digital works of these authors will be incorporated into the new publication.

For the educational track we may want to explore the route of relating the play's storyline to a contemporary context, for instance, by posing the following question: to what extent are family relations among the sixteenth-century Danish royalty different from relations among present-day royalty, about which, we can reasonably expect, schoolchildren know a lot, given the excessive media coverage that members of the royal family receive, in addition to what they might have read in novels that take this theme as a leitmotif. Here, for instance, the aforementioned theme of the psychology of a boyhood deprived from a father figure can become relevant and thus be duly treated. (Note that the beauty of a network consists in the ability not only to refer to other studies in a footnote but also, in principle, to incorporate the entire source to which a reference has been made, thereby making it an integral part of the discourse.)[13] At the same time, we can make some side-steps into the historical basis of the Hamlet family and its relationship to older sagas, which creates a direct connection to the scholarly trail, where these references might be discussed as well.[14]

*Third module: Context*
In the next module, the introduction and the description of the research are welded into the larger framework of our example of authoring specific research projects.

The new scholarly text may put an emphasis here on identifying and analyzing the stories that somehow may have influenced the writing of *Hamlet*. The linking to or incorporation of electronic resources available on the Internet is relatively straightforward. However, in this, we may be confronted by the possibility of manuscripts that deal with sixteenth-century issues being physically scattered around the world. Old manuscripts that may have influenced Shakespeare, directly or indirectly, might be lost since he started researching the material for his play. We have to find them in order to be able to argue that Shakespeare used them or not. Copies or versions of relevant sources could be in libraries or even in private collections. If so, part of the research environment can be a digital library of indexed and hopefully scanned documents. As long as the digitisation projects of archives remain incomplete, physical visits to them will be necessary. This means that in the research environment, strong emphasis must be given to searching and retrieving techniques. The methodologies used will be fully described in this module with pertinent references to the tools and software used. The example of discovering the sources for *Hamlet* can even be cast as an exercise in defining the methodological requirements for a study of old manuscripts and books, partly overlapping with actual methods for old texts comparison and analysis and partly as a 'Catalogue raisonné' of sources that go beyond solely bibliographic metadata.

In the educational track, we see a real opening for integrating multimedia in education. To build on an earlier example, here, the basis for comparison between the Danish Hamletian court and present-day royalty, forms a starting point and outline for discussing various royal cultures. This outline, which is the core of this module, is obviously based on historical as well as popular sources, including the avalanche of motion pictures that try to be faithful to the director's and producer's best knowledge of the period. A link between the educational and the scholarly is also easily made if we give students the exercise to search for relevant and reliable information on the subject. For this assignment, the students might be asked to try out two different ways of obtaining the necessary information – by using the scholarly track within the current electronic resource and by searching on the Internet. This might be an excellent opportunity for them to experience directly the difficulties associated with online research, which often relies on key-word search (think of words such as 'royalty', which, of course, can also mean a percentage of the sales price or net profit for authors, or 'family', which is really a catch-all for everything that has a relationship with something else).

*Fourth module: Development of own research activities*
In the context of a scholarly research project, the informed user might find the modules discussed thus far to contain rather well-known matter. In the fifth module, however, the scholarly author's own research activities are reported. Here, the sleuth, as it were, tries to resolve the research quest of module two, within the given context (module three). Here is the place to discuss findings on the basis of the methodologies described in the previous module. The scholarly author may have found serious works that might or even must have influenced Shakespeare, such as the *Oresteia* and *Gesta Danorum* and the works of Aeschylos and Saxo Grammaticus. Here is where the author can compare the various sources, and so it is in this module that we touch on the field of scholarly annotated editions of *Hamlet*. Contrary to traditional practice, extensive quotes from old works need not be just cut and pasted. In a hypertext environment, we can incorporate the quotations in such a way that the reader will be able to switch between the full-text quoted source and our electronic resource on *Hamlet* and can continue reading the quoted source as long as he or she pleases. It goes without saying that typing the hyperlinks will give the reader a clue as to why he or she should follow it. In a bidirectional typed-hyperlink system, the same reader can then switch again, if need be, from this source text to another treatise, by a different author, that deals with the same source. The whole point is that switching lanes is a well-structured and reasoned activity thanks to the very structured nature of our electronic resource.

For the educational track, say that we now have drawn up a historical overview of royal parental cultures and want to compare this with modern royal families. As Hamlet is a northern European, the most obvious example that comes to mind is the British queen, Elizabeth ii, and her son Charles, who, it is rumoured, is not on the friendliest of terms with his own father, Prince Philip, though the latter is still around and still happily married to her, as far as we are given to believe. In the Netherlands, we have Queen Beatrix and her son Willem, and the two, at least from what is publicly known, seem to enjoy a good relationship.

*Fifth module: Conclusions*

After introducing the research topic and describing the research process and the context in which the research project was carried out, the meat on the bone is the presentation of the conclusions that the author of the educational or scholarly text finally arrived at. In the scientific investigations, we conclude that Shakespeare's *Hamlet* is clearly inspired by older sources; in particular, Shakespeare based *Hamlet* on the legend of *Amleth*, preserved by the thirteenth century chronicler Saxo Grammaticus in his *Gesta Danorum* as subsequently retold by the sixteenth century scholar François de Belleforest. He may have also drawn on, or perhaps written, an earlier (hypothetical) Elizabethan play known today as the *Ur-Hamlet*.

In the educational track, we can argue, for instance, that parent-children, and in particular mother-son, relations are strongly determined by the social-historical context. These psychological conclusions can be connected to other studies, classic as well as modern, where this issue is at stake. In the first half of the twentieth century, when psychoanalysis was at the height of its influence, its concepts were applied to *Hamlet*, notably by Sigmund Freud (on dreams and the Oedipal desire for his mother; Freud 1913), Ernest Jones (1949), and Jacques Lacan et al. (1977); these studies have sometimes influenced theatrical productions, too. So in a comparative study of parent-children relations among the royalty, such studies might be helpful.

*Sixth module: Overview of other authors*

In this module, we look back on our own conclusions and examine what others have said on the same subject. Here, each reference to others will have a distinct rhetorical meaning. This makes the notion of typed hyperlinks immediately clear: we agree or disagree with or call in to rescue or debunk other authors' analyses and conclusions.

In the scholarly track, we are confronted, for instance, by an array of sources claiming that the sixteenth-century author François de Belleforeston was the sole source for the *Hamlet* play, as Shakespeare, and other contemporaries, might not have had access to older sources and so were not aware of them. But, as little is known about Shakespeare's life, many theories have been put forward about who he 'really' was, given his simple background. One of the most well known of these propositions is that it was Francis Bacon who wrote *Hamlet* (*Britannica*, 1911). At present, the so-called Oxfordians, who are convinced that Edward de Vere, the seventeenth Earl of Oxford, used Shakespeare's name for his literary works, contest all other candidates, including William himself (http://www.shakespeare-oxford. com/). So, in fact the whole validity of the question 'who influenced Shakespeare' can be challenged.

In the educational track, we are confronted by the fact that we have dealt with protestant royalty, whereas the Roman Catholic Church claims eternal family values that transcend social-economical circumstances (John-Paul II, 1981). Hence, we have to bring this into the discourse, as it is an important ingredient for understanding the full range of parental relationships among royalty.[15]

*Seventh module: Future research*
As in every narrative, life goes on in the 'ever after'. The scholarly track may end with the evergreen catchall that more research is needed, and digitising more archives is imperative in order for this research to be carried out. The educational track, in turn, may recommend further research into the family dynamics of non-protestant royalty, such as Catholics and Muslims, for instance.

## 5 Conclusions

Above, we have tried to illustrate that digitally born works need a new structure in order for users not to drown in the data stream but rather take a deep dive and return with the pearls. Electronic tools will be of great importance for changing the nature of authorship and incorporating a work in the totality of electronic works. We schematise our example discussed above in Table 1.

Table 1

| Original Linear text | Educational modular text | Scholarly modular text | Argumentational Scheme |
|---|---|---|---|
| *Enter KING CLAUDIUS, QUEEN GERTRUDE, HAMLET, POLONIUS, AERTES, VOLTIMAND, CORNELIUS, Lords, and Attendants* KING CLAUDIUS Though yet of Hamlet our dear brother's death The memory be green, and that it us befitted To bear our hearts in grief and our whole kingdom To be contracted in one brow of woe, Yet so far hath discretion fought with nature That we with wisest sorrow think on him, Together with remembrance of ourselves. Therefore our sometime sister, now our queen, The imperial jointress to this warlike state, Have we, as 'twere with a defeated joy,-- With an auspicious and a dropping eye, With mirth in funeral and with dirge in marriage, In equal scale weighing delight and dole,-- Taken to wife: nor have we herein barr'd Your better wisdoms, which have freely gone, etc. | Parent-children relations were different in the past | On which sources is *Hamlet* based? | Introduction |
| | Let us compare royalty now and in 16th-century Denmark | Try and find earlier potential sources and influences | Outline of the research process |
| | Prince Charles is angry at his mother too | In libraries, we find *Oresteia* and *Gesta Danorum* | Environment/ Context |
| | An outline of various royal cultures | Manuscripts are scattered in repositories around the world | Development of own research activities |
| | Some parent-children relations are historically determined | Shakespeare is clearly inspired by the sources mentioned | Conclusions made on the basis of the research |
| | The Roman Catholic Church upholds eternal family values | Others claim the only source was the 16th-century author François de Bellefo-reston | Reviewing other authors' results and ideas on the same subject; |
| | We will look further at non-protestant royalty | A further inter-textual analysis is required | Thoughts on further/future research |

New technologies enable new ways of offering a message to the reader. So, just as film became an inspiration for storytelling on paper, the use of hypertext and Internet-based features has become commonplace in modern writing of all kinds (see, e.g., Lightman's fascinating novel *The diagnosis* (2000), where e-mail exchanges are clearly distinguished, and not only typographically, from the rest of the text).

However, the shift to the digital medium heralds a really new stage with two interwoven developments: the usage of the very new medium itself as substrate and network, on the one hand, and the metaphors in style that the new media provides, on the other. In this essay, we have dealt with the first thread by pointing out how in the new digital environment we can write quite differently from just mimicking paper forms. It is already amply clear (see also Cramer, this volume) that hypertext novels are not the success that their advent led many to believe they were. It is worthwhile to research further to what extent the lack of structure plays havoc, as well as to establish the degree to which the limitations of a strict modular structure are commensurate with that shortfall. As we have asserted, storytelling is characterised by many repetitions and iterations, and in that sense, modularisation might become too rigid a change of style, as repetition of an argument normally serves to enhance persuasion. This will be a serious issue in any attempt to make school courses modular; each module must in and of itself remain a comprehensive and self-contained exposé.

Another important novelty is that we can write texts that relate to one another and have cross-references, such as we tried to show with the two modes of discussing one classical play. In an educational environment, this can lead to various reading paths within one structured resource: one reading along the main lines and supplementary reading paths, where more detailed discussions are available. Take the well-known phrase in science books: 'after some algebra we obtain'; in a hypertext environment, the full mathematical digression can be part of the text (as a pop-up) and only displayed on request, for instance in preparations for an exam. The same idea can be applied to extra explanations on *Hamlet*, such as sources discussing sexual morals in the sixteenth century or Shakespeare's peculiar grammar and vocabulary. The ability to follow various reading paths in the network of modules will become essential.

In other words apart from new 'post-novel' narratives in hyperspace, digital techniques allow the juxtaposition of multiple versions, studies, and elaborations of a story. This helps enrich the way we convey a message, as contextual and background information can grow in time, not making the original a so-called 'living document', but rather creating a living habitat for the narrative. In such a habitat, new works can incorporate existing modules and need not just review what has already been published. With the bidirectional typed hyperlinks, new and old works become one fertile playgroup for structured learning and scholarly communication.

Finally, unbounding the book in this way is useful not only in the educational and scholarly realm, but also for the fiction and entertainment public, because of the new ways in which it allows stories to be (re-)told.

## Acknowledgement

We thank the people who read and commented on the draft, in particular Keith Jones, Kees Snoek, and Adriaan van der Weel for their conscientious reading and helpful comments.

## Notes

1    Elsewhere we analysed the relationship between contemporary technology and its metaphorical expression in the story line of novels. Interestingly, we noticed that the backbone of the storyline remains in most cases the same; independently of the media used (Boef and Kircz, in preparation).

2    Obviously, this new way of structuring material will need to tie in with digital preservation and annotation efforts of existing texts and archives of source material.

3    Some important developments include changes in rhythm and rhyme to ease reading, increased sentence lengths, and the capability to refer to and from pages in a thick volume.

4    Adrian Johns has challenged Eisenstein forcefully on the issue of the transformative role of technology in his *The nature of the book* (Johns, 1998), and this has led to an interesting exchange of opinions (Eisenstein 2002a and 2002b; Johns 2002). The present authors fully endorse the Eisensteinian point of view.

5    In researching digital writing, it is important not to mix a critique or working around the limitations of existing tools, such as Microsoft Word, with the essential task of developing new 'system requirements' for writing and reading aids and tools.

6    Also on the way text is expressed and how the internal structure of a narrative and its presentation into a medium make deep inroads in the societal way of dealing with text and information, see e.g. of Goody (1986), Martin (1988), and Olson (1996). At every stage of implementing a new technology we have to take the change of use of the content into account, just as human consciousness changed considerably after the invention of writing (Ong 1983, 78). This contribution is not the place to dwell on this point more deeply, but just consider the cultural difference between the almost sacred value of an old book full of ancient wisdom and the whole of Chinese, Christian, Hindu, Islamic, Jewish, etc. mythology at one's Wikipedia fingertips.

7    For scientific e-born journal editing, see the proceedings of the sole international cross-disciplinary conference on this subject so far, which took place in 2001 and provides many examples, ranging from Comparative Law to Chemistry: *Change and continuity in scholarly communications* <http://web.archive.org/web/20051104080029/wwwoud.niwi.knaw.nl/ccsc/index.htm >. Interestingly, the pace of change in full e-journals in traditional fields is slow, as recent research shows (Mayernik 2007).

8    It is of great sociological interest to note that it was the stripped-down, simplified grammar of HTML that enabled the explosion of web pages. After it found its natural Waterloo, it was surpassed by the SGML 'dialect' XML (eXtensible Markup Language).

9    Of special importance is the parallel development of the Text Encoding Initiative (TEI), whose 'chief deliverable is a set of Guidelines which specify encoding methods for machine-readable texts, chiefly in the humanities, social sciences and linguistics' (http://www.tei-c.org/index.xml).

10  Note that in the field of academic publishing, links between works and their references are now globally implemented using the Digital Object Identifiers (DOI), a unique and most successful collaboration (http://www.doi.org/) between fiercely competing publishing houses.

11  This method for capturing the rhetoric of a scholarly publication is one of various attempts to do so (for an overview, see Buckingham Shum et al. 2012).

12  To illustrate the importance of this issue, we share an episode from one of the current authors' own past: the 1963 (10th) Dutch edition of *Hamlet*, which was published by the Dutch educational publisher Wolters and was a required high school reading at that time, included the following note, translated here into English: 'The text has been slightly expurgated'.

13  With concerns over copyright persisting, despite attempts at alternative systems of attribution, the described scheme might work best if implemented, for instance, within the licence system of a university library system or in a Creative Commons Licence environment.

14  In his article: 'The main literary types of men in the Germanic hero-sagas', Van Sweringen makes a division between, among others: The hostile kinsman, The avenger; split into: The father, The Son and The Brother, and The Traitor (Sweringen 1915). We provide this old reference not because we know that it is the most relevant one, but to show that with the help of a good online university library, we can dig up many lost treasures and review them. In this reference the quests of parental relationships as well as the mythological aspects thereof are discussed.

15  We can entertain, for the sake of argument, the possibility that the historical Hamlet, if he ever existed, was Catholic. However, in 1537, Denmark became a Lutheran country, and Shakespeare lived from 1564 till 1616 in Anglican England. Hamlet and his friend Horatio attended the Lutheran University of Wittenberg. Moreover, the role of the only priest (in act v) is minimal and purely formal. Hence, Shakespeare's Hamlet is certainly protestant.

# About the authors

ARIANNE BAGGERMAN studied history at Erasmus Universiteit Rotterdam. In 2001 she was awarded a grant by NWO for her research project 'Controlling time and shaping the Self: education, introspection and practices of writing in the Netherlands 1750-1914'. Her publication *Kind van de toekomst. De wondere wereld van Otto van Eck (1790-1798)* (Wereldbibliotheek 2005), co-written with Rudolf Dekker was in 2006 awarded the dr. Wijnaendts Francken prize of the Maatschappij der Nederlandse Letterkunde and in 2008 the Martinus J. Langeveld prize of the Universiteit van Utrecht. Baggerman is a member of the editorial board of *Quaerendo. A Quarterly Journal from the Low Countries Devoted to Manuscripts and Printed Books.* In 2006 she launched an international book series, Egodocuments and History published by Brill, of which she is co-editor. She teaches history at Erasmus Universiteit Rotterdam and she was in 2009 appointed professor in the history of publishing and book trade at the Universiteit van Amsterdam.

http://www.eshcc.eur.nl/english/personal/baggerman/

AUGUST HANS DEN BOEF studied literature at Leiden University and was until 2012 a teacher-researcher at de Institute for Media and Communication, Hogeschool van Amsterdam on the relation between news journalism and recent developments in the society, social, political and technological. He is a writer on modern fiction and history, politics and religion, and rock music. He is Dutch Freethinker of the year 2010 and the author of a.o. *Nederland seculier!*, *God als hype* and (forthcoming) and *Haat als deugd*.

FLORIAN CRAMER is applied research professor for the impact of new technology on art and design professions & program director of the research center Creating 010, Rotterdam University of Applied Sciences, critical writer on arts and media, developer of the Parallel University at WORM, the Rotterdam-based Institute of Avantgardistic Recreation. Publications include: *Exe.cut[up]able Statements: poetische Kalküle und Phantasmen des selbstausführenden Texts*, Wilhelm Fink, 2012. His book *Anti-Media: Ephemera on speculative arts* is be published in the Institute of Network Cultures series of NAi Uitgevers, 2013.

ALAIN GIFFARD has been the Information Technologies director of the TGB, the brainchild behind the digital library of the Bibliothèque Nationale de France, the deputy director of the Institut Mémoires de l'Edition Contemporaine (IMEC), the information society advisor to the Minister of Culture and Communication, and the president of the inter-ministerial commission for public access to Internet. He has recently carried out a report on digital readership and on 'industrial reading' for the Department of Culture and Communication. He is conducting a study on Hugues de Saint Victor, XII century philosopher and teacher. Alain Giffard has published articles and essays on hypertext, digital readership, and on cultural practices related to the Internet. A large part of these texts are on his French blog. He is president of Alphabetville, active member of Ars Industrialis, and a collaborator of the Centre international de Poésie Marseille.

> http://alaingiffard.blogs.com/
> http://alaingiffard.wordpress.com/

JOOST KIRCZ is a scientific researcher and professional in academic publishing, specializing in the design and implementation of electronic publishing experiments and products. During 16 years at Elsevier Science, he held various positions, including publisher of the distinguished physics programme (under the North-Holland imprint). In 1998, he founded Kircz Research Amsterdam (KRA), an independent research and consultancy company in Publishing. From 1992, he held various positions as a visiting scientist at the University of Amsterdam, presently at the Information and Language Processing Systems Group. From 2006-2010 he was part-time Lector (professor) and is presently director of research of Electronic Publishing at the Create-It applied research group of the University of Applied Science Amsterdam.

> www.kra.nl

CORINA KOOLEN is a PhD student in Digital Humanities at the University of Amsterdam and a lecturer at the Book and Digital Media Studies programme at Leiden University.

> http://www.looksinbooks.nl/

MIHA KOVAČ is head of digital development at Mladinska knjiga publishing and full professor at the Department of Library and Information Science and Book Studies at the University of Ljubljana, Slovenia. In 1985, he became Editor-in-Chief of Mladina, the only opposition weekly in then-socialist Slovenia, which was still part of Yugoslavia at that time. After 1988, he moved into book publishing and worked as editorial director in the two largest Slovene publishing houses, DZS and Mladinska knjiga. In 2000 he left professional book publishing and started to lecture at University of Ljubljana. He also worked as a consultant to textbook publishers in Slovenia, Serbia and Montenegro and participated as a textbook specialist in the World Bank Mission in Georgia (former Soviet Union). Between 2005-2009 he edited the Slovene edition of *National Geographic Magazine*. Between 1990 and 2004 he published more than 500 columns on Slovene political and cultural life in Slovene daily and weekly press. In august 2009, he returned to Mladinska knjiga as a publisher and resumed to work there as head of digital development in 2012. At the same time he keeps teaching at the University of Ljubljana. He is author of four books on book history and book publishing. In 2008, his first book in English *Never Mind the Web. Here Comes the Book* was published by Chandos in Oxford. http://mihakovac.cgpublisher.com

ANNE MANGEN is associate professor at The National Centre for Reading Education and Research, University of Stavanger, Norway. The title of her doctoral dissertation (Norwegian University of Science and Technology, 2006) was *New Narrative Pleasures: A Cognitive-Phenomenological Study of the Experience of Reading Digital Narrative Fiction*. Her research interests include experiential/phenomenological and (neuro)psychological impact of the interfaces and affordances of digital technologies on reading and writing, and she is currently doing empirical studies of literary reading in print and on e-books (Kindle) and tablets (iPad). She has been a visiting scholar at Xerox PARC (Palo Alto Research Center), USA; LinCS, University of Gothenburg, Sweden; L'Institut de Neurosciences Cognitives, CNRS, Aix-Marseille Université, France; and University of Alberta, Canada.

BERNHARD RIEDER is Assistant Professor of New Media at the University of Amsterdam. His research interests focus on the history, theory, and politics of software, more particularly on the role of algorithms in social processes and in the production of knowledge. As a researcher and software developer at the Digital Methods Initiative, he works on tool-based methods for studying online data.
   He keeps a blog at http://thepoliticsofsystems.net.

RAY SIEMENS is Canada Research Chair in Humanities Computing and Distinguished Professor in the Faculty of Humanities at the University of Victoria, in English and Computer Science, and visiting Senior Research Fellow in the Department of Digital Humanities at King's College London. He is founding editor of the electronic scholarly journal *Early Modern Literary Studies*, and his publications include, among others, *Blackwell's Companion to Digital Humanities* (with Schreibman and Unsworth), *Blackwell's Companion to Digital Literary Studies* (with Schreibman) and *Mind Technologies: Humanities Computing and the Canadian Academic Community* (with Moorman). He directs the Digital Humanities Summer Institute and the Electronic Textual Cultures Lab and serves as Vice President of the Canadian Federation of the Humanities and Social Sciences for Research Dissemination, recently serving also as Chair of the international Alliance of Digital Humanities Organisations' Steering Committee and as Chair of the Modern Language Association's Committee on Information Technology.
   http://web.uvic.ca/~siemens

BOB STEIN has been engaged with electronic publishing full-time since 1980, when he spent a year researching and writing a paper for Encyclopedia Britannica: 'EB and Intellectual Tools of the Future'. In 1984 he founded The Criterion Collection, a critically acclaimed series of definitive films, which included the first supplementary sections and director commentaries and introduced the letterbox format. He also founded the Voyager Company, which in 1989 published one of the first commercially viable CD-ROMs, *The CD Companion to Beethoven's Ninth Symphony*. In 1992 Voyager published the first electronic books, including Douglas Adams' *Hitchhikers Guide to the Galaxy* and Michael Crichton's *Jurassic Park*. In 2004 The Macarthur Foundation provided a generous grant with which Stein founded the Institute for the Future of the Book a small think & do tank aimed at exploring and influencing the evolution of new forms of intellectual expression. In 2005 the Institute published the first 'networked books', which were instrumental in the recognition of the important shift to social reading and writing as discourse moves from printed pages to networked screens. Currently Stein and his partners are building a comprehensive platform for social reading.

http://www.futureofthebook.org/

ADRIAAN VAN DER WEEL is Bohn extraordinary professor of Modern Dutch Book History at the University of Leiden, lecturing in the department of Book and Digital Media Studies. He has also taught at Utrecht University and William and Mary College, Williamsburg. His research interests are in the field of Book Studies, concentrating on the digitisation of textual transmission, publishing studies, and scholarly communication. He is editor of a number of book series on these subjects, and European articles editor of Digital humanities quarterly. His latest book is *Changing our textual minds: Towards a digital order of knowledge* (Manchester: Manchester UP, 2011).

http://www.let.leidenuniv.nl/wgbw/research/Weel_research.html

# References

Aaltonen, Mari, Petri Mannonen, Saija Nieminen, and Marko Nieminen. 2011. 'Usability and compatibility of e-book readers in an academic environment: A collaborative study'. IFLA *Journal* 37: 1, 16-27.

Ackerman, Rakefet, and Morris Goldsmith. 2011. 'Metacognitive regulation of text learning: On screen versus on paper'. *Journal of experimental psychology: applied* 17: 1, 18-32.

Adema, Janneke. 2011. 'Notes on unbound books – a conference report (part II)'. *Open reflection blog*, 09 July. http://openreflections.wordpress.com/2011/07/02/notes-on-unbound-books-percentE2percent8opercent93-a-conference-report-part-ii/.

Agre, Philip. 2003. 'Information and institutional change: The case of digital libraries'. In *Digital library use: Social practice in design and evaluation* edited by Ann P. Bishop, Nancy A. Van House, Barbara P. Buttenfield. Cambridge, MA: MIT Press.

— 1994. 'Surveillance and capture: Two models of privacy'. *Information society* 10: 2, 101-127.

Alamargot, Denis, David Chesnet, Christophe Dansac, and Christine Ros. 2006. 'Eye and pen: A new device for studying reading during writing'. *Behavior research methods* 38: 1, 287-299.

Anderson, Chris. 2004. 'The long tail'. *Wired*, October, accessed 9 October 2012 http://www.wired.com/wired/archive/12.10/tail.html.

Angrosh, M.A., Stephen Cranefield, and Nigel Stanger. 2012. 'Contextual information retrieval in research articles: Semantic publishing tools for the research community'. *Semantic web: Interoperability, usability, applicability, accessed 1 May 2012*. http://www.semantic-web-journal.net/content/contextual-information-retrieval-research-articles-semantic-publishing-tools-research-commun.

Baccino, Thierry. 2004. *La lecture électronique*. Grenoble: Presses Universitaires de Grenoble.

Baggerman, Arianne. 2011a. *Over leven, lezen en schrijven: De bandbreedte van boekgeschiedenis*. Amsterdam: Vossiuspers.

— 2011b. 'Lost time: memory and time-management in Dutch nineteenth century egodocuments'. In *Controlling time and shaping the self: The rise of autobiographical writing since the seventeenth century* edited by Anne Baggerman, Rudolf Dekker, Michael Mascuch. Leiden, Netherlands: Brill.

Barrett, Edward. 1988. *Text, context and hypertext*. Cambridge, MA: MIT Press.

— 1989. *The society of text*. Cambridge, MA: MIT Press.

— 1992. *Sociomedia*. Cambridge, MA: MIT Press.

Bauerlein, Mark. 2008. *The dumbest generation: How the digital age stupefies young Americans and jeopardizes our future (Or, don't trust anyone under 30)*. New York: Penguin.

Baumer, Eric, Mark Sueyoshi, and Bill Tomlinson. 2008. 'Exploring the role of the reader in the activity of blogging'. In *Proceeding of the twenty-sixth annual SIGCHI conference on human factors in computing systems*, 1111-1120. Florence, Italy: ACM.

Bennett, Sue, and Karl Maton. 2010. 'Beyond the "digital natives" debate: Towards a more nuanced understanding of students' technology experiences'. *Journal of computer assisted learning* 26, 321-331.

Bennett, Sue, Karl Maton, and Lisa Kervin. 2008. 'The "digital natives" debate: A critical review of the evidence'. *British journal of educational technology* 39: 5, 775-786.

Berkhout, Karel. 2011. 'Als een dorpsplein op de campus'. NRC Handelsblad, 29 November.

Berners-Lee, Tim, and R. Cailliau. 1990. 'WorldWideWeb: Proposal for a HyperText project', Cern Internel memo. http://www.w3.org/Proposal.html.

Bevington, David. 2011. Murder most foul. Hamlet through the ages. Oxford: Oxford University Press.

Bier, Eric, Lance Good, Kris Popat, and Alan Newberger. 2004. 'A document corpus browser for in-depth reading'. In Proceedings of the 4th ACM/IEEE-CS joint conference on Digital libraries, 87-96. Tuscon, Arizona: ACM.

Blair, Ann. 2010. Too much to know: Managing scholarly information before the modern era. New Haven: Yale University Press.

Boef, August Hans den, and Joost Kircz. 'The usages of new technologies in story writing', in preparation.

Bolter, Jay D. 1991. Writing space: The computer, hypertext and the history of writing. Mahwah, NJ: Lawrence Erlbaum Associates.

Bottini, Thomas, Pierre Morizet-Mahoudeaux, and Bruno Bachimont. 2011. 'A model and environment for improving multimedia scholarly reading practices'. Journal of intelligent information systems 37: 1, 39-63.

Bowman, Laura L., Laura. E Levine, Bradley M. Waite, and Michael Gendron. 2010. 'Can students really multitask? An experimental study of instant messaging while reading'. Computers & education 54: 4, 927-931.

Bradshaw, Tom, and Bonnie Nichols. 2004. Reading at risk: A survey of literacy reading in America. Washington, DC: National Endowment for the Arts. www.nea.gov/research/ReadingatRisk.pdf, accessed 9 October 2012.

Bridle, James. 2011a, accessed 9 October 2012, http://shorttermmemoryloss.com.

— 2011b. 'Encoded experiences'. In I read where I am: Valiz with graphic design museum, edited by Mieke Gerritzen, Geert Lovink, and Minke Kampman. http://www.ireadwhereiam.com/.

Britannica. 1911. 'The Shakespeare-Bacon theory,' Encyclopaedia Britannica, 11th edition, Volume XXIV, John George Robertson, Cambridge University Press, pp. 786-787. A shortened version available at http://www.britannica.com/EBchecked/topic/537853/William-Shakespeare/232444/Understanding-Shakespeare.

Buckingham Shum, Simon, Tim Clark, Anita de Waard, Tudor Groza, Siegfried Handschuh and Ágnes Sándor. 2010. Scientific discourse on the semantic web: A survey of models and enabling technologies. Accessed 1 May 2012. http://people.kmi.open.ac.uk/sbs/2010/12/semantic-web-scientific-discourse-survey/.

Burger, Hendrik. 1949. Leeuwarder jeugdherinneringen, 18. Amsterdam: J.H. de Bussy.

Burhanna, Kenneth J., Jamie Seeholzer, and Joseph Salem Jr. 2009. 'No natives here: A focus group study of student perceptions of web 2.0 and the academic library'. The journal of academic librarianship 35: 6, 523-532.

Bush, Vannevar. 1945. 'As we may think'. Atlantic monthly, July.

Cain, Kate, and Jane Oakhill. 2004. 'Reading comprehension difficulties'. In Handbook of children's literacy, edited by Terezinha Nunes and Peter Bryant, 313-338. London: Kluwer Academic Publishers.

Caporossi, Gilles, Denis Alamargot, and David Chesnet. 2004. 'Using the computer to study the dynamics of the handwriting processes'. Lecture notes in computer science 3245, 73-78.

Carr, Nicholas. 2010. The shallows: What the Internet is doing to our brains, 141-142. New York and London: W.W. Norton & Company.

Carruthers, Mary J. 1990. The book of memory: A study of memory in medieval culture. Cambridge: Cambridge University Press.

Cataldo, Maria G., and Jane Oakhill. 2000. 'Why are poor comprehenders inefficient searchers? An investigation into the effects of text'. *Journal of educational psychology* 92: 4, 791-799.

Cavallo, Guglielmo. 1999. 'Between Volumen and Codex: Reading in the Roman World'. Lydia Cochrane, trans. *A history of reading in the West*, Guglielmo Cavallo and Rogier Chartier (eds.), 64-99. Cambridge: Polity.

Cavallo, Guglielmo, and Roger Chartier, ed. 2003. *A history of reading in the West*. Amherst: University of Massachusetts Press.

Cayley, John. 'Book Unbound'. *Postmodern Culture* 7: 3. Accessed October 2011. http://muse.jhu. edu/journals/postmodern_culture/v007/7.3cayley.html.

Chartier, Roger. 1994. *The order of books: Readers, authors, and libraries in Europe between the fourteenth and eighteenth centuries*. Palo Alto, CA: Stanford University Press.

Clark, Giles, and Angus Phillips. 2008. *Inside book publishing*. London/New York: Routledge.

Cockburn, Andy, Amy Karlson, and Benjamin B. Bederson. 2009. 'A review of overview+detail, zooming, and focus+context interfaces'. ACM *Computing Surveys* 41: 1, 1-31.

Cohen, Alexander. 1936. *Van anarchist tot monarchist*, 33-34. Amsterdam: De Steenuil.

Cohen, Philip. 1996. 'Is there a text in this discipline? Textual scholarship and American literary studies'. *American literary history* 8: 4, 728-744.

Conklin, Jeff. 1987. *Hypertext: An introduction and survey*. IEEE-Computer, September 20, 17-41.

Coover, Robert. 1994. 'The end of books'. *The New York Times Book Review*, 21 June.

Cope, Bill and Angus Phillips. 2006. *The future of the book in the digital age*. Oxford: Chandos.

Cortenraad, Hans W. 2009. *Centraal boekhuis: Logistiek van boeken in veranderend perspectief* Amsterdam: Amsterdam University Press.

Cull, Barry W. 2011. 'Reading revolutions: Online digital text and implications for reading in academe'. *First Monday* 16: 6. http://firstmonday.org/htbin/cgiwrap/bin/ojs/index.php/fm/article/view/3340/2985.

Darnton, Robert. 1999. 'The New Age of the Book'. *The New York review of books*, 18 March.

— 2009. 'Google and the future of books'. *The New York review of books*, 56: 2. February.

— 2009. *The case for books: Past, present and future*, 69. New York: PublicAffairs.

— 2011. 'Six reasons Google Books failed'. *The New York review of books blog*, 28 March, accessed 9 October 2012. http://www.nybooks.com/blogs/nyrblog/2011/mar/28/six-reasons-google-books-failed.

De la Flor, Grace, Marina Jirotka, Paul Luff, John Pybus, and Ruth Kirkham. 2010. 'Transforming scholarly practice: Embedding technological interventions to support the collaborative analysis of ancient texts.' *Computer supported cooperative work (CSCW)* 19: 3, 309-334.

De wetenschappelijke bibliotheek op weg naar 'the cloud'. UKB Beleidsplan 2011-2015 ('The academic library on its way to 'the Cloud'. UKB policy plan) 2011.

Dempsey, Lorcan. 2011. 'When the books leave the building: The future of research libraries, collections, and services'. *The Lorcan Dempsey weblog on libraries, services, and networks*. 26 October. http://orweblog.oclc.org/archives/002106.html.

Derrida, Jacques. 2005. *Paper machine (cultural memory in the present)*. Translated by Rachel Bowlby. Palo Alto, CA: Stanford University Press.

DeStefano, Diana, and Jo-Anne LeFevre. 2007. 'Cognitive load in hypertext reading: A review'. *Computers in human behavior* 23: 3, 1616-1641.

Dijck, José van. 2010. 'Search engines and the production of academic knowledge'. *International journal of cultural studies* 13: 6, 574-592.

Doctorow, Cory. 2006. 'GAM3R 7H3ORY: a networked book on games'. Review of *GAM3R 7H3ORY* by McKenzie Wark. *Boing Boing*, 24 May. http://boingboing.net/2006/05/24/gam3r-7h3ory-a-netwo.html.

Domela Nieuwenhuis, Ferdinand. 1910. *Van christen tot anarchist*, 14. Gedenkschriften van F. Domela Nieuwenhuis. Amsterdam.

Doueihi, Milad. 2011. *La grande conversion numérique; suivi de Rêveries d'un promeneur numérique*. Paris: Editions du Seuil.

— 2011. *Pour un Humanisme numérique*: Paris: Editions du Seuil.

Douglas, Mary. 2008. 'Writing a blurb'. In Giles Clark and Angus Phillips (eds.) *Inside book publishing*. London/New York: Routledge.

Drucker, Johanna. 2004. *The century of artists' books*. New York: Granary Books.

— 2011. 'Diagrammatic writing and the poetics of relations', Institute for Modern and Contemporary Culture, accessed 10 October 2012. http://archivingcultures.org/mot/451.

Duffy, Gerald G., and Susan E. Israel (eds.). 2009. *Handbook of research on reading comprehension*. New York: Routledge.

Eco, Umberto, and Jean-Claude Carrière. 2011. *This is not the end of the book: A conversation curated by J.P. de Tonac*. Translated by Polly McLean. London: Harvill Secker.

Eemeren, van Frans H., and Rob Grootendorst. 1992. *Argumentation, communication and fallacies. A pragma-dialectical perspective*. Lawrence Erlbaum ass. Publ.

Eisenstein, Elizabeth L. 1979. *The printing press as an agent of change: Communications and cultural transformations in early modern Europe*, 2 volumes. Cambridge: Cambridge University Press.

— 2002a. 'An unacknowledged revolution revisited'. *The American historical review*, 107: 1, 87-105.

— 2002b. [How to acknowledge a revolution]: Reply'. *The American historical review*, 107: 1, 126-128.

Eklundh, Kerstin S. 1992. 'Problems in achieving a global perspective of the text in computer-based writing'. *Instructional science* 21: 1, 73-84.

— 1994. 'Linear and nonlinear strategies in computer-based writing'. *Computers and composition* 11: 3, 203-216.

Eklundh, Kerstin Severinson, and Henrry Rodriguez. 2004. 'Coherence and interactivity in text-based group discussions around web documents'. In *Proceedings of the 37th Annual Hawaii International Conference on System Sciences* 4. Washington, DC: IEEE Computer Society.

Erickson, Thomas. 2008. "Social' systems: Designing digital systems that support social intelligence'. *AI and society* 23: 2, 147-166.

Evans, Mariah D.R., Jonathan Kelley, Joanna Sikora, and Donald J. Treiman. 2010. 'Family scholarly culture and educational success: Books and schooling in 27 nations'. *Research in social stratification and mobility* 28: 2, 171-197.

Ferrari, Jan, and Nanette Pfliester. 2011. 'Why do we still need microfilm?' *Microform & digitization review* 40: 2, 77-78.

Fitzpatrick, Kathleen. 2007. 'CommentPress: New (social) structures for new (networked) texts'. *Journal of electronic publishing* 10: 3. http://quod.lib.umich.edu/j/jep/3336451.0010.305?rgn=main;view=fulltext.

Foucault, Michel. 1988. *Technologies of the self: A seminar with Michel Foucault*. Edited by Luther H. Martin, Huck Gutman, and Patrick H. Hutton. Amherst, MA: University of Massachusetts Press.

— 2001a. *Dits et écrits, tome 2: 1976-1988*. Paris: Gallimard.

— 2001b. *L'Herméneutique du sujet*. Paris: Gallimard-Seuil.

Fox, Annie B., Jonathan Rosen, and Mary Crawford. 2009. 'Distractions, distractions: Does instant messaging affect college students' performance on a concurrent reading comprehension task?' *CyberPsychology & behavior* 21: 1, 51-53.

Freud, Sigmund. 1913. *The interpretations of dreams*. New York: The Macmillan Company.

Gee, James Paul. 1988. 'Discourse systems and aspirin bottles: On Literacy'. *Journal of education* 170: 1, 27-40.

Geertz, Clifford. 1973. *The interpretation of cultures*. New York: Basic Books.

Genette, Gérard. 1982. *Palimpsestes: La littérature au second degré*. Paris: Seuil.

— 1987. *Paratexts: Thresholds of interpretation*. Cambridge: Cambridge University Press.

— 1987. *Seuils*. Paris: Seuil.

Gibson, James J. 1979. *The ecological approach to visual perception*. Boston: Houghton Mifflin.

Giesecke, Michael. 1998. *Der Buchdruck in der frühen Neuzeit*. Frankfurt: Suhrkamp.

Giffard, Alain. 1997. 'Petites introductions à l'hypertexte'. In *Banques de données et hypertextes pour l'étude du roman*. Edited by Nathalie Ferrand. Paris: Presses Universitaires de France.

— 2008. 'La lecture numérique à la Bibliothèque de France'. In *L'Edition du manuscrit*, edited by Aurèle Crasson. Academia Bruylant.

— 2009. 'Des lectures industrielles'. In Industrialis, *Pour en finir avec la mécroissance: Quelques réflexions d'ars industrialis* by Bernard Stiegler, Alain Giffard, and Christian Fauré. Flammarion.

— 2011. 'Critique de la lecture numérique: *The shallows* de Nicholas Carr'. *Bulletin des bibliothèques de France*, 5. http://bbf.enssib.fr/consulter/bbf-2011-05-0071-013.

— 2011. 'Digital readings, industrial readings'. In *Going digital: Evolutionary and revolutionary aspects of digitization*, edited by Karl Grandin. Nobel Symposia, The Royal Swedish Academy of Sciences.

Golden Notebook Project, The. Accessed 10 October 2012, http://thegoldennotebook.org.

Goldman, Susan R., Arthur C. Graesser, and Paul van den Broek, Eds. 1999. *Narrative comprehension, casuality, and coherence: Essays in honor of Tom Trabasso*. Mahwah, NJ: Lawrence Erlbaum Associates.

Goody, Jack. 1986. *The logic of writing and the organization of society*. Cambridge: Cambridge University Press.

Gough, Philip B. 1995. 'The new literacy: Caveat emptor'. *Journal of research in reading* 18: 2, 79-86.

Gradmann, Stefan, and Jan Meister. 2008. 'Digital document and interpretation: Re-thinking 'text' and scholarship in electronic settings'. *Poiesis & praxis* 5: 2, 139-153.

Graesser, Arthur C., and Gordon H. Bower. 1990. *Inferences and text comprehension*. San Diego: AP Academic Press, Inc.

Graesser, Arthur C., Murray Singer, and Tom Trabasso. 1994. 'Constructing inferences during narrative text comprehension'. *Psychological review* 101: 3, 371-395.

Graesser, Arthur C., Keith K. Millis, and Rolf A. Zwaan. 1997. 'Discourse comprehension'. *Annual review of psychology* 48, 163-189.

Grafton, Anthony, *The footnote: A curious history*, Harvard University Press, 1997.

— 1999. 'The Humanist as Reader'. In *A history of reading in the West*, Guglielmo Cavallo and Rogier Chartier (eds.), 179-212. Cambridge: Polity.

— 2008. *Codex in crisis*, 2nd edition, 60. New York: The Crumpled Press.

Grafton, Anthony, and Jeffrey Hamburger. 2010. 'Save the Warburg Library'. *The New York review of books*, 30 September.

Guédon, Jean-Claude, and Boudewijn Walraven. 2008. 'Who will digitize the world's books?' *New York review of books*, 14 August. http://www.nybooks.com/articles/archives/2008/aug/14/who-will-digitize-the-worlds-books.

Gustafsson, Jan-Eric, and Monica Rosén. 2005. *Förändringar i läskompetens 1991-2001: en jämförelse över tid och länder*. Göteborg: Göteborgs Universitet (University of Gothenburg).

Haakman, David. 2011. 'Nu ook strengere regels Apple voor e-book apps'. *NRC.nl*, 1 February.

Haas, Christina. 1996. *Writing technology: Studies on the materiality of literacy*. Mahwah, NJ: Lawrence Erlbaum Associates.

Haptic, Julien. 2011. 'Paper phone prototype opens door to flexible, interactive computing'. *EE Times Europe*, 9 May.

Harmsze, Frédérique. 2000. *A modular structure for scientific articles in an electronic environment*. PhD Thesis. Amsterdam: University of Amsterdam. http://dare.uva.nl/record/78293.

Havelaar, Just. 1926. *De weg tot de werkelijkheid*, 47. Arnhem.

Helsper, Ellen J., and Rebecca Eynon. 2010. 'Digital natives: Where is the evidence?' *British educational research journal* 36: 3, 503-520.

Hembrooke, Helene, and Geri Gay. 2003. 'The laptop and the lecture: The effects of multitasking in learning environments'. *Journal of computing in higher education* 15: 1, 46-64.

Hillesund, Terje. 2010. 'Digital reading spaces: How expert readers handle books, the web and electronic paper'. *First monday* 15: 4.

Hinckley, Ken, Morgan Dixon, Raman Sarin, Francois Guimbretiere, and Ravin Balakrishnan. 2009. 'Codex: a dual screen tablet computer'. In *Proceedings of the 27th international conference on human factors in computing systems*, 1933-1942. Boston, MA: ACM.

Hoadley, Christopher M., and Peter G. Kilner. 2005. 'Using technology to transform communities of practice into knowledge-building communities'. *SIGGROUP Bulletin* 25: 1, 31-40.

Holland, Norman. 1992. *The critical I*. New York: Columbia University Press.

Hornbæk, Kasper, Benjamin B. Bederson, and Catherine Plaisant. 2002. 'Navigation patterns and usability of zoomable user interfaces with and without an overview'. *ACM transactions on computer-human interaction*, 362-389. Print.

Hugh of St. Victor. 1939. *Hugonis de Sancto Victore Didascalicon de studio legendi: A critical text*. Edited by Charles Henry Buttimer. Washington, DC: Catholic University Press.

Hughes, Lorna M. 2004. *Digitizing collections: Strategic issues for the information manager*, 51-52. London: Facet Publishing.

Human Media Lab. 2010. 'Press release: Revolutionary new paper computer shows flexible future for smartphones and tablets'. Accessed 30 October 2011. http/www.hml.queensu.ca/paperphone.

Hwang, Jane, Jaehoon Jung, and Gerard Jounghyun Kim. 2006. 'Hand-held virtual reality: A feasibility study'. In *Proceedings of the ACM symposium on virtual reality software and technology*, 356-363. Limassol, Cyprus: ACM.

Inhoff, Albrecht W., and Andrew M. Gordon. 1997. 'Eye movements and eye-hand coordination during typing'. *Current directions in psychological science* 6, 153-157.

Institute for the Future of the Book, The. 2012. 'Commentpress: A wordpress theme and plugin for social texts'. http://www.futureofthebook.org/commentpress/.

Iyengar, Sunil. 2007. *To read or not to read: A question of national consequence*. Washington, DC: National Endowment for the Arts, accessed 9 October 2012. www.nea.gov/research/ToRead_ExecSum.pdf.

Jacobsen, Wade C., and Renata Forste. 2011. 'The wired generation: Academic and social outcomes of electronic media use among university students'. *CyberPsychology, behavior, & social networking* 14: 5, 275-280.

Johns, Adrian. 1998. *The nature of the book*. Chicago: University of Chicago Press.

— 2002. 'How to acknowledge a revolution'. *The American historical review* 107: 1, 106-125.

Johnson, Steven B. 2005. *Everything bad is good for you: How today's popular culture is actually making us smarter*. New York: Riverhead Books/Penguin.

John-Paul II. 1981. *Familiaris Consortio.* http://www.vatican.va/holy_father/john_paul_ii/apost_exhortations/documents/hf_jp-ii_exh_19811122_familiaris-consortio_en.html.

Jónasdóttir, Katrín Björg. 2012. 'The inevitable e-book evolution: Analysing the role of the technology sector in the evolution of e-books'. Unpublished MA thesis, August, Leiden University.

Jones, Chris, Ruslan Ramanau, Simon Cross, and Graham Healing. 2010. 'Net generation or digital natives: Is there a distinct new generation entering university?' *Computers & education* 54: 3, 722-732.

Jones, Ernest. 1949. *Hamlet and Oedipus: A classic study in the psychoanalysis of literature.* London: Victor Gollanz Ltd.

Judd, Terry, and Gregor Kennedy. 2011. 'Measurement and evidence of computer-based task switching and multitasking by 'Net Generation' students'. *Computers & education* 56: 3, 625-631.

Kaiser, David. 2012. 'A tale of two textbooks: Experiments in genre'. ISIS 103: 1, 126-138. http://www.jstor.org/stable/10.1086/664983.

Kendrick, Michelle. 2001. 'Interactive technology and the remediation of the subject of writing'. *Configurations* 9: 2, 231-251.

Kintsch, Walter. 1998. *Comprehension: A paradigm for cognition.* Cambridge: Cambridge University Press.

Kircz, Joost G. 1991. 'Rhetorical structure of scientific articles: The case for argumentational analysis in information retrieval'. *Journal of documentation* 47: 4, 354-372. http://www.kra.nl/Website/Artikelen/Rhet-structure.pdf.

— 1998. 'Modularity: The next form of scientific information presentation?' *Journal of documentation* 54: 2, 210-235. http://www.kra.nl/Website/Artikelen/Jdoc98.htm.

Kircz, J.G., and F.A.P. Harmsze. 2000. 'Modular Scenarios in the Electronic Age'. Conferentie Informatiewetenschap 2000. Doelen, Rotterdam 5 april 2000. *Proceedings Conferentie Informatiewetenschap 2000. De Doelen Utrecht (sic), 5 april 2000,* P. van der Vet and P. de Bra (eds.), 31-43. http://www.kra.nl/Website/Artikelen/mod2k.html.

Kirschenbaum, Matthew. 2007. 'How reading is being reimagined'. *Chronicle of higher education* 54: 15, B20.

— 2007. *Mechanisms: New media and the forensic imagination,* Cambridge: MIT Press.

Kirschner, Femke, Liesbeth Kester, and Gemma Corbalan. 2011. 'Cognitive load theory and multimedia learning, task characteristics and learning engagement: The current state of the art'. *Computers in human behavior* 27: 1, 1-4.

Knorr-Cetina, Karin. 1999. *Epistemic cultures: How the sciences make knowledge.* Cambridge, MA: Harvard University Press.

Kovač, Miha. 2008. *Never mind the web: Here comes the book.* Oxford: Chandos Publishing.

— 2011. 'The end of codex and the disintegration of communication circuit of the book'. *Logos* 22: 1.

Kress, Gunther. 2003. *Literacy in the new media age.* London/New York: Routledge.

Lacan, Jacques, Jacques-Alain Miller, and James Hulbert. 1977. 'Desire and the interpretation of desire in Hamlet'. *Yale French studies,* 55/56, 11-52.

Lam, Shun Leung, Paul Lam, John Lam, and Carmel McNaught. 2009. 'Usability and usefulness of eBooks on PPCs: How students' opinions vary over time'. *Australasian journal of educational technology* 25: 1, 30-44.

Landow, George P. 1992. *Hypertext.* Baltimore, MD: Johns Hopkins University Press.

— 1992. 'Hypertextual Derrida, poststructuralist Nelson?' In George P. Landow, *Hypertext: The convergence of contemporary critical theory and technology.* Baltimore, MD: Johns Hopkins University Press.

— 1997. *Hypertext 2.0 (Rev., amplified ed.).* Baltimore, MD: Johns Hopkins University Press.
— 2003. 'The paradigm is more important than the purchase'. In *Digital media revisited: Theoretical and conceptual innovation in digital domains,* edited by Gunnar Liestøl, Andrew Morrison, and Terje Rasmussen. 35-64. Cambridge, MA: MIT Press.
— 2006. *Hypertext 3.0: Critical theory and new media in an era of globalization.* Baltimore: Johns Hopkins University Press.
Le Bigot, Nathalie, Jean-Michel Passerault, and Thierry Olive. 2009. 'Memory for words location in writing'. *Psychological research* 73, 89-97.
Leeuw, Aart van de. 1914. *Kinderland.* Amsterdam.
Leitch, Cara. 2009. '*Social networking tools for professional readers in the humanities*'. Whitepaper, unpublished.
Liesaputra, Veronica, Ian H. Witten, and David Bainbridge. 2009a. 'Creating and reading realistic electronic books'. *Computer* 42: 2, 72-81.
— 2009b. 'Searching in a book'. *Research and advanced technology for digital libraries: Lecture notes in computer science* 5714, 442-446.
Lightman, Alan. 2000. *The diagnosis.* London: Bloomsbury.
Ligthart, Jan. 1950. *Jeugdherinneringen.* Groningen/Djakarta.
Lin, Lin. 2009. 'Breadth-biased versus focused cognitive control in media multitasking behaviors'. *PNAS – Proceedings of the National Academy of Sciences of the United States of America* 106: 37, 15521-15522.
Lin, Lin, Tip Robertson, and Jennifer Lee. 2009. 'Reading performances between novices and experts in different media multitasking environments'. *Computers in the schools* 26: 3, 169-186.
Liu, Alan, David Durand, Nick Montfort, Merrillee Proffitt, Liam R.E. Quin, Jean-Hughes Rety, Noah Wardrip-Fruin. 2005. 'Born again bits: A framework for migrating electronic literature'. Electronic Literature Organization. Accessed October 2011. http://eliterature.org/pad/bab.html.
Liu, Chung-Chu, and Shiou-Yu Chen. 2005. 'Determinants of knowledge sharing of e-learners'. *International journal of innovation and learning* 2: 4, 434-445.
Liu, Ziming. 2008. *Paper to digital: Documents in the information age.* Westport, CT/London: Libraries Unlimited (A member of the Greenwood Publishing Group).
— 2006. 'Reading behavior in the digital environment'. *Journal of documentation* 61: 6.
Loizides, Fernando, and George R. Buchanan. 2008. 'The myth of find: User behaviour and attitudes towards the basic search feature'. In *Proceedings of the 8th ACM/IEEE-CS joint conference on Digital libraries,* 48-51. Pittsburgh, Pennsylvania: ACM.
Luhn, Hans-Peter. 1959. 'Auto-encoding of documents for information retrieval systems'. In *Modern trends in documentation* edited by Martha Boaz, 45-58. London: Pergamon Press.

Macdonald, Janet. 2004. 'Developing competent e-learners: The role of assessment'. *Assessment & evaluation in higher education* 29: 2, 215-226.
Mackey, Margaret. 2007. *Literacies across media: Playing the text* (second ed.). London/New York: Routledge.
— 2011. 'The embedded and embodied literacies of an early reader'. *Children's literature in education: An international quarterly.* 42: 4, 289-307.
Mangen, Anne. 2008. 'Hypertext fiction reading: Haptics and immersion'. *Journal of research in reading* 31: 4, 404-419.
— 2010. 'Point and click: Theoretical and phenomenological reflections on the digitization of early childhood education'. *Contemporary issues in early childhood* 11: 4, 415-431.
Mangen, Anne, and Theresa S.S. Schilhab. 2012. 'An embodied view of reading: Theoretical considerations, empirical findings, and educational implications'. In *Skriv! Les!* Synnøve Matre & Atle Skaftun (eds.). Trondheim: Akademika. 285-300.

Mangen, Anne, and Jean-Luc Velay. 2010. 'Digitizing literacy: Reflections on the haptics of writing'. In *Advances in haptics*. Mehrdad H. Zadeh (ed.) Vienna: IN-TECH web, 385-402.

Manguel, Alberto. 1996. *A history of reading*. London: HarperCollins.

— 2004. 'Turning the page'. In *The future of the page* edited by Peter Stoicheff and Andrew Taylor, 27-35. Toronto: University of Toronto Press.

Marlow, Cameron, Mor Naaman, Danah Boyd, and Marc Davis. 2006. 'HT06, tagging paper, taxonomy, Flickr, academic article, to read'. In *Proceedings of the seventeenth conference on Hypertext and hypermedia*, 31-40. Odense, Denmark: ACM.

Marshall, Catherine. C. 2005. 'Reading and interactivity in the digital library: Creating an experience that transcends paper'. In *Digital library development: The view from Kanazawa* edited by Deanna Marcum and Gerald George, 127-145. Westport: Libraries Unlimited.

Marshall, Catherine C., and A. J. Bernheim Brush. 2004. 'Exploring the relationship between personal and public annotations'. In *Proceedings of the 4th ACM/IEEE-CS joint conference on Digital libraries*, 349-357. Tuscon, AZ: ACM.

Marshall, Catherine C., and Sara Bly. 2005. 'Turning the page on navigation'. Paper presented at the ACM/IEEE-CS joint conference on Digital libraries, Denver, CO.

Martin, Henri-Jean. 1988. *The history and power of writing*. Chicago: University of Chicago Press.

Mayer, Richard E. 2001. *Multimedia learning*. Cambridge: Cambridge University Press.

Mayernik, Matthew. 2007. 'The prevalence of additional electronic Features in pure e-journals,' *Journal of electronic publishing* 10: 3. http://dx.doi.org/10.3998/3336451.0010.307.

McDonald, David W. 2003. 'Recommending collaboration with social networks: A comparative evaluation'. In *Proceedings of the SIGCHI conference on Human factors in computing systems*, 593-600. Ft. Lauderdale, FL: ACM.

McGann, Jerome. 2004. 'Marking texts of many dimensions'. In *A companion to Digital Humanities*, edited by Susan Schreibman, Ray Siemens, and John Unsworth. Oxford: Blackwell. http://www.digitalhumanities.org/companion/.

McKenzie, Don F. 1999. *Bibliography and the sociology of texts*. Cambridge: Cambridge University Press.

McNamara, Danielle S., ed. 2007. *Reading comprehension strategies: Theories, interventions, and technologies*. New York/London: Lawrence Erlbaum Associates.

Mees, Willemine (1887-1967), National Archive, Family Archive Fruin (2.21.222) Netherlands. 116.

Miall, David S. 1999. 'Trivializing or liberating? The limitations of hypertext theorizing'. *Mosaic: a journal for the interdisciplinary study of literature* 32: 2, 157.

Miall, David S. and Teresa Dobson. 2001. 'Reading hypertext and the experience of literature'. *Journal of digital information* 2: 1.

Michel, Jean-Baptiste, Yuan Kui Shen, Aviva P. Aiden, Adrian Veres, Matthew K. Gray, The Google Books Team, Joseph P. Pickett, Dale Hoiberg, Dan Clancy, Peter Norvig, Jon Orwant, Steven Pinker, Martin A. Nowak, and Erez Lieberman Aiden. 2011. 'Quantitative analysis of culture using millions of digitized books'. *Science* 331: 6014, 176-182.

Middelberg, Gerrit. (1846-1916) NA II, Family Archive Middelberg (2.21.232) Netherlands. 21, 20.

Milne, David, and Ian H. Witten. 2008. 'Learning to link with Wikipedia'. In *Proceeding of the 17th ACM conference on Information and knowledge management*, 5090518. Napa Valley, CA: ACM.

Misner, Charles W., Kip S. Thorne and John Archibald Wheeler. 1973. *Gravitation*. San Francisco: W.H. Freeman and Company.

Montfort, Nick and Noah Wardrip-Fruin 2004. 'Acid-free bits: Recommendations for long-lasting electronic literature'. *Electronic literature organization*. Accessed October 2011. http://eliterature.org/pad/afb.html.

Moreno, Roxana, and Richard Mayer. 2007. 'Interactive multimodal learning environments'. *Educational psychology review* 19: 3, 309-326.

Moretti, Franco. 2000. 'Conjectures on world literature'. *New left review* 1, January-February.

— 2005. *Graphs, maps, trees: Abstract models for literary history.* London and New York: Verso.

Morineau, Thierry, Caroline Blanche, Laurence Tobin, and Nicolas Gueguen. 2005. 'The emergence of the contextual role of the e-book in cognitive processes through an ecological and functional analysis'. *International journal of human-computer studies* 62: 3, 329-348.

Muller, Femina Geertruida Henriette (1826-1909). Aletta (Instituut voor Vrouwengeschiedenis). 1907. EGO 113 Memoirs of Femina G.H. Muller, copy. Amsterdam.

Nagtglas, Frederik (1821-1902). 1977. 'Mijn leven', *Archief.* Mededelingen van het Koninklijk Zeeuwsch Genootschap der Wetenschappen.

Nationale Coalitie Digitale Duurzaamheid, Toekomst voor ons digitaal geheugen (2). 2010. Strategische agenda voor duurzame toegankelijkheid. Den Haag.

NEA. 2009. *Reading on the rise: A new chapter in American literacy.* Washington, DC: National Endowment for the Arts, Office of Research & Analysis. Accessed 9 October 2012. www.nea.gov/research/readingonrise.pdf.

Nelson, Ted. 1980. *Literary machines.* Sausalito, CA: Mindful Press.

— 1999. 'Xanological structure, needed now more than ever: Parallel document, deep links to content, deep versioning, and deep re-use'. *ACM comput. surv.* 31, 4es: 33 December. DOI=10.1145/345966.346033 http://doi.acm.org/10.1145/345966.346033.

Ni, Tao, Doug A. Bowman, and Jian Chen. 2006. 'Increased display size and resolution improve task performance in information-rich virtual environments'. *Proceedings of graphics interface.* Quebec, Canada: Canadian Information Processing Society. 139-146.

Nyce, James M., and Paul Kahn. 1991. *From memex to hypertext: Vannevar Bush and the mind's machine.* Waltham, MA: Academic Press.

O'Reilly, Tim. 2005. 'What Is web 2.0.: Design patterns and business models for the next generation of software'. Accessed 9 October 2012, http://oreilly.com/web2/archive/what-is-web-20.html.

OECD. 2011. PISA 2009 Results: Students on line: Digital technologies and performance (Volume VI): OECD.

Olson, David R. 1996. *The world on paper: The conceptual and cognitive implications of writing and reading.* Cambridge: Cambridge University Press.

Ong, Walter J. 1982. *Orality and literacy: The technologizing of the word.* London: Methuen.

Ophir, Eyal, Clifford Nass, and Anthony D. Wagner. 2009. 'Cognitive control in media multitaskers'. *PNAS – Proceedings of the National Academy of Sciences of the United States of America* 106: 37, 15583-15587.

Paape, Gerrit. 1792. *Mijne vrolijke wijsgeerte in mijne ballingschap.* Hilversum, Verloren 1996.

Parkes, M.B. 1999. 'Reading, coying and interpreting a text in the early Middle Ages'. *A history of reading in the West.* Guglielmo Cavallo and Rogier Chartier (eds.), 90-102. Cambridge: Polity.

Pearson, P. David. 2009. 'The roots of reading comprehension instruction'. In *Handbook of research on reading comprehension* edited by Susan E. Israel and Gerald G. Duffy, 3-31. New York: Routledge.

Pedró, Francesc. 2007. 'The new millennium learners: Challenging our views on digital technologies and learning'. *Nordic journal of digital literacy* 2: 4, 244-264.

Petrucci, Armando. 1999. 'Reading to read: A future for reading'. In *A history of reading in the West,* edited by Guglielmo Cavallo and Roger Chartier. Amherst, MA: University of Massachusetts Press.

Phillips, Angus. 2007. 'How books are positioned in the market'. In *Judging a book by its cover* by Nicole Matthews and Nickianne Moody. Aldershot, UK: Ashgate.

Piolat, Annie, Jean-Yves Roussey, and Olivier Thunin. 1997. 'Effects of screen presentation on text reading and revising'. *International journal of human-computer studies* 47: 4, 565-589.

Piolat, Annie, Thierry Olive, and Ronald T. Kellogg. 2005. 'Cognitive effort during note taking'. *Applied cognitive psychology* 19: 3, 291-312.

Prensky, Marc. 2001. 'Digital natives, digital immigrants'. *On the horizon* 9, 1-6.

Prins, Adriaan P. 1958. *Ik ga m'n eige baan*. Amsterdam.

Proust, Marcel, and John Ruskin. 2011. *On reading*. Translated by Damion Searls. London: Hesperus Press.

Qayyum, Muhammad Asim. 2008. 'Capturing the online academic reading process'. *Information processing & management* 44: 2, 581-595.

Ribière, Myriam, Jérôme Picault, and Sylvain Squedin. 2010. 'The sBook: Towards social and personalized learning experiences'. In *Proceedings of the third workshop on research advances in large digital book repositories and complementary media*, 3-8. Toronto, ON, Canada: ACM.

Rouvroy, Antoinette, and Tomas Berns. 2009. 'Le corps statistique'. *La pensée et les hommes* 53: 74, 2009.

Rowlands, Ian, David Nicholas, Peter Williams, Paul Huntington, Maggie Fieldhouse, Barrie Gunter, Richard Withey, Hamid R. Jamali, Tom Dobrowolski, and Carol Tenopir. 2008. 'The Google generation: The information behaviour of the researcher of the future'. *Aslib proceedings: new information perspectives* 60: 4, 290-310.

Saenger, Paul. 1999. 'Reading in the Middle Ages'. *A history of reading in the West*, Guglielmo Cavallo and Rogier Chartier (eds.), 120-148. Cambridge: Polity.

Saint-Gelais, Richard, and Rene Audet. 2003. 'Underground lies: Revisiting narrative in hyperfiction'. In *Close reading new media: Analyzing electronic literature*, edited by Jan Van Looy and Jan Baetens, Leuven: Leuven University Press.

Salomon, Gavriel. 1993. 'No distribution without individuals' cognition: A dynamic interactional view'. In *Distributed cognitions: Psychological and educational considerations* edited by Gavriel Salomon, 111-138. Cambridge: Cambridge University Press.

Sandusky, Robert J., and Carol Tenopir. 2008. 'Finding and using journal-article components: Impact of disaggregation on teaching and research practice'. *Journal of the American Society for Information Science and Technology* 59: 6, 970-982.

Schaper, J.H. 1933-1935. *Een halve eeuw van strijd: Herinneringen van J.H. Schaper, lid van de Tweede kamer der Staten-Generaal*. Groningen, Wolters.

Schols, Marjon, Marion Duimel, and Jos de Haan. 2011. *Hoe cultureel is de digitale generatie? Het Internet gebruik voor culturele doeleinden onder schoolgaande tieners*. Den Haag: Sociaal en Cultureel Planbureau, 91.

Schreibman, Susan. 2002. 'Computer-mediated texts and textuality: Theory and practice'. *Computers and the humanities* 36: 3, 283-293.

Schreibman, Susan, Ray Siemens, John Unsworth, eds. 2004. *A companion to the Digital Humanities*. Hoboken, NJ: Wiley-Blackwell Publishing.

Sellen, Abigail J., and Richard H.R. Harper. 2002. *The myth of the paperless office*. Cambridge, MA: MIT Press.

Shapiro, Lawrence A. 2010. *Embodied cognition*. New York: Routledge.

Shatzkin, Mike. 2011. *The Shatzkin files*. Kobo.

Shillingsburg, Peter. 2009. 'How literary works exist: Convenient scholarly editions'. *Digital humanities quarterly* 3: 3. http://digitalhumanities.org/dhq/vol/3/3/000054/000054.html.

Siegenthaler, Eva, Pascal Wurtz, Per Bergamin, and Rudolf Groner. 2011. 'Comparing reading processes on e-ink displays and print'. *Display* 32, 268-273.

Siemens, Ray, Claire Warwick, Stan Ruecker, and the INKE Research Group. 2008. 'Codex redux: Books and new knowledge environments'. *Proceedings of the BooksOnline 2008 workshop at ACM 17th Conference on information and knowledge management (CIKM 2008)*. New York: ACM.

Siemens, Ray, Cara Leitch, Analisa Blake, Karin Armstrong, and John Willinsky. 2009a. 'It may change my understanding of the field: Understanding reading tools for scholars and professional readers'. *Digital humanities quarterly* 3: 4.

Siemens, Ray, Claire Warwick, Richard Cunningham, Teresa Dobson, Alan Galey, Stan Ruecker, Susan Schreibman, and the INKE team. 2009b. 'Codex ultor: Toward a conceptual and theoretical foundation for new research on books and knowledge environments'. *Digital Studies/Le champ numérique* 1: 2.

Siemens, Ray, Mike Elkink, Alastair McColl, Karin Armstrong, James Dixon, Angelsea Saby, Brett D. Hirsch, and Cara Leitch. 2010. 'Underpinnings of the social edition? A narrative, 2004-9, for the Renaissance English Knowledgebase (REKn) and Professional Reading Environment (PReE)'. In *Online humanities scholarship: the shape of things to come*, edited by Jerome McGann, 401-460. Houston: Rice University Press.

Siemens, Ray, Teresa Dobson, Stan Ruecker, Richard Cunningham, Alan Galey, Claire Warwick, Lynne Siemens, a.o. 2011. 'HCI-book? Perspectives on E-book research, 2006-2008 (Foundational to Implementing New Knowledge Environments)'. *Papers of the Bibliographical Society of Canada/Cahiers de la Société bibliographique du Canada* 49: 1, 35-89

Siemens, Ray, Meagan Timney, Cara Leitch, Corina Koolen, and Alex Garnett, with the ETCL, INKE, and PKP Research Groups. 2012. 'Toward modeling the social edition: An approach to understanding the electronic scholarly edition in the context of new and emerging social media'. *Literary and linguistic computing* 27: 4, 445-461. http://web.uvic.ca/~siemens/pub/2011-SocialEdition.pdf.

Skaf-Molli, Hala, Claudia Ignat, Charbel Rahhal, and Pascal Molli. 2007. 'New work modes for collaborative writing'. In *International conference on enterprise information systems and web technologies*, edited by Narayana Swamy Kutti and Bobby Granville, 176-182. ISRST.

'Sluiting bibliotheken is een sociale ramp'. 2011. *Algemeen Dagblad*, 31 October.

Small, Gary and Gigi Vorgan. 2008. *iBrain: Surviving the technological alteration of the modern mind*. New York: HarperCollins.

Squires, Claire. 2007. *Marketing literature*. London: Palgrave Macmillan.

Stein, Bob. 2011. 'Social reading'. In *I read where I am*. Edited by Mieke Gerritzen, Geert Lovink, and Minke Kampman. Valiz with graphic design museum, http://www.ireadwhereiam.com/.

Stiegler, Bernard. 1994. 'Machines à écrire et matières à penser'. *Genesis: Revue internationale de critique génétique* 5.

Stock, Brian. 1996. *Augustine the reader: Meditation, self-knowledge, and the ethics of interpretation*. Cambridge, MA: Harvard University Press.

Strand, Ginger. 2008. 'Keyword: evil. Google's addiction to cheap electricity'. *Harper's Magazine*, March.

Stross, Randall. 2008. *Planet Google: One company's audacious plan to organize everything we know*. New York: Free Press.

Sweet, Anne P., and Catherine E. Snow. 2003. *Rethinking reading comprehension*. New York: Guilford Press.

Sweringen, Grace Fleming van. 1915. 'The main literary types of men in the germanic hero-sagas'. *The journal of English and Germanic philology* 14: 2, 212-225. http://www.jstor.org/stable/27700658.

Tapiero, Isabelle. 2007. *Situation models and levels of coherence*. New York: Lawrence Erlbaum Associates.

Tapscott, Don. 1998. *Growing up digital: The rise of the net generation*. New York: McGraw-Hill.

— 2009. *Grown up digital: How the net generation is changing your world*. New York: McGraw-Hill.

Tashman, Craig S., and W. Keith Edwards. 2011. 'LiquidText: a flexible, multitouch environment to support active reading'. In *Proceedings of the 2011 annual conference on Human factors in computing systems*, 3285-3294. Vancouver, BC, Canada: ACM.

Tenner, Edward. 1996. *Why things bite back: Technology and the revenge of unintended consequences*. New York: Vintage.

Therriault, David J., and Gary E. Raney. 2002. 'The representation and comprehension of place-on-the-page and text-sequence memory'. *Scientific studies of reading* 6: 2, 117-134.

Thompson, Evan. 2007. *Mind in life: Biology, phenomenology, and the sciences of mind*. Cambridge, MA: Harvard University Press.

Timmerman, Aegidius W. 1983. *Tim's herinneringen*. Edited by Harry Prick. Amsterdam.

Tol, Maarten van der. 2001. 'Abstracts as orientation tools in a modular electronic environment'. *Document design* 2: 1, 76-88. An earlier version available at http://www.kra.nl/Website/Artikelen/mvdt/mvdt-dd01.htm.

Varela, Francisco J., Evan Thompson, and Eleanor Rosch. 1991. *The embodied mind: Cognitive science and human experience*. Cambridge, MA: MIT Press.

Vassiliou, Magda, and Jennifer Rowley. 2008. 'Progressing the definition of "e-book"'. *Library hi tech* 26: 3, 355-368.

Veen, Wim, and Ben Vrakking. 2006. *Homo zappiens: Growing up in a digital age*. London: Network Continuum Education.

Virbel, Jacques. 1993. 'Reading and managing texts on the BNF station'. In *The digital world: Text-based computing in the humanities*, edited by Paul Delany and George P. Landow. Cambridge, MA: MIT Press.

Virilio, Paul. 1988. *La machine de vision: Essai sur les nouvelles techniques de représentation*. Paris: Galilée.

Waard, Anita de, and Joost Kircz. 2008. 'Modeling scientific discourse: Shifting perspectives and persistent issues'. Leslie Chan and Susanna Mornati (eds.), 234-245. ELPUB2008. *Open scholarship: Authority, community, and sustainability in the age of web 2.0 – proceedings of the 12th international conference on electronic publishing*, 25 27 June. http://elpub.scix.net/cgi-bin/works/Show?234_elpub2008.

Wark, McKenzie. 2006. 'GAM3R 7H30RY: Version 1.1'. Accessed 10 October 2012, http://www.futureofthebook.org/gamertheory .

Warwick, Claire, Ray Siemens, and Stan Ruecker. 2008. 'Codex redux: books and new knowledge environments'. In *Proceedings of the 2008 ACM workshop on Research advances in large digital book repositories*, 29-32. Napa Valley, California: ACM.

Weel, Adriaan van der. 2003. 'Is a book still a book when it is not a printed artifact?' *Logos* 14: 1, 22-26.

— 2010a. 'E-roads and I-ways: a sociotechnical look at user acceptance of e-books'. *Logos* 21: 3-4.

— 2010b. 'New mediums: new perspectives on knowledge production'. In *Text comparison and digital creativity*, edited by Wido Th. van Peursen, Ernst Thoutenhoofd, and Adriaan van der Weel, 253-268. Leiden: Brill.

— 2011a. *Changing our textual minds: Towards a digital order of knowledge*. Manchester: Manchester University Press.

— 2011b. 'De lezer ontletterd'. In *Boeketje boekwetenschap: over de (on)natuurlijkheid van schrijven, drukken en lezen, Dr. P.A. Tiele-stichting* by Arianne Baggerman, Paul Hoftijzer, Gerard Unger, and Adriaan van der Weel, 26-31. Amsterdam: Amsterdam University Press.

— 2011c. 'Explorations in the libroverse'. In *Nobel symposium 147 Going digital: Evolutionary and revolutionary aspects of digitization* edited by Karl Grandin, 32-46. Stockholm: Centre for History of Science.

Weinberger, David. 2008. *Everything is miscellaneous: The power of the new digital disorder*. New York. Holt Paperbacks.

Wengelin, Åsa, Mark Torrance, Kenneth Holmqvist, Sol Simpson, David Galbraith, Victoria Johansson, and Roger Johansson. 2009. 'Combined eyetracking and keystroke-logging methods for studying cognitive processes in text production'. *Behavior research methods* 41: 2, 337-351.

Wereld, Afscheid van de. 2010. *De autobiografie van Boudewijn Donker Curtius, 1746-1832*, edited by Maarten W. van Boven. Haarlem. Egodocumenten 25: 37.

Wikipedia contributors. 'HyperCard'. *Wikipedia, The Free Encyclopedia*. Accessed October 2011. http://en.wikipedia.org/w/index.php?title=HyperCard&oldid=453304040.

Wischenbart, Rüdiger. 2008. 'Ripping the cover: Has digitization changed what's really in the book?' *Logos* 13: 1.

Wolf, Maryanne. 2007. *Proust and the squid: The story and science of the reading brain*. New York: HarperCollins.

Woody, William Douglas, David. B. Daniel, and Crystal A. Baker. 2010. 'E-books or textbooks: Students prefer textbooks'. *Computers & education* 55, 945-948.

Yoon, Dongwook, Yongjun Cho, Kiwon Yeom, and Ji-Hyung Park. 2011. 'Touch-bookmark: A lightweight navigation and bookmarking technique for e-books'. In *Proceedings of the 2011 annual conference extended abstracts on Human factors in computing systems*, 1189-1194. Vancouver, BC: ACM.

Zwaan, Rolf A. 1993. *Aspects of literary comprehension: A cognitive approach*. Amsterdam/Philadelphia: J. Benjamins Publishing.

— 1996. 'Toward a model of literary comprehension'. In *Models of understanding text* edited by Bruce K. Britton & Arthur C. Graesser, 241-255. Mahwah, NJ: Lawrence Erlbaum Associates.

Zwaan, Rolf A., Mark C. Langston, and Arthur C. Graesser. 1995. 'The construction of situation models in narrative comprehension: An event-indexing model'. *Psychological science* 6: 5, 292-297.

Zwaan, Rolf A., and Gabriel A. Radvansky. 1998. 'Situation models in language comprehension and memory'. *Psychological bulletin* 123: 2, 162-185.